Redefining the Supreme Court's Role

Redefining THE Supreme Court's Role

A THEORY OF MANAGING
THE FEDERAL JUDICIAL PROCESS

SAMUEL ESTREICHER · JOHN SEXTON

YALE UNIVERSITY PRESS · NEW HAVEN AND LONDON

Designed by Sally Harris
and set in Times Roman type by
Huron Valley Graphics, Inc.
Printed in the United States of America by
Vail-Ballou Press, Binghamton, N.Y.

Library of Congress Cataloging-in-Publication Data

Estreicher, Samuel.
    Redefining the Supreme Court's role.

    Bibliography: p.
    Includes index.
    1. United States. Supreme Court. 2. Justice,
Administration of—United States. I. Sexton, John.
II. Title.
KF8748.E87 1986   347.73'26   86–9247
                    347.30735
ISBN 0–300–03733–3 (alk. paper)
ISBN 0–300–03734–1 (pbk.: alk. paper)

The paper in this book meets the guidelines for
permanence and durability of the Committee on
Production Guidelines for Book Longevity
of the Council of Library Resources.

10 9 8 7 6 5 4 3 2 1

for
Aleta and Michael
Lisa and Jed

Contents

We began working on the study that became the New York University Supreme Court Project after we heard a speech at NYU Law School given by former Judge Shirley Hufstedler, a speech she titled "The Quiet Collapse: The Crumbling of the Federal Appellate Structure." Though admirers of Judge Hufstedler, we observed that the claims she made for a new national appellate court rested on empirical premises that neither she nor others had established. Moreover, we observed that those premises did not correspond with our own earlier experience as Supreme Court law clerks—Estreicher for Justice Powell in the 1977 Term, and Sexton for Chief Justice Burger in the 1980 Term.

This initial skepticism notwithstanding, we began our study with no bias for or against the proposed new court. Indeed, if we harbored any bias, it would have been in favor of the proposed new court, because the Justices for whom we had clerked were supporters of it.

We began our study in earnest in 1983, and its complete results are found in volume 59 of the *New York University Law Review*. The endeavor would not have been possible without the extraordinary work of three successive boards of *Law Review* editors, the active encouragement of Dean Norman Redlich of the law school, and the financial assistance of the New York University Law Center Foundation Faculty Research Program and the New York University Law Review Alumni Association.

x   **Preface**

Many individuals contributed greatly to the study that forms
the basis of this book—including at various stages Richard
Bernstein and Shirley Gray, who coordinated the project, made
it come together, and typed draft after draft of the study and
this book. We are deeply indebted to both of them. We also are
grateful to Michael Broyde for preparing the index with characteristic care and skill, and to our colleagues Anthony Amsterdam, Brookes Billman, Norman Dorsen, Rochelle Dreyfuss,
Eleanor Fox, Jeffrey Gordon, Andreas Lowenfeld, Robert
McKay, William Nelson, Norman Redlich, Steven Reiss,
Ricky Revesz, Lawrence Sager, and Linda Silberman, each of
whom took the time to read and comment on the manuscript.
Attorneys Sanford Caust-Ellenbogen, Daniel Chazin, David
Drueding, and Alan Morrison also provided valuable criti-
cisms of early drafts.

And last, but most important, we thank our wives, Aleta
Estreicher and Lisa Goldberg, attorneys in their own right, who
each read and commented on our work and (along with our
sons, Michael and Jed) put up with our maddening schedules
and work habits.

Redefining the Supreme Court's Role

Chapter 1

The Need for a New Vision of the Court

The popular view of the Supreme Court of the United States is exactly what its name implies. It is the High Court of Justice, the ultimate guarantor of the rule of law, ever ready to correct the errors of subordinate courts and ensure a just result in each case. The image of the innocent death-row inmate saved from execution by an eleventh-hour order from the Court is a powerful one—but simply an aspect of the generally held view that the Justices are there for any litigant willing to take his case "all the way to the Supreme Court."

Myth often captures Truth, but the myth of the Supreme Court as the ultimate error-corrector is fundamentally misleading—at least as applied to the Court of the 1980s. Today's Court sits at the top of a multilayered, regionally diverse judicial system that decides more cases in a week than the Court could decide in a decade. Given such numbers, it is impossible for the Court to intervene in any way in more than an inappreciable fraction of the cases brought to American courts. Thus, in 1982, 280,000 cases were filed in federal trial courts[1] (perhaps an equal number in state courts raising federal claims); the Supreme Court was asked to review approximately 5000 cases[2] and the Justices heard and decided only 151.[3]

Whether or not the Supreme Court ever was truly a court of errors, it self-consciously ceased playing that role with the passage of the Judiciary Act of 1925. In advocating the so-called "Judges' Bill," which relieved the Court of most of its obliga-

1

tory jurisdiction, Chief Justice Taft stressed that "The function of the Supreme Court is conceived to be, not the remedying of the particular litigant wrong, but the consideration of cases whose decision involves principles, the application of which are of wide public or governmental interest."[4] Chief Justice Vinson echoed these views when he said, some years later: "The Supreme Court is not, and never has been, primarily concerned with the correction of errors in lower court decisions."[5]

No sophisticated observer would argue that the Court today sits merely to correct error at the behest of disappointed litigants; yet even some serious students of the Court have failed to adjust their conception of its role to fit modern reality. Nowhere is this more evident than in the debate over proposals for creation of a new national court of appeals, now often called an Intercircuit Tribunal (ICT), that would sit below the Supreme Court and above the present federal courts of appeals and state supreme courts for the purpose of promulgating nationally binding law in cases referred to it by the Supreme Court. Advocates of the ICT argue that the new court is needed because the Supreme Court cannot handle its workload. But they rarely attempt to specify what the Court's mandatory responsibilities are or to demonstrate that the Court is not adequately handling those responsibilities.

Moreover, any vision ICT advocates project that offers assistance in defining the Court's workload is nearly as unrealistic as the popular myth of the Court as the ultimate error-corrector. These ICT proponents[6] assert that the Court sits to impart authoritative guidance and "coherence" to national law—a proposition with some surface appeal. But a glance at the figures on the number of cases implicating federal law handled annually by American courts is enough to establish a stark reality: even if it were desirable for the Supreme Court to intervene wherever there is "incoherence" in federal law, and one could be certain that a ruling by the Court would always clarify or improve the law (propositions we dispute), the Court (with or without an ICT) could never intervene in a sufficient number of cases to remove incoherence from federal law.

The Supreme Court has the capacity to decide a limited number of cases, and an ICT would increase the Court's ability to influence the outcome—though not decide—a few dozen more. Most would put the maximum number of cases the Justices can decide each year somewhere between 125 and 175 (or between 14 and 19 majority opinions per Justice),[7] and even the most ardent ICT proponents acknowledge that the new court would decide only an additional 40 to 50.[8] Any meaningful definition of the Court's role must begin by recognizing the limitations imposed by these numbers.

In 1983, as the campaign for an ICT gathered momentum, we were struck by the fact that the case for the new court was being made at a level of abstraction and bald assertion—with advocates simply declaring that the Court was now not able to hear all of the cases that it should hear, but without identifying precisely which cases those were (that is, without specifying the role of the Supreme Court within our judicial system).

For example, in testimony before the House Subcommittee on Courts, Erwin Griswold, the former Dean of the Harvard Law School and a major proponent of the ICT proposal, argued that a "workload problem" existed because the Supreme Court could not by itself produce a sufficient amount of nationally binding law.[9] He offered *Mellon Bank v. United States*[10] as a "paradigm case" to illustrate the need for the proposed ICT. This case raised the question whether a bequest to a nonprofit cemetery association qualifies for a deduction under the Internal Revenue Code. Justice O'Connor, joined by Justices Blackmun and Powell, had dissented from the denial of certiorari in the case. Griswold argued that an ICT would provide a needed nationally binding rule in *Mellon Bank* and cases like it. But even Justice O'Connor's dissent conceded that the decision of the Third Circuit in *Mellon Bank* conformed to the decisions and analyses of *all* other federal courts to have faced the issue. In short, we presently have a uniform rule! It is just that Justice O'Connor, two of her colleagues, and Griswold believe the rule to be the wrong rule. And, presumably, if the ICT (composed, after all, of the same kind of circuit judges who, in the view of Justice O'Connor and Dean Griswold, have been getting it wrong all along) were to announce the same rule as the Third

Circuit, Justice O'Connor and the dean would press Supreme Court for review of the ICT's decision.

If *Mellon* is an example of a case that the Supreme Court but for lack of capacity should hear, then probably most rulings on federal law issuing from lower courts would qualify. That such a conception of the Supreme Court leads to a diagnosis of system failure is hardly surprising, but the conception teaches little about the Supreme Court's workload or the role of the Supreme Court in our judicial system.

In order to move the debate beyond mere rhetoric and conclusion, we decided to test—in a way it had never been tested before—the assertion that the Court was not hearing the cases it should hear. First, we would develop a theory of the Court's role, and, concomitantly, a theory of how it should select cases for plenary consideration (that is, how it should identify which cases require the Court's intervention). Second, we would apply our theory to the cases brought to the Court in a Term in which a serious workload problem was alleged by ICT advocates to exist. The application of the theory to the cases would tell us two things: (1) whether, given our conception of the Court's role, all of the cases heard by the Justices that year truly demanded their attention, and, (2) whether there were cases the Court did not hear that it should have heard. The results of our effort became the NYU Supreme Court Project, a two-year effort conducted in conjunction with the editors of the *New York University Law Review*. The full project occupies 1253 pages in volume 59 of that journal.[11] This book presents the findings of the project in a manner more accessible to the non-lawyer, with additional material exploring some of the broader implications of our study.

We propose in this book what we call a managerial model of the Supreme Court's responsibilities. Recognizing that the Court has a finite capacity to hear cases, we argue that the Court's principal objectives in selecting cases for plenary consideration should be to establish clearly and definitively the contours of national legal doctrine once the issues have fully "percolated" in the lower courts, to settle fundamental inter-branch and state-federal conflicts, and to encourage the state and federal appellate courts to engage in thoughtful decision-making, mindful of their own responsibility in the national lawmaking process. Following our managerial model, the Court would not select cases because of the presence of error or the ostensible importance of the substantive issue involved. For the Supreme Court to take a case, there should be some structural basis for suspending the strong presumption of regularity that ordinarily should attach to the decisions of subordinate actors in the judicial system (for example, where lower courts had reached contrary results on the legal issue in question); the decision to review the case would *not* turn on whether the Justices agreed or disagreed with the result reached by the lower court.

We do not claim that our vision is the only possible one. Nor do we doubt the seductiveness of the more sophisticated version of the error-correction (or coherence) model of the Court's role advanced by some ICT proponents. Indeed, the Justices themselves feel a strong impulse to shoulder the burden of clarifying the law whenever they see ambiguity in it. Why else, for example, would the Court's response to a hypothetical question raised by Justice Rehnquist about the liability of officials who *negligently* deprived persons of civil rights[12] have led to a ten-year search for a case that might provide an answer?[13] But the seductive pull of this model does not prove its wisdom, for five years after the Court reached the issue in a 1981 case,[14] the Justices returned to the question and retracted much of what they had said.[15] And it remains unclear how much coherence their decisions have brought to the area.

Similar examples in other areas abound. We advance just one more, from a subject which we both teach. The Court has shown an extraordinary propensity in recent years to consider questions of personal jurisdiction (the authority of a court to hear a suit against a particular defendant).[16] Although the rules here work tolerably well, and the cases invariably turn on fact-specific applications of the broadly gauged standards first announced in the landmark case *International Shoe Co. v. Washington*,[17] the Justices appear to be granting review largely out of intellectual fascination with these issues. Having attempted a

grand resynthesis in *Shaffer v. Heitner,*[18] they have felt compelled each year to hear an additional case or two in an effort to
clarify questions left open or created by the previous Term's
handiwork. The result has not been a more predictable or more
coherent body of law.

On our vision of the Court's role, the Court would not have
heard the more than half-a-dozen cases it took ostensibly for
the sole purpose of resolving Justice Rehnquist's hypothetical
question, or many of the nearly dozen recent personal jurisdiction cases. Rather, it would have avoided the attendant waste of
time and energy, for the Court's job, in our view, is not to
search for interesting (or even "important") questions. The
Court's mission is to manage the process of national lawmaking,
intervening only when a nationally binding resolution that it is
uniquely capable of providing is called for in a given year.

Our findings for the 1982 Term indicate that under our criteria a significant portion of the time and energies of the Supreme
Court is being misdirected:

- Nearly one-fourth of the cases granted review by the Court in
  the 1982 Term had no legitimate claim on the Court's time
  and resources.

- Only 48 percent of the cases granted review in the 1982 Term
  were cases that *had* to be heard by the Court that year. Thus,
  over half of the Court's docket was discretionary.

- Significantly less than 1 percent of the cases denied review
  during the 1982 Term were cases that should have been heard
  by the Court that year.

At least in one recent term, the Court had the capacity to hear
and decide all of the cases that required its attention that year,
and it enjoyed a substantial measure of additional capacity for
other cases.

The problem, in our view, is one of unrealistic expectations,
not docket capacity. The vision of the Court as error-corrector,
though vaguely comforting, breeds frustration among those who
do not gain a hearing despite their perception that error requiring review has occurred in their cases. Similarly, the vision of the

Court as national codifier sitting to eliminate incoherence wherever it crops up is equally unsatisfying; the occasions seemingly requiring the Court's intervention for this purpose are also innumerable, and the confidence that the Court's resolution will enhance the certainty and coherence of federal law, rather than prematurely cut short the process of lower-court exploration, rests on no firmer foundation. Either set of expectations fosters the belief that a workload crisis exists and diverts the Court from performing undistractedly the managerial role that is uniquely its province and that the federal system urgently requires.

When we first began thinking about the ICT controversy, we had no a priori view on the need for such a new court—or on the existence *vel non* of a workload problem at the Supreme Court. We did believe that it was senseless to talk about creating a new court to address the Court's workload problem without developing a vision of what its workload should be. Once we had developed the vision, the alleged workload problem— and the need for an ICT—disappeared. We do not gainsay that the Justices work very hard and feel under considerable pressure to decide cases that they presently do not hear. The problem is not one of workload, however, but of role definition.

Chapter 2

The Evolution of Our
Present Judicial Structure

Article III of the Constitution mandates the establishment of only one court (the Supreme Court); it leaves to Congress the discretion to establish such inferior federal courts as it deems appropriate.[1] Thus, the structure of the federal judicial system does not have to be what it is today—and for years it was not.

In the Judiciary Act of 1789,[2] Congress created a six-member Supreme Court with five Associate Justices presided over by a Chief Justice.[3] The 1789 measure also created two "inferior Courts"—the federal district courts (at least one in each state) and the federal circuit courts (three for the nation).[4] Although the Supreme Court and the district courts were staffed by permanent judges, the circuit courts were not. Instead, each circuit court sat twice a year in each district in the circuit and consisted of the district judge for that district and two Supreme Court Justices.[5] The district courts had only original jurisdiction, whereas the circuit courts had both original and limited appellate jurisdiction.[6]

In its early days, the Supreme Court did not enjoy the prestige and influence that it commands today. Indeed, when the Supreme Court first convened in New York City on February 2, 1790, only four of the six Justices—Chief Justice John Jay of New York and Associate Justices William Cushing of Massachusetts, James Wilson of Pennsylvania, and John Blair of Virginia—bothered to come. Associate Justice John Rutledge of South Carolina did not attend a session of the Court from the date of his appointment until he resigned in 1791, although he did serve on the circuit courts in South Carolina and Georgia. And Robert Hanson Harrison of Maryland declined his appointment as an Associate Justice to become Chancellor of his state's equity courts.[7]

During the first year of its existence, the Court sat for only twelve days and decided no cases.[8] From 1790 to 1801, only 87 cases were entered on its appellate docket—an average of less than 8 per year![9] More than 40 percent of the cases brought before the Court were admiralty suits.[10]

During this period the Justices complained bitterly about what was then their workload problem—the burdens of "riding circuit." For example, Justice Iredell complained that he had to ride 1900 miles on one circuit, in addition to an 1800-mile round trip to get to his starting point! He argued that "no Judge can conscientiously undertake to ride the Southern Circuit constantly, and perform the other parts of his duty."[11] In 1792, the Justices wrote a letter to President Washington complaining in "strong and explicit terms" of their "burdensome" circuit-riding duties.[12] This letter—probably the first attempt at lobbying by the Justices—resulted in a 1793 amendment to the Judiciary Act requiring only one Justice to attend the sessions of each circuit court.[13]

The first attempt to restructure the federal judiciary was the short-lived Judiciary Act of 1801.[14] The 1801 measure, partly in response to protests from the Justices that circuit-riding was still too burdensome,[15] authorized the appointment of sixteen permanent circuit judges.[16] Of course, this so-called Midnight Judges' Act was not principally inspired by the Justices' workload difficulties. It was primarily the product of a long and bitter political dispute between the ruling Federalists, whose judicial appointments reflected Federalist political and constitutional ideals, and the Jeffersonian Republicans, who feared that Federalist judges would import British common law doctrines incompatible with republicanism.[17] In 1801, just after new Federalist judges had been appointed to fill the sixteen circuit court positions, Thomas Jefferson became President. He and his fellow Republicans quickly pressed to repeal the 1801 law and eliminate the circuit judgeships.[18] Soon thereafter, Congress passed the Judiciary Act of 1802, which increased the number of circuits and relieved the Justices of some circuit-riding responsibilities by providing that circuit court panels could consist of a single judge.[19] Thereafter, circuit court panels often consisted simply of a district judge.

The Justices continued to perceive their circuit-riding responsibilities as a significant burden, which was only aggravated by the expanding business of the Court. In 1803, a startling (by eighteenth-century standards) 51 cases were docketed at the Court, and by 1810 the number had increased to 98.[20] In 1812, as a result of complaints regarding the "considerable delay and injury . . . occasioned to suitors . . . from the increased business of the Supreme Court," a committee was appointed in the House of Representatives "to investigate what alterations were necessary in the judicial system of the United States,"[21] but no legislation ensued. Again, in 1824, President Monroe urged in his annual message to Congress that the Justices "be exempted from every other duty than those which are incident to that high trust," but Congress took no action.[22] As the country grew, though, and the number of circuits increased, some relief came in the form of progressive enlargement of the Court: in 1807, Congress increased the number of circuits and Justices to seven;[23] in 1837, to nine;[24] and in 1863, to ten.[25]

In 1866, President Andrew Johnson attempted to appoint his Attorney General, Homer Stanbery, to the vacancy created by the death of Associate Justice John Catron. Congress responded by reducing the Court's size from ten to seven, effective with the next two vacancies,[26] depriving Johnson of one actual and two potential nominations. Justice Stephen J. Field, who had been appointed to the Court in 1863, is the only person to have filled a tenth seat. Although at least one commentator has viewed the reduction in the size of the Court as politically motivated,[27] others have suggested that the 1866 measure reflected the Justices' belief that a ten-member Court was too large to conduct business efficiently.[28]

After Congress passed the 1866 measure, attrition did reduce the number of Justices to eight, but in 1869 the number of Justices was again increased to nine,[29] a change that Henry Abraham has characterized as a "gift" to the recently elected President Ulysses S. Grant.[30] Since then, the Court has stabilized at nine members. Congress in 1869 also authorized the appointment of one circuit judge for each circuit and provided that a Supreme Court Justice need sit with the circuit court only once every two years in each district within his circuit.[31]

As the nineteenth century progressed, the Supreme Court fell farther and farther behind in its work—building up at times a three-year backlog.[32] In 1845, the Court was able to dispose of only 64 cases out of the 173 then pending.[33] The court began its 1870 term with 630 cases on its docket, and by 1890 the number had increased to 1816.[34] This dramatic surge was due in large part to the fact that, as of 1875, the lower federal court exercised general "federal question jurisdiction" (jurisdiction over all cases arising under the federal Constitution, laws, and treaties).[35]

Not until 1891 did Congress finally respond in a meaningful way to the Justices' pleas. That year it passed the Circuit Courts of Appeals Act,[36] which created nine appellate courts—placed between the federal trial courts and the Supreme Court, and staffed with permanent circuit judges—and, for the first time, gave the Supreme Court some limited discretion over which cases it would hear.[37] These reforms provided only temporary relief, for by the end of the First World War the Supreme Court again found itself behind in its work, largely because of a vast increase in the amount of public litigation.[38]

Soon after the war, former President William Howard Taft became Chief Justice. Taft's interest in the judiciary was of long standing: he had been both a Yale law professor and one of the first judges of the circuit courts of appeals, and had campaigned extensively to restructure the federal judiciary.[39] Taft promptly assumed the leadership of the movement for further judicial reform. Working in conjunction with the chairmen of the House and Senate Judiciary committees, Taft appointed Justices Day, Van Devanter, and McReynolds to assist in drafting reform legislation.[40] Justice Sutherland participated informally in drafting the bill, and eventually all of the Justices reviewed, approved, and publicly endorsed it for submission to Congress.[41] These efforts culminated in the passage of the so-called "Judges' Bill" in 1925.[42]

At the time, the Justices' participation in the legislative process was considered unusual, although not unprecedented. Justice Horace Gray had previously drafted a report for the Court, at the request of Chief Justice Melville W. Fuller, setting forth recommendations for legislative proposals that eventually led to the Circuit Court of Appeals Act in 1890–91.[43] By contrast, Chief Justice Edward D. White, Taft's predecessor, had asked his colleagues not to take any active public role in working for legislation, and had refused to do so himself.[44] In the case of the Judges' Bill, however, the Justices publicly acknowledged authorship, and the House Judiciary Committee voted to express its "deep obligation to the Chief Justice and Justices of the Supreme Court for their help not only in preparing this bill but explaining it thoroughly."[45]

The Judges' Bill radically altered the Court's function, converting what had been a largely mandatory jurisdiction into a predominantly certiorari (or discretionary) docket. The bill thus enshrined a concept long held by the Justices: the Court's primary role was to decide cases of national importance, not to sit as a court of last resort for disappointed and determined litigants. Moreover, by dramatically enlarging the number of cases in which review was discretionary, the Judges' Bill made it unnecessary for the Justices to return repeatedly to Congress for help in controlling the Court's docket.

The Judges' Bill generated only token opposition. Senator Thomas Walsh, a leading member of the Democratic minority on the Judiciary Committee, argued: "To deny a litigant a right to present to the Supreme Court a question arising under the laws of Congress . . . except by writ of certiorari to be issued upon written application supported by briefs, but without oral argument, is all but to compel him to abide by chance alone, with the odds all against him."[46] Even Walsh, though, abandoned his opposition when he realized that the bill commanded overwhelming support among members of both houses of Congress.[47]

Felix Frankfurter and James M. Landis, at that time the preeminent students of the Court's procedures and jurisdiction, welcomed the Judges' Bill: "The history of the Supreme Court since the Civil War shows a steady atrophy of ordinary private litigation and growing preoccupation by the Court with public law. In freeing the Court for litigation of national and public importance, the Act of 1925 furthered that tendency."[48] Frankfurter and Landis even expressed reservations about whether the reforms were far-reaching enough to absorb what they predicted would be dramatic increases in the Court's workload.[49] In their view, more litigation inevitably would mean more applications for Supreme Court review, and the discretionary system adopted in 1925 would require the Justices to devote an increasing amount of time to reviewing petitions.[50]

History has vindicated this prediction. The average number of cases filed each year in the Supreme Court, calculated by decade, was 737 in the 1920s, 940 in the 1930s, 1223 in the 1940s, 1516 in the 1950s, 2639 in the 1960s, and 3683 in the 1970s.[51] In the 1980 Term, 4174 cases were filed; in the 1981 Term, there were 4422.[52] Until recently, however, the Court has succeeded in keeping pace with its work or at least has avoided appealing to Congress for further assistance. With one exception, no major legislative alteration of the federal judiciary was proposed in the ensuing five decades.

The one serious attempt to alter the structure of the Supreme Court during this period was President Franklin D. Roosevelt's 1937 proposal for authority to appoint additional Justices (up to a maximum of six) whenever an incumbent failed to retire after reaching the age of seventy.[53] The underlying motivation for this initiative was undoubtedly Roosevelt's frustration with the invalidation by the Justices—six of whom were over seventy years old—of early New Deal legislation, and the fear that his entire legislative program was in peril at the hands of this superannuated, conservative Court.[54] But in an effort to market the plan to Congress, he argued that an increase in the membership of the Court was necessary to enable the Court to keep pace with its work. Pointing out that the number of Justices had remained at nine since 1869, Roosevelt asserted that "the personnel of the Federal judiciary is insufficient to meet the business before them."[55]

Roosevelt's "Court-packing" plan was strongly opposed by all the Justices, both conservative and liberal.[56] Although he refused to testify before the Senate Judiciary Committee, which held hearings on the proposal, Chief Justice Charles Evans Hughes wrote in a letter to Senator Burton K. Wheeler, an opponent of the plan, that "[t]he Supreme Court is fully abreast of its work," and that "[t]he present number of justices is thought to be large enough so far as the prompt, adequate, and efficient conduct of the work of the Court is concerned."[57]

The opposition of the Justices to Roosevelt's proposal undermined the judicial-efficiency argument that had been advanced in its favor. Ultimately the Court reversed its unpopular stand on the New Deal legislation, and President Roosevelt was able, through the appointments power, to begin shaping the Court to his liking. Thus the political impetus for the proposal disappeared, and the Court-packing bill was recommitted to the Senate committee, from which it never again emerged.[58]

Chapter 3

Recent Proposals
for Change

The debate over the Supreme Court's workload was rekindled with the appointment of Chief Justice Warren Burger in 1969. Following Chief Justice Taft's example, Burger quickly donned the mantle as the leader of the federal judiciary, responsible for overseeing the workings of the judicial branch and identifying needed reforms.[1] More important, he moved to raise public concern over the Court's ability to handle an ever-increasing number of requests for review. In addresses to the American Bar Association and to other professional and academic organizations, the Chief Justice repeatedly questioned the Court's capacity to handle its increasing caseload while maintaining high standards of decisionmaking. For example, in 1973 he told the ABA:

> Until someone perfects an eight- or nine-day week or a thirty-hour day, the enormous increase in the Court's work over the past twenty years must produce undue stress somewhere and ultimately affect the quality of the product. To wait to do something about this problem until someone can empirically demonstrate that three or four thousand cases cannot be processed as well as one thousand is not my conception of how we on the Court should fulfill our responsibility to the Court as an institution.[2]

In previous years, other Justices had commented, wearily, wryly, or in despair, on the growing burden they had to

shoulder.[3] Not for fifty years, however, had a sitting Justice—
let alone a Chief Justice—so vigorously and publicly expressed
his conviction that the Court urgently needed help.[4]

Chief Justice Burger did not simply make public statements
on the subject. In 1971 he appointed a Study Committee on the
Caseload of the Supreme Court, chaired by Paul A. Freund of
the Harvard Law School.[5] After a year of study and deliberation, the Freund Committee agreed that the Supreme Court
faced a workload crisis and proposed several recommendations,
most of them uncontroversial. Among these were:

1. The elimination by statute of three-judge district courts and
   direct review of their decisions in the Supreme Court; the
   elimination also of direct appeals to the Court in ICC and
   antitrust cases; and the substitution of certiorari for appeal in
   all cases where appeal is now the prescribed procedure for
   review in the Supreme Court.

2. The establishment by statute of a nonjudicial body whose
   members would investigate and report on complaints of prisoners, both collateral attacks on convictions and complaints
   of mistreatment in prison. Recourse to this procedure would
   be available to prisoners before filing a petition in a federal
   court, and to the federal judges with whom petitions were
   filed.

3. Increased staff support for the Supreme Court in the Clerk's
   office and the Library, and improved secretarial facilities for
   the Justices and their law clerks.[6]

The committee rejected many suggested solutions, including
(1) providing more law clerks for the Justices; (2) establishing a
senior screening staff to identify cases that the Justices should
consider accepting for review; (3) making Supreme Court review of certiorari petitions conditional upon certification from
the court below; (4) excluding certain classes of cases from the
Court's jurisdiction; (5) limiting the Court's jurisdiction to cases
presenting constitutional issues; (6) dividing the Court into panels to increase its capacity to hear cases; (7) creating a special-

ized court of criminal appeals; (8) creating specialized courts of administrative appeals; and (9) creating a new appellate court between the Supreme Court and the present courts of appeals to decide cases referred to it by the Supreme Court and, in some cases, on direct appeal from lower courts.[7]

The committee gave "most serious consideration" to one other proposal that it eventually rejected: establishing a National Court of Review (NCR) to review rulings of the federal courts of appeals and state supreme courts. This NCR would have consisted of fifteen judges sitting as three panels (one civil, one administrative, and one criminal) of five judges each. Once the NCR had declined to hear a case, there would have been no recourse to the Supreme Court. If, however, the NCR had heard and decided a case, the Supreme Court would have discretionary jurisdiction by writ of certiorari. Moreover, the Supreme Court would have had the ability (although, in the committee's view, it would have exercised it rarely) to hear a case by writ of certiorari before the NCR or a court of appeals rendered judgment. The committee expected such an NCR to hear approximately 450 cases a year. From these, the Supreme Court would select its own limited docket, supplemented with the rare case taken before judgment below was entered. Though the concept of an NCR intrigued the Freund Committee, it concluded that the proposal was too drastic for the moment.[8] In the committee's view, the NCR would not have relieved the Supreme Court of its most oppressive burden: the screening of certiorari petitions function. Furthermore, the Freund Committee believed that the proposed referral court gradually would have transformed the Supreme Court into a constitutional court, isolating it from the "other major aspects of national law."[9]

The Freund Committee did, however, recommend that a National Court of Appeals (NCA) be created, and this recommendation unleashed a storm of controversy. The proposed NCA was to consist of seven judges, drawn on a rotating basis from the federal courts of appeals, serving staggered three-year terms. Its functions were to include:

(1) screening all petitions for certiorari and appeals that would at present be filed in the Supreme Court, referring the most review-worthy (perhaps 400 or 450 per Term) to the Supreme Court (except as provided in clause (2)), and denying the rest; and (2) retaining for decision on the merits cases of genuine conflict between circuits (except those of special moment, which would be certified to the Supreme Court). The Supreme Court would determine which of the cases thus referred to it should be granted review and decided on the merits in the Supreme Court. The residue would be denied, or in some instances remanded for decision by the National Court of Appeals.[10]

The Freund Committee's proposal triggered immediate, widespread, and passionate criticism from lawyers, legal scholars, political scientists, appellate judges, and—most important for the proposal's future—three sitting Justices and retired Chief Justice Earl Warren.[11] In the face of this withering attack, the Freund NCA languished and eventually was abandoned.

On the heels of the Freund Committee Report, Congress in October 1972 created the Commission on Revision of the Federal Court Appellate System (Hruska Commission).[12] The Hruska Commission's mandate was far broader than the Freund Committee's: to review the structure, internal procedures, boundaries, and jurisdiction of the courts of appeals, and to propose changes to improve their functioning.[13]

The Hruska Commission issued two reports. The first recommended that the boundaries of the circuits be redrawn, and met with little criticism.[14] The second urged the creation of an NCA far different from the Freund NCA.[15] The Hruska NCA would have heard only cases referred to it by the Supreme Court or transferred to it by the courts of appeals.[16] The Supreme Court still would initially have screened its petitions for certiorari, but it could have referred as many cases as it wished to the Hruska NCA.[17] The Hruska Commission believed that its proposal would have permitted the Supreme Court to continue to control the development of federal law without having to decide lesser issues that could be relegated to another court.[18]

The Hruska NCA also would have had jurisdiction over cases referred to it by one of the courts of appeals for the purpose of obtaining "a nationally binding decision at the first level of appellate review."[19] A case in any of the following three categories would have been eligible for such referral:

(1) The case turns on a rule of federal law and federal courts have reached inconsistent conclusions with respect to it; or

(2) The case turns on a rule of federal law applicable to a recurring factual situation, and a showing is made that the advantages of a prompt and definitive determination of that rule by the National Court of Appeals outweigh any potential disadvantages of transfer; or

(3) The case turns on a rule of federal law which has theretofore been announced by the National Court of Appeals, and there is a substantial question about the proper interpretation or application of that rule in the pending case.[20]

The Hruska NCA could have refused the transfer of any case either because the case was unworthy of review or because it needed to control the size of its own docket.[21] Standards and procedures for transfer would have been promulgated just as the Supreme Court promulgates its rules, with the assistance of an advisory committee.[22] The Supreme Court could have reviewed, by petition for certiorari, any of the Hruska NCA's decisions.[23]

The Hruska Commission rejected the idea of staffing an NCA with judges from the existing courts of appeals. It preferred instead the stability of a separate panel with its own institutional identity as well as "a process of selection designed to achieve the highest level of quality in its incumbents."[24] For similar reasons, the Commission rejected the idea of a temporary, experimental panel.[25] The Hruska NCA was to have had seven judges appointed by the President and confirmed by the Senate.[26]

In spite of criticism from Justices, attorneys, and scholars,[27] the Hruska Commission's proposal fared better at first than had the Freund NCA; legislation to establish the Hruska NCA was promptly introduced in Congress.[28] The proposals died, however, as criticism and inertia once again stymied change.[29]

The lesson to draw from this history is that sweeping changes in the structure of the federal judiciary have not been forthcoming without a consensus among the Justices and the scholarly and legal communities that a problem of sufficient magnitude exists. As Robert L. Stern, a member of the Freund Committee, and Eugene Gressman explained in their treatise on Supreme Court practice:

> Firm if not unanimous support from the Court appears to be one prerequisite to the adoption of [major revisions of the structure of the federal judiciary], coupled with a convincing demonstration by the Court itself that it is incapable of handling its workload or that litigants are being prejudiced by an undue delay in the Court's resolution of their cases. Indeed, a consensus among the bar, the commentators, and the Court as to both problems and solutions seems to be essential to judicial reform. That consensus is not yet evident, even as to whether there is a workload problem much less what should be done about it.[30]

This lack of consensus brought about the failure of the proposals advanced in the 1970s for restructuring the federal judiciary.

Proposals for reform resurfaced in the 1980s and began to make some progress by 1983. On June 29, the Subcommittee on Courts of the Senate Judiciary Committee approved legislation creating an "Intercircuit Tribunal of the United States Courts of Appeals."[31] The Senate bill was introduced by Senators Robert Dole, Howell Heflin, and Strom Thurmond. As originally proposed, the Dole-Heflin-Thurmond ICT would consist of the Chancellor of the United States, who would be a sitting court of appeals judge serving at the pleasure of the Chief Justice, and twenty-six circuit judges, either active or senior. Each circuit's judicial council would appoint two judges to serve on the new court for five years. The court would sit in panels of five judges. The Senate bill would also abolish the Supreme Court's remaining mandatory appellate jurisdiction.

The House soon followed suit. In September 1984, the Subcommittee on Courts, Civil Liberties and the Administration of Justice of the House Judiciary Committee sent to the full committee a slightly different ICT proposal.[32] The House bill, introduced by Congressman Robert Kastenmeier and eighteen co-sponsors, proposed an ICT consisting of twenty-six judges, drawn from the current courts of appeals, who would sit in panels of seven. No two judges from the same circuit could sit on the same panel. Although the Supreme Court would refer cases to it, the new court could refuse to review particular cases so referred unless specifically directed to do so by the Supreme Court. Its decisions would be binding on all lower federal courts and on state courts as well. The new court would exist for five years; continuation of this experiment after that time would require new legislation.

Renewed enthusiasm for the ICT no doubt was sparked by Chief Justice Burger's February 1983 address to the American Bar Association.[33] For over a decade, the Chief Justice had spotlighted the growth in the Court's workload. In his 1983 ABA address, however, he called it "perhaps the most important single, immediate problem facing the judiciary"; in his view, the Court was facing "almost a tidal wave" of business compared to its workload when he first became Chief Justice.[34] Moreover, he argued that the number of filings was only part of the problem: "Over the last 30 years or more the content and complexity of the cases have changed drastically, and often there are few precedents to guide the courts in these new areas. These wholly new kinds of cases that are reaching the courts reflect changes in our increasingly complex society and changes in the relationships of government to individuals."[35]

The Chief Justice explained that because he detected no consensus during the 1970s on a solution to the workload problem, he "had no choice but to await events, keep a watchful eye on the docket, and from time to time draw the subject to [the bar's] attention."[36] By 1983, however, the problem had become so severe that the time was ripe for a specific plan of action:

I advocate an interim step which would provide immediate relief and also provide a concrete experience and information on which decisions can be made. I propose that, without waiting for any further study, a special, but temporary panel of the new United States Court of Appeals for the Federal Circuit be created. This special temporary panel,

which I now propose, could be added to that court for administrative purposes. It should have special and narrow jurisdiction to decide all intercircuit conflicts and a limited
five-year existence.[37]

As proposed, the Chief Justice's panel would have twenty-six
judges, two from each of the current courts of appeals. Subpa-
nels of seven or nine judges would sit for six months to one year
to "hear and decide all intercircuit conflicts and possibly, in
addition, a defined category of statutory interpretation cases."[38]
Such a panel could, in the Chief Justice's estimate, "take as
many as 35 to 50 cases a year from the argument calendar of the
Supreme Court,"[39] thereby enabling the Court to reduce its
calendar to 100 cases per Term. The Supreme Court would
retain certiorari jurisdiction over cases heard by the ICT, but
the Chief Justice expressed confidence that the Court would
rarely, if ever, need to review cases decided by the experimental panel.

The Chief Justice repeated his call for a temporary ICT in his
1984 annual report on the judiciary.[40] He modified his original
proposal, however, by suggesting that the ICT be composed of
"[n]ine judges selected by the Supreme Court [who] would
come to Washington, perhaps for a two-week session twice each
year."[41] Subsequently, other minor modifications have been
made in both the Chief Justice's proposal and the bills introduced in Congress. None of these changes is relevant for our
purposes.

In the two years since the Chief Justice first announced his
proposal for change, several of the other Justices have taken a
public position on these questions.[42] Seven of the eight Associate Justices have voiced concern about the Court's caseload,
although they have disagreed over whether a new national court
is necessary.[43] Among the sitting Justices, only Justice Harry
Blackmun has been silent during the period since the Chief
Justice's 1983 ABA address. In a 1975 letter to Senator Hruska,
however, Justice Blackmun acknowledged that the Court was
seriously overworked and proposed abolishing the Court's remaining mandatory appellate jurisdiction, creating an experi-

mental NCA, and abolishing or redefining diversity jurisdiction
(the grant to federal courts of jurisdiction to hear suits between
citizens of different states, even though the rights sued upon are
created by state law).[44]

Justices White, Powell, Rehnquist, and O'Connor have
squarely endorsed the ICT concept.[45] Justice White has also suggested several possible reforms that are variations of well-known
themes: (1) creating an NCA along the lines of the Hruska Commission proposal; (2) dividing the Supreme Court's workload
between two Supreme Courts (one for constitutional and the
other for statutory cases, or one for civil and the other for criminal cases); and (3) creating specialized courts of appeals.[46]

Justice Stevens, in contrast, has countered that an ICT
"would do nothing to alleviate the workload of [the Supreme]
Court" and would only "increase the burdens of our already
over-worked Courts of Appeals."[47] He has also taken issue with
some of his colleagues' diagnosis of the problem, maintaining
that the Court itself is largely to blame because it often grants
review in cases that it need not hear: "A willingness to allow the
decisions of other courts to stand until it is *necessary* to review
them is not a characteristic of this Court when it believes that
error may have been committed."[48] Nevertheless, Justice Stevens has urged the creation of an NCA (more like the Freund
Committee's version) to select cases for the Supreme Court,[49]
and in the absence of an alternative solution, requiring the vote
of five Justices rather than four (the "Rule of Four") for a grant
of certiorari.[50]

Although both Justice Brennan[51] and Justice Marshall[52] have
acknowledged the existence of a workload problem of sorts,
each has reiterated his earlier opposition to proposals for new
courts that would be given some of the authority now exercised
by the Supreme Court. Like Justice Stevens, Justice Brennan
has challenged the diagnosis offered by ICT advocates: the
Court "too often take[s] cases that present no necessity for
announcement of a new proposition of law but where we believe only that the court below has committed error."[53] In 1982,
he agreed for the first time that the creation of specialized
courts of appeals should be seriously considered[54] but would not

endorse an ICT exercising general jurisdiction or one that would usurp the Supreme Court's responsibiltiy for selecting cases to review.[55] In a somewhat different vein, Justice Marshall has argued that the primary problem lies in the Court's summary treatment of too many cases.[56]

The recent proposals reveal a widely shared perception that the Court faces increasing difficulties in dealing with the thousands of cases brought to it each Term. Yet although many Justices, judges, lawyers, and scholars[57] have advocated the creation of a new national appellate tribunal, there is little agreement on the form or function of such a body.[58] The Chief Justice's 1983 ABA proposal is, however, sufficiently representative to serve as a paradigm for studying all of the major proposals for an NCA or ICT. We therefore will focus our attention on it in this study, and will not concern ourselves with the minor modifications made in the Chief Justice's proposal after 1983.

Chapter 4

The Contours of
the Present Debate

The basic argument advanced by ICT proponents is that the Supreme Court is simply so overworked that it cannot adequately perform its functions.[1] The overwork claim requires some definition because, although the number of applications for review is beyond the Court's control and has increased sharply over the years,[2] the number of cases accepted for review *is* within the Court's control. More precisely stated, the basic overload argument is that the volume of cases brought to the Court forces the Justices to choose among three undesirable options: compromising performance in individual cases by hearing more cases than they can comfortably adjudicate, refusing to decide cases that should be decided, or radically curtailing the time spent identifying cases meriting review (and thereby increasing the likelihood of error in the selection process). Presumably, we are left with either an intolerable number of unresolved conflicts among the courts of appeals[3] or a shortage of authoritative guidance to the lower courts on important questions of federal law.[4]

The Debate over the Freund NCA

The Freund Committee and its supporters saw the crux of the problem as the vastly increased number of petitions for certiorari. The Committee noted that "cases that would have been decided on the merits a generation ago are passed over by the

Court today" and that "consideration given to the cases actually decided on the merits is compromised by the pressures of processing the inflated docket of petitions and appeals."[5] These pressures were impeding the Court's performance of its unique functions:

> Any assessment of the Court's workload will be affected by the conception that is held of the Court's function in our judicial system and in our national life. We accept and underscore the traditional view that the Supreme Court is not simply another court of errors and appeals. Its role is a distinctive and essential one in our legal and constitutional order: to define and vindicate the rights guaranteed by the Constitution, to assure the uniformity of federal law, and to maintain the constitutional distribution of powers in our federal union.[6]

The Freund Committee's conception of the Court's role led it to advocate the creation of an NCA that would shape the Supreme Court's docket. By relieving the Court of the burden of case selection, the Freund NCA would have left the Court free to deliberate, consider, and decide cases in opinions drafted with the greatest possible care and attention.

Critics of the Freund NCA maintained that case selection was too important a function to delegate to others.[7] For example, former Chief Justice Warren declared that the purpose of the certiorari screening process was "to permit the Court not only to achieve control of its docket but also to establish our national priorities in constitutional and legal matters."[8] Warren also criticized the Freund Committee and its report on other grounds. He faulted the committee's composition: the Chief Justice had appointed no sitting or retired Justices or lower court judges as members.[9] He then complained of its procedures: the Freund Committee had failed to interview any former Justices, and its meetings tended to be "highly secret," "closed," and "sporadic."[10] His major criticism, though, was that an NCA would damage or destroy the public perception of the Supreme Court as an institution "open to all people and to all claims of injustice . . . always there to right the major wrongs . . . and to advance and protect our precious constitutional liberties and privileges."[11] In contrast, the Freund NCA offered only "the final judgment of a chance group of unknown and temporary subordinate judges."[12]

Reflecting on the failure of the Freund NCA, former Judge Shirley Hufstedler commented that "[a]lthough there are many candidates for nomination as the exterminators of the [Freund NCA], that award may have been won accidentally by the Freund Committee" itself,[13] by virtue of its recommendation that the Freund NCA control the Supreme Court's docket.[14] Because the screening decisions of the Freund NCA would not have been reviewable by the Supreme Court (except by NCA referral), opponents argued that the new court "effectively would cut off from Supreme Court review those cases in which the principle involved might not be of general significance but in which specific individual liberties might have been compromised."[15] Moreover, since in the great majority of cases the Justices would be unable to issue dissents from denials of certiorari, both individual litigants and the Supreme Court bar would be deprived of the important signals often provided by those opinions.[16]

The Debate over the Hruska NCA

In large part because its congressional mandate directed it to focus on the federal judiciary generally rather than on the Supreme Court alone, the Hruska Commission examined the Court's burgeoning caseload in the context of a nationwide increase in litigation. Thus the Commission did not dwell on the quality of the Court's opinions, as had the Freund Committee, but rather emphasized the Court's role in resolving intercircuit conflicts and in fostering the development of a coherent body of national law: "The United States Supreme Court is today the only court with the power to hand down judgments which constitute binding precedents in all state and federal courts. It is charged with maintaining a harmonious body of national law through its power of review of the judgments in cases brought before it by way of certiorari and appeal."[17] According to the commission, the Court's ability to perform this role was increasingly placed in question by the explosive growth in federal law:

> [W]hile the scope of federal regulatory legislation—typically including provisions for judicial review—has been steadily broadening, the number of definitive decisions interpreting that legislation has been diminishing. What this means, in absolute figures, is that in each term the Supreme Court can be expected to hand down no more than 80, and perhaps as few as 55, plenary decisions in all areas of federal non-constitutional law. The question is whether this number of decisions is adequate to meet the country's needs for authoritative exposition of recurring issues of national law.[18]

The commission concluded that the Supreme Court was already operating at its limits, and that proposals to persuade the Court to accept more cases for review would be pointless.[19]

Stressing that "the primary focus of our inquiry has not been the burden on the Supreme Court," but rather "to determine whether the need for definitive declaration of the national law in all its facets is being met, and, if it is not being met, how best to assure that it will be met,"[20] the Hruska Commission identified four consequences of "the failure of the federal judicial system to provide adequate capacity for the declaration of national law."[21] First, intercircuit conflicts were left unresolved; second, resolution of such conflicts was unnecessarily delayed; third, the Supreme Court was being forced to resolve relatively unimportant conflicts; and fourth, the shortage of clearly articulated national rules of decision was producing uncertainty and incoherence in federal law, even where intercircuit conflicts had not squarely emerged.[22]

These considerations shaped the structure of the Hruska NCA, which was to be an overflow court, handling cases that merited some form of nationally binding review but not necessarily Supreme Court consideration. Even this circumscribed proposal encountered opposition, however,[23] and some of its supporters embraced it only with reservations.[24]

Opponents generally did not dispute either the statistical evidence of a mounting caseload or the problems that this caseload posed for the Supreme Court and the legal system. Instead, they argued that the Hruska NCA would not solve the Court's workload problem. Indeed, William Alsup predicted that the Hruska NCA would add to the Court's burden: first, by requiring the Supreme Court to decide which cases to refer to the Hruska NCA and which to retain; second, by forcing the Court to police the nationally binding decisions of the Hruska NCA; third, by compelling the Justices to devote increased attention to requests for review of decisions made by the Hruska NCA; and fourth, by encouraging applications for review that otherwise would not be made.[25]

Alsup also argued that the Hruska NCA could not succeed because of the play of three irreconcilable factors—"the frequency of review by the Supreme Court of decisions of the National Court of Appeals, the number of important decisions referred to the new court, and the degree of certainty such decisions would achieve."[26] Because "[t]he frequency of review will determine the degree of finality and certainty" of Hruska NCA decisions, the Court would not be able to refer many important cases to the Hruska NCA without either frequently exercising review power over those cases (thus not appreciably lessening its workload) or conceding some of its authority to the Hruska NCA, thereby "diminish[ing] the authority and position of the Supreme Court in our political system."[27]

The Hruska NCA also was criticized because it had failed to address some nettlesome precedural problems. For example, the commission had not specified the procedure by which the Supreme Court would refer cases to the Hruska NCA.[28] And the very existence of a referral practice would have complicated doctrine relating to the Supreme Court's jurisdiction. Since all cases referred to the new court would have been channeled through the Court, the propriety of the Hruska NCA's referral jurisdiction would have hinged upon the propriety of the Supreme Court's initial jurisdiction. Jurisdictional issues often are not apparent at the time the cases first reach the Supreme Court, but surface at argument or even after submission. Unless the Court took it upon itself to uncover and solve such ques-

tions before referral (expending some of the very judicial resources that the new court was designed to conserve), the
Hruska NCA inevitably would have had to promulgate doctrine
about the Supreme Court's jurisdiction.[29]

The Debate over the Chief Justice's Proposal and the Current Congressional Bills

In the late 1970s, after it had become clear that neither the
Hruska Commission's nor the Freund Committee's proposals
would become law, reformers generated a plethora of wildly
different suggestions for courts, panels, and tribunals, both permanent and temporary. Once Chief Justice Burger proposed an
ICT and responsive bills were introduced in the House (H.R.
1970) and Senate (S. 645), however, the debate began to focus
on these concrete proposals.[30]

The arguments advanced by proponents of the current pro-
posals closely resemble those made earlier for creating an
NCA. For example, Daniel J. Meador of the University of
Virginia acknowledged:

> There are two related problems: the overload on the Supreme
> Court and the inability of the federal judiciary to render a suffi-
> cient number of definitive and clarifying appellate decisions
> having nationwide binding effect. Even if I were not indepen-
> dently persuaded of these difficulties, I would be content to
> abide by the judgment of some of the best thinkers on the
> American legal scene since the mid-20th century.[31]

Meador, like other ICT proponents, further asserted that in the
years since the Freund Committee and Hruska Commission
reports were published, the case for a new appellate court has
become even stronger.[32]

Even opponents of an ICT seem to accept the premise that
the federal judiciary, particularly the Supreme Court, faces a
serious problem. For instance, although it opposed current proposed legislation creating an ICT, the Association of the Bar of
the City of New York expressed its willingness to support other
ways to address the workload situation: "We have little doubt

that the Supreme Court, if not presently overburdened, has reached the limits of its capacity to deal with its substantial caseload. Thus, we look forward to supporting legislative innovations that will reduce the Court's caseload and allow for the expeditious disposition of cases that merit Supreme Court action."[33]

Because ICT proponents have assumed without question the need for a new appellate court, they focus on details—whether the new court should be temporary or permanent; whether the judges should be specially appointed or drawn from the circuit judges; whether the judges of the new court should sit in rotating panels of five, seven, or nine judges, or whether they should serve staggered terms on a single court; and whether the new court's jurisdiction should be restricted to intercircuit conflicts or whether it should be more general.

Similarly, opponents of an ICT offer the same criticisms earlier advanced against the Freund and Hruska NCAs—the likelihood that a new court, as a fourth tier of the federal judiciary, would cause delay and actually increase the Supreme Court's workload; the instability of a court staffed by panels of rotating judges; the undesirability of conferring the power to appoint or designate the judges of the new court on any one person, or even on the Supreme Court; the possibility that a temporary panel might become, by inertia, a permanent addition to the judiciary; the absence of any urgent problem posed by unresolved intercircuit conflicts; and the advisability of trying less severe and sweeping reforms before creating a new appellate court.[34]

Current debate is characterized by two features: broad agreement that the federal judiciary, particularly the Supreme Court, faces a workload crisis, and repetition of the same arguments that were made during the debate over the Freund and Hruska NCAs. But the underlying assumption that there is a significant workload problem is rarely examined.

Chapter 5

Assessments of the Court's Workload

From the steep increase in the number of applications for Supreme Court review, NCA and ICT advocates too readily jump to the conclusion that the Court is being taxed beyond its capacity. The number of filings may not be a barometer of workload at all. For example, Justice Brennan has said:

> For my own part, I find that I don't need a great deal of time to perform the screening function—certainly not an amount of time that compromises my ability to attend to decisions of argued cases. I should emphasize that the longer one works at the screening function, the less onerous and time-consuming it becomes. Unquestionably the equalizer is experience, and for experience there can be no substitute, not even a second court.[1]

And, of course, some cases have such obvious merit (or lack thereof) that the Court spends little time in deciding whether to review them. Moreover, a comparative judgment is required, for the Court may not have been working at full capacity in previous years, or perhaps it was using its full capacity but hearing cases it did not have to hear. And the Court's capacity for work might increase over time with the addition of support personnel and such technological aids as word processing.

Pointing to the rise in filings, ICT advocates have simply assumed that the Court's workload now outstrips the Justices' capacity to perform their essential tasks. Few have tested this assumption, and those who have tried have conducted their studies in a manner that does not readily permit evaluation of their findings. Public debate has proceeded at an abstract level, with reformers assuming that a problem exists and their critics either sidestepping or baldly rejecting their assumption.

The Freund Committee Report, for example, made only a cursory examination of the Court's workload.[2] Because it did not provide any detailed analysis or explanation, its data have limited value. For instance, although one of the major problems identified by the committee was that the Justices had failed to resolve a number of intercircuit conflicts, the report did not attempt either to count the unresolved conflicts or to identify any specific examples.[3]

Two subsequent studies attempted to address this shortcoming. The first was an analysis by Floyd Feeney of the University of California at Davis, undertaken at the request of the Hruska Commission and designed to determine how often the Court denied review of intercircuit conflicts.[4] Feeney studied about two-thirds of the paid cases that the Court was asked to review during the 1971 and 1972 terms. He concluded that each Term the Court failed to review between 65 and 70 direct conflicts— "those [cases] in which the decisions deal with the same explicit point and reach contradictory results."[5] When Feeney corrected for procedural defects (such as the lack of final judgment), he reduced the number of unresolved direct conflicts per Term to between 45 and 55. After he eliminated duplications and conflicts resolved through circuit realignment by the time that certiorari was denied, Feeney was able to bring the number to between 30 and 36.[6]

Feeney identified another class of cases, that of "strong partial conflict," which included cases "in which the decision below is in the same general area of the law as some other case and where the implications of the doctrine followed in one case would compel an opposite result in the other."[7] Feeney's remaining two categories of cases were "weak partial conflict" ("where the conflict is more attenuated than in the strong partial category") and "no genuine conflict."[8] Feeney estimated that about 50 strong partial conflicts per Term were denied review. Once again correcting for serious procedural defects, duplications, and the like, he reduced the number of strong partial conflicts left unresolved each Term to between 22 and 24,[9] giving a total of between 50 and 60 unresolved direct and strong partial conflicts each Term.[10] Feeney also concluded that these figures would probably increase proportionately with the number of filings.[11]

Unfortunately, Feeney's study cannot be viewed as the final word on the subject. Some of the difficulties stem from his presentation of data; others flow from the methodology, which was largely shaped by his mandate from the Hruska Commission. Still others are the result of a failure to address several important questions.

First, the Feeney study, as reprinted in the Hruska Commission Report, does not disclose the data that form the basis for its conclusions. The published study fails to provide even a complete list of the cases alleged to be unresolved intercircuit conflicts. The reader is offered only a few illustrative cases.[12] It is thus impossible to evaluate Feeney's claim that there are between 50 and 60 unresolved "direct" and "strong partial" conflicts each Term, because the relevant cases are not identified. Similarly, although Feeney provides tables listing the number of unresolved conflicts in various subject areas,[13] the cases in these categories are not identified either. One cannot determine whether the unresolved conflicts are confined largely to one or two discrete areas of the law and require only one or two specialized national appellate courts rather than a broad-based NCA. Through Feeney's cooperation, we were able to obtain a list of the cases he found to present unresolved intercircuit conflicts. Under our supervision, these cases were reexamined as part of the NYU Supreme Court Project by a member of the *Law Review,* Michael Shenberg, who found that 13 square conflicts existed in 1972—far fewer than Feeney reported.[14]

Second, by assuming that all unresolved conflicts should be addressed and resolved by the Supreme Court, Feeney did not entertain the possibility that in certain circumstances the Supreme Court might properly decline to review petitions presenting unresolved conflicts. We believe that the federal judicial system—consisting, as it does, of several courts of appeals unbound by each other's decisions—reveals in its very structure that a degree of conflict is desirable, at least in the short run (see chapter 6). By leaving courts of appeals free independently to decide issues already decided by other courts of appeals or state courts, the system encourages the percolation of legal issues.[15] Feeney's own statistics cast doubt on his conclusion that the unresolved conflicts he identified evidence a failure by the Court to discharge its responsibilities: indeed, about three-fourths of these conflicts were resolved, either by the Court or by some other means, within three years.[16] Moreover, the survey of practitioners conducted by the Hruska Commission did not reveal significant concern over unresolved conflicts.[17]

Third, Feeney's study was confined to the narrow task of investigating the unresolved conflicts that the Supreme Court refused to hear. The study did not attempt to determine whether the Court was reviewing cases that it did not need to review and so made no evaluation of the Court's use or misuse of its decisional capacity.

Finally, Feeney's study did not try to identify the reasons that the Court might be failing to hear unresolved conflicts (or granting review in cases it need not hear). In part Feeney's omission stemmed from the Hruska Commission's uncritical assumption that the fundamental illness of the federal judicial system was the workload crisis, and that any other observed malady could most naturally be explained as merely another symptom of the same illness. In making this assumption, however, the commission (and hence the Feeney study) ignored the possibility that the workload problem could itself be a symptom of a different underlying problem—the lack of clearly defined criteria to guide the Supreme Court's case selection. Feeney also ignored the possibility that the organizational and political dynamics of the Court itself may be an important contributing factor. In short, the Feeney study neither identified the causes of the symptoms it sought to discover, nor advanced appropriate reforms.

Shortly after Feeney's work was made public, Dean Gerhard Casper and then Professor Richard Posner of the University of Chicago published their study, *The Workload of the Supreme*

Court, which examined the 1974 Term; a later article investigating the 1975 and 1976 Terms supplemented this work.[18] Casper and Posner offered a detailed and sophisticated statistical analysis of the Court's caseload, with special attention to the caseload rise in specific subject-matter categories. Rejecting a major premise of both the Freund Committee and the Hruska Commission,[19] they vigorously denied "the simplistic impression that caseload changes are caused solely by broad social trends external to the legal system,"[20] arguing that other factors, including the relative costs of litigation and of settlement, the uncertainty of the law, and the amount of previous litigation in an area, are equally important determinants of the increasing propensity to seek Supreme Court review.[21] For Casper and Posner, the caseload growth is, "to a large extent, a product of changes in the law."[22] For example, they found that "[t]he decisive factor in the growth of the Supreme Court's criminal caseload may have been the Criminal Justice Act of 1964, which provided for appellate representation, at public expense, of persons convicted of federal crimes."[23]

Again, distancing themselves from the Freund and Hruska inquiries, Casper and Posner stipulated that changes in the number of filings and cases decided do not prove or disprove the existence of a workload problem. "Our analysis is consistent with, although it does not compel acceptance of, the proposition that the Court's caseload is excessive and will remain so unless Congress takes measures to reduce it. Indeed, an important implication of the analysis is that, should the Court's caseload level off or even decline in the coming years, this would *not* refute the existence of a serious problem—the caseload may simply become so large in relation to the Court's ability to decide cases that litigants are discouraged from seeking review by the low probability of obtaining it."[24]

In evaluating the impact of caseload growth on the Court's ability to function effectively, Casper and Posner isolated three possible areas of concern: (1) the increase in applications might reduce the time available to screen each application, thus increasing the number of errors in the screening process; (2) the rise in filings might reduce the time available for considering and deciding cases granted review, thus diminishing the quality of the Court's decisions; and (3) the Court's limited capacity to review cases might cause it to deny review, as a deliberate policy, in cases in which review would have been appropriate.[25]

Turning first to the effect of caseload growth on the Court's screening function, Casper and Posner attempted to translate the *number* of petitions for review into the *time* spent on screening them. Their calculation, admittedly based on "indirect methods of estimation," led them to conclude that the amount of time each Justice spent on screening had risen only moderately since 1956—from approximately four to approximately six hours per week. More important, as measured by various indices of error, such as the number of dismissals of cases as having been improvidently granted, there had been "no discernible reduction in the efficiency with which the screening function is performed."[26]

Next, Casper and Posner considered the impact of caseload growth on the quality and quantity of Supreme Court opinions. They found that the Court's output—measured by the number of signed majority opinions—had risen only moderately since 1956 and was no higher than it had been in 1940. On the average, each Justice wrote about half as many majority opinions as did a federal court of appeals judge. Casper and Posner disputed the prevailing assumption that the Court's cases were now more difficult than they had been twenty or thirty years before. Even if the Court's average case was more difficult than in years past, "it does not follow that the time required to decide the cases has increased substantially."[27] Assuming that most of the time devoted to deciding a case was spent writing the opinion, and that the length of the opinion was a function of time available for study and deliberation, Casper and Posner concluded that the growth of the caseload had not adversely affected the quality of the Court's work: "[T]he pressures of time have not caused the Court to reduce the length of its opinions below some optimal level. Such an effect would have shown up . . . as a reduction over time in the average length of opinions, but no such trend is discernible. It thus does not appear that the Court is slighting its opinion-writing responsibilities as a result of time pressures."[28]

Finally, Casper and Posner considered "whether the principal adverse effect of the caseload increase [was] to prevent the Court from accepting for review cases that ought to receive judicial attention beyond the level of the state supreme court or federal court of appeals."[29] Acknowledging that the percentage of petitions granted review by the Court had decreased over time,[30] they conceded that this might mean that some cases denied review today would have been granted in the past. Even if that were so, it did not necessarily follow that cases were being denied review inappropriately; the Supreme Court in the earlier period may have been reviewing cases that did not merit review.

Assuming that there was no acute need for further appellate review of cases in which the circuits were in agreement, Casper and Posner tried to determine the incidence of unresolved conflicts. Using research assistants to examine 10 percent of the applications for review on the Court's docket for each of the years studied, they found that the number of cases in which the petitioners alleged an unresolved conflict had grown only moderately, and that the actual number of unresolved conflicts— cases in which the lower courts acknowledged a conflict or where research assistants agreed with the petitioner's assertion that a conflict existed—had remained constant over the period studied. According to their calculations, 3.9 percent of the applications for review filed with the Court during the Terms they studied involved a genuine conflict.[31] Most of these were accepted for review. In only 1.3 percent of the cases studied did the Court decline review where a conflict was present.[32]

When Casper and Posner examined the overall impact of the growth in the Court's caseload on the three areas isolated for review, they found that despite "statistical evidence that the increase in the caseload over the last 20 years has resulted in a significant, though perhaps moderate (especially when the increase in the number of law clerks is taken into account), increase in the time required by the Justices to screen the applications for review,"[33] they could find "no statistical basis for a definite inference that the growth of the caseload has as yet substantially impaired [the Court's ability to discharge its responsibilities effectively]."[34] Consequently, they concluded, neither the Freund NCA nor the Hruska NCA was necessary.[35]

Although Casper and Posner presented an impressive statistical study of the Court's caseload, their work, too, is not completely satisfying. First, its methodology is sometimes questionable. For example, in assessing the Court's work on cases accepted for review, they assumed that the length of the Court's opinions correlated to the time spent in preparing them. This is an assumption obviously open to question. Perhaps, as Judge Posner apparently now recognizes,[36] more time devoted to organizing and editing could result in shorter, and better, opinions.

Second, their data provide only a comparative judgment of the Court's performance. Casper and Posner sought to measure the impact of the Court's workload indirectly by comparing performance levels with an earlier, presumably less harried time. But they could not determine whether the Court was overworked or underworked in the base period. At best, their study tells us only whether the Court was spending more or less time on certain tasks than it was spending on those tasks at an earlier time.

Third, since Casper and Posner offer a general statistical presentation, no individual cases are presented or discussed. As with the Feeney study, therefore, the reader cannot easily evaluate the underlying data. The reader does not know, for example, which cases were found by Casper and Posner to present genuine conflicts. The reader is therefore unable to determine whether their list is overinclusive or underinclusive, but must accept the authors' word for the reliability of their findings.

Fourth, like Feeney, Casper and Posner did not attempt to determine whether the Court was granting review in a significant number of cases that it did not need to hear. They thus do not focus on the possibility that the Court's case selection process may be an important cause of the perception, if not the reality, of the Court's workload problem.

Notwithstanding Feeney's and Casper and Posner's work, the

empirical premises underlying the debate over the Court's putative workload problem remain largely untested. What is needed
is an articulation of the Court's mandatory and discretionary
responsibilities, a set of criteria for evaluating case selection,
and measures of the Court's performance derived from an application of such criteria to a reasonably representative period,
conducted in a manner that allows the reader to examine the
data independently.

Chapter 6

A Managerial Theory of
the Supreme Court's Docket:
Criteria for Case Selection

Confronting Our Ambivalence in Defining the Court's Agenda

We enter a forbidding thicket. Because the Constitution provides for only "one Supreme Court," and then stipulates only a modest indefeasible original jurisdiction, many constituencies compete for the Court's limited appellate resources. Civil liberties advocates stress the importance of reviewing decisions rejecting claims of individual liberty.[1] Government lawyers emphasize the need for Supreme Court review of rulings interfering with the workings of the modern regulatory state. Corporate counsel contend that all decisions imposing substantial regulatory costs on the private sector or thwarting significant commercial enterprise merit the Court's attention. Others bemoan the Court's reluctance to seize a particular vehicle for doctrinal clarification or expansion. From each quarter, for different reasons, we hear that the Court is not taking cases that it should be hearing—or that it is deciding cases, drawn from other sectors, that it need not have heard.

There is more here than a difference of perspective. Writing and thinking about the Court is marked by an unwillingness or inability to resolve conflicting visions of the Court's responsibilities. Virtually all agree that the modern Court can no longer serve as the tribunal of last resort, ensuring that justice is done in any given case.[2] But this point is grudgingly acknowledged. Many of the same commentators persist in asserting that our system is fundamentally awry because the Court cannot or will not intervene in every case raising important issues of federal law.[3] Critical analysis invariably has failed to meet head-on the implications of the facts that we no longer have a Supreme Court of last resort, that we cannot recreate one by establishing new courts, and that an increasingly complex, federalized society demands systematic thinking about how best to use the scarce resources of the Supreme Court.

This tension between the promise that the Court may hear all important federal questions and the reality that it cannot do so is reflected in Supreme Court Rule 17:

> A review on writ of certiorari is not a matter of right, but of judicial discretion, and will be granted only when there are special and important reasons therefor. The following, while neither controlling nor fully measuring the Court's discretion, indicate the character of reasons that will be considered.
>
> (a) When a federal court of appeals has rendered a decision in conflict with the decision of another federal court of appeals on the same matter; or has decided a federal question in a way in conflict with a state court of last resort; or has so far departed from the accepted and usual course of judicial proceedings, or so far sanctioned such a departure by a lower court, as to call for an exercise of this Court's power of supervision.
> (b) When a state court of last resort has decided a federal question in a way in conflict with the decision of another state court of last resort or of a federal court of appeals.
> (c) When a state court or a federal court of appeals has decided an important question of federal law which has not been, but should be, settled by this Court, or has decided a federal question in a way in conflict with applicable decisions of this Court.[4]

Rule 17 implies that conflicts—whether among the federal courts of appeals, the state courts of last resort, or federal courts of appeals and state courts of last resort—present a strong claim for review. But in the study period we have chosen (the 1982 Term), "conflict" appeared as a justification for a grant of certiorari in only about 35 percent of the cases: 69 cases (or 42 percent) presented intercourt conflicts, only 57 of which (or 34 percent) were properly granted on a conflict rationale.[5]

Rule 17 is indeterminate with respect to other potential grounds for review. Conflict with Supreme Court precedent, if viewed in the narrow sense of head-on clashes with prior rulings, would clearly warrant a grant of certiorari, but such cases are few and far between: we identified only five such cases out of the 164 on the docket.[6] The rule also indicates that review is appropriate in cases calling for "an extraordinary exercise" of the Court's power of supervision, but the very language used suggests that this is a narrow category of cases. Thus, Rule 17 accounts for most of the nonconflict cases heard by the Court under the open-ended residual category of "important question[s] of federal law which [have] not been, but should be, settled by this Court."

It is, of course, vaguely comforting that the Court is free to grant certiorari whenever a particular petition strikes it as meritorious, thus making the Court potentially available for all significant questions of federal law. With this view, however, the perception of overload is inevitable. For the Court to assume, and for students of the Court to insist upon, an unrealistic set of responsibilities is to ensure dissatisfaction and, more important, to forestall careful thinking about what the Court should be doing with its limited decisional capacity. What is needed, we submit, is a realistic vision for the Court—one capable of yielding a manageable yet principled agenda while responsive to fundamental premises of the system.

We are mindful of the warning of Robert Stern and Eugene Gressman, two noted authorities on the Court: "Any attempt to restate [the criteria of Rule 17] with greater precision is somewhat temeritous, particularly in view of the Court's warning that the reasons stated in the rule are 'neither controlling nor fully measuring the court's discretion.' Frequently the question whether a case is 'certworthy' is more a matter of 'feel' than of precisely ascertainable rules."[7] Nonetheless, we think it is possible to improve significantly upon the generalities of Rule 17 and provide a more useful guide to the Court's exercise of discretion in handling its certiorari docket. Simply as a matter of national policy, it is important that various conceptions of the role of the Supreme Court in our judicial system be subjected to a process of public debate, in the hope that a clearer definition of the Justices' responsibilities will emerge. More precise criteria for case selection would probably reduce the Court's screening burden by reducing the number of petitions filed. A system encouraging the filing of petitions that would not be filed if the review criteria were clearly articulated unnecessarily inflicts costs on both litigants and the Court.

Our enterprise is confessedly heuristic. We cannot hope to develop a set of criteria that will satisfy all students of the Court. It should be possible, however, to develop a vision of the Court's role based on what the Court can realistically be expected to do, whether or not new national courts are grafted onto the system. We offer a conception of the Court's docket and responsibilities that, we hope, will further national understanding of the Court, aid assessment of the arguments for an ICT, and help the Supreme Court begin the process of self-conscious management of its decisional resources.

We assume for present purposes that Congress will repeal all obligatory appeals,[8] leaving the Court formally with a wholly discretionary jurisdiction. Of course, the Court would still retain obligatory original jurisdiction in certain cases, such as disputes between states. This portion of the Court's docket is very small, and through the use of devices such as the appointment of special masters occupies even less time than the number of cases would suggest.[9]

Our task, then, is to think carefully about the kinds of cases the Court ordinarily should hear, the kinds of cases it may hear, and the kinds of cases it ordinarily should not hear. Accordingly, we suggest that the Court's docket can be viewed as having three parts. One part, termed here the *priority docket,* consists of those cases the Court ordinarily should hear when they arise, irrespective of the Justices' own assessment of their significance. A second, presumably larger segment, termed the *discretionary docket,* encompasses cases that the Court may appropriately, but need not, hear in any given year. Some cases are certworthy simply because they provide the Court with vehicles for major advances in the development of federal law. The final part of the Court's docket, termed here the *improvident grant* segment, consists of those cases that lack the attributes to place them on the priority or discretionary dockets.

This three-part conception of the Court's docket facilitates empirical consideration of two major arguments for a new national appellate court. The first allegation—that the Court is overloaded by having to hear more cases than its capacity for quality decisionmaking can accommodate—assumes that every case granted review merits Supreme Court consideration. Cases are not interchangeable, and we are aware that not all petitions present the same claim on the Court's resources. Other factors that bear on the Court's ability to render quality decisions, such as the sheer weight of the screening burden, are also not addressed in this study. Nevertheless, we think that inquiry into whether the Court is hearing cases that do not merit its consideration advances evaluation of the overload argument. Our hypothesis—that about 20 to 25 percent of the cases chosen for plenary review represent improvident grants— if correct, compels at least a reevaluation of the Court's case selection procedures. Of course, even if it is shown that the Court is granting review in cases it need not hear, there could still be a work overload problem, for the Court could be denying review in an equal or even greater number of cases that it should hear.

This second contention—that because the Court is occupied with other tasks, it is unable to resolve all of the conflicts among lower courts that come to its attention—is directly tested by our examination of the cases denied review. Moreover, if the Court is now hearing cases that it need not hear, removing such cases from the docket would allow the Court additional appellate capacity for deciding intercircuit conflicts presently left unresolved.

We do not address directly what might be called the "incoherence" argument—that, because it is occupied with other tasks, the Court is unable to generate enough decisions to bring coherence to federal law, even if all head-on conflicts are resolved. It certainly is conceivable that the number of cases requiring such authoritative guidance might exceed the number of improvident grants. In our view, whether or not the incoherence argument ultimately has any force, it has not yet been offered with sufficient specification to command attention in this study. Proponents of a new national court who seize upon this contention should first define what they mean by "incoherence," provide some quantitative assessment of the problem, explain how the Court might identify and be required to refer such cases to an NCA or an ICT, and demonstrate how an additional layer of appellate capacity, national yet nonfinal, would minimize incoherence without generating new sources of doctrinal instability. Aside from identifying, in Chapter 10, some of the costs of creating a new national court, our contribution to consideration of the incoherence claim is an assessment of the hypothesis that a significant portion of the Court's capacity is presently misused and might be devoted more productively to other types of cases.

This study also does not directly address the argument that, whatever the objective reality, the Court feels overwhelmed by its responsibilities and would appreciate the ability to influence, through referral to a new national appellate court, a number of cases that it presently lacks the capacity to hear. If these cases are not already captured by our priority docket conception, it remains to be shown why they must be decided in any given year. We also do not know whether this subjective perception attributed to the Justices would persist even after meaningful criteria for case selection and accompanying procedures were developed that would permit a self-conscious management of the Court's docket, or indeed whether the perception would persist even after creation of a new court. In sum, while our study does not refute it, we submit that this claim, too, is insufficiently specified.

We do not consider here the implications of the caseload explosion in the federal district courts and courts of appeals.[10] To our knowledge, the ICT proposals are not advanced as a cure or palliative for this problem. Although we suggest in our concluding chapter that the Court as manager can take important steps to improve the performance, both actual and perceived, of the lower courts, we agree with Judge Posner that the problem, if any, lies in the explosive growth in federal law and is immune to solution by creation of new courts, unless we are prepared radically to bureaucratize the federal judiciary.

A Vision of the Court's Role

Basic Assumptions

We hope to found our analysis of the Court's docket on widely held perceptions of the Court's responsibilities. We accept and underscore the traditional view that the Supreme Court is not simply another court of errors and appeals.[11] Although we agree with the Freund Committee's general vision—"to define and vindicate the rights guaranteed by the Constitution, to assure the uniformity of federal law, and to maintain the constitutional distribution of power in our federal system"[12]—we do not think that the Court's role is to ensure the correctness of *all* rulings in a given year on issues of federal law, or even to ensure the correctness of all rulings issuing that year on *significant* issues of federal law. Such a role, if taken seriously, seems hardly possible in today's world, whether or not new layers of intermediate appellate review are created, and, even if possible, ignores the benefits of percolation in the lower courts to the process of creating sound, nationally binding law.

Some learned students of the Court may find this last proposition difficult to accept. For example, former Judge Shirley Hufstedler finds it disquieting that the Court is able to supervise no more than 1 percent of the rulings of the federal courts of appeals.[13] Former Dean Griswold characterizes this situation as involving the "rationing of justice."[14] Certainly sophisticated observers like Hufstedler and Griswold understand that, even with the aid of a new court, the Supreme Court cannot hope to police every important ruling on federal law. Yet their indictment of current arrangements and their proposals for change exhibit a continuing unwillingness to abandon a vision of the Court's role that, however well it fitted an earlier time, makes little sense in today's increasingly federalized, complex, litigious society with its elaborate, multitiered, regionally diverse system of federal and state courts.

Although the Court is responsible for maintaining the uniformity of federal law, we do not think that the Court must act to eradicate disuniformity as soon as it appears. From the absence of a rule of intercircuit stare decisis (federal law announced by one circuit is not binding precedent on another),[15] and the presence of state and federal courts free to disagree with one another though operating in the same geographic jurisdiction, we derive a basic premise that disuniformity, at least in the short run, may be tolerable and perhaps beneficial. It may be that such disuniformity was an unintended byproduct of a geographically dispersed, decentralized judicial structure;[16] but it is a feature that has endured, we submit, because the system's commitment to uniformity is qualified by a policy in favor of intercircuit experimentation. Disagreement in the lower courts facilitates percolation—the independent evaluation of a legal issue by different courts. The process of percolation allows a period of exploratory consideration and experimentation by lower courts before the Supreme Court ends the process with a nationally binding rule. The Supreme Court, when it decides a fully percolated issue, thus has the benefit of the experience of those lower courts, often yielding concrete information about how a particular rule will "write," its capacity for dealing with varying fact patterns, and the merits of alternative approaches. Irrespective of docket capacity, the Court should not be compelled to intervene solely to promote uniformity when further percolation or experimentation is desirable. As the Supreme Court recently observed, in a ruling permitting the United States to relitigate adverse findings reached in prior litigation with third parties: "Allowing only one final adjudication would deprive this Court of the benefit it receives from permitting several courts of appeals to explore a difficult question before this Court grants certiorari."[17]

A Managerial Model of the Supreme Court

We propose an alternative model of the Court's responsibilities—one that embodies traditional premises of the legal system, makes affirmative use of the existing infrastructure of federal and state courts, and ensures a manageable agenda for the Court regardless of any expansion of the body of federal law or surge in the number of petitions filed for review. We believe that the Court should recognize the inappropriateness of the nineteenth-century model of direct intervention and move toward a view of its role as manager of a system of courts involved in the development of sound, nationally binding federal law.

The Court's authority and responsibility flow from its unique position as the only institution in our society capable of an authoritative, final judicial resolution of a controversy governed by federal law. In constitutional law, the finality of the Court's decisions is virtually unshakable (despite occasional overruling of precedent).[18] Even the Court's rulings on statutory and common law questions enjoy practical finality, given the deference accorded such resolutions (stare decisis) and the hurdles that lie in the path of legislative action in our system. Justice Jackson captured an important insight in his famous epigram: "We are not final because we are infallible, but we are infallible only because we are final."[19]

The Court, however, cannot and should not seek to arrest the law's development at each available opportunity. Nor should it be expected to do so. First, the Court simply cannot issue definitive rulings on every important federal question appearing on its docket—unless, of course, we are prepared to expand its membership and bureaucratize its processes so radically that we are left with a vastly different institution. Second, quite aside from considerations of docket capacity (which are important and will persist whether or not new national courts are created) the Court should act with great care before it finally resolves a question of federal law.

The managerial metaphor may trouble readers who find it inapposite to a court of law. This conceptual transformation of the Court's position in the legal system occurred long ago, and was arguably codified by the 1925 Judiciary Act. A Court with a discretionary jurisdiction and a limited capacity to grant plenary review—whether or not new intermediate courts are established—must exercise its power so as to maximize its influence over the development of law within the limits of its resources.

The reality of scarce resources dictates that the Court conceive of its role not in isolation, as an oracle issuing definitive rulings on national law, but as a manager of a process of federal law adjudication in which important responsibilities are assigned to the state courts and federal courts of appeals.

The Court can, and should, establish and police a framework for the delegation to and the exercise of responsibility by lower courts. Except in special situations justifying immediate intervention, however, the Court as manager should accord a presumption of regularity and validity to the decisions of state and lower federal courts. A wise manager delegates responsibilities to subordinates and, when there is no indication that something is awry, does not intervene. To do otherwise is to denigrate the authority of subordinate actors, diminishing their own sense of responsibility and ultimately increasing the manager's tasks as well as the overall workload. The Supreme Court as manager would trust the subordinate actors in the judicial system, intervening only when some structural signal (such as a persistent conflict between subordinates) indicated a problem requiring correction.

That the decisions of lower courts, both state and federal, should enjoy a presumption of regularity is a time-honored precept often forgotten in the debate over proposals for a new court. Today, the vast majority of lower court rulings are not reviewed by the Supreme Court—and would continue to be unreviewed even if we added a new national court. Our multi-tiered court system inherently reposes confidence in the decisions of the state supreme courts and the federal courts of appeals—courts populated by judges who are presumed to be acting in good faith and who, like the Supreme Court Justices, take oaths to uphold the Constitution and laws of the United States. The presumption of regularity lies at the core of our vision of the Supreme Court as manager.

Our system is already committed in substantial measure to the principle of percolation. Otherwise there would be no justification for the absence of intercircuit stare decisis. Similarly, state and federal courts daily engage in a process of "dialectical federalism"[20] wherein state courts are not bound by the holdings of lower federal courts in the same geographic area. But more than past practice and the structure of the judicial system support a policy of awaiting percolation before Supreme Court intervention. A managerial conception of the Court's role embraces lower court percolation as an affirmative value.[21] The views of the lower courts on a particular legal issue provide the Supreme Court with a means of identifying significant rulings as well as an experimental base and a set of doctrinal materials with which to fashion sound, binding law. Moreover, the process of percolation encourages the lower courts to act as responsible agents in developing national law.

Circuit courts usually do not blindly follow the holdings of other circuits, but when they reach conflicting conclusions, they do so knowing that other points of view are possible and need to be addressed. As Judge Posner writes,

> An issue that provokes a conflict among the circuits that is not immediately eliminated by one circuit's receding from its previous position is likely to involve a difficult legal question; and a difficult question is more likely to be answered correctly if it is allowed to engage the attention of different sets of judges deciding factually different cases than if it is answered finally by the first panel to consider it.[22]

Seemingly inconsistent positions can sometimes be harmonized in a carefully reasoned opinion. Rather than always spawning incoherence in the law, as the Hruska Commission and the Feeney study suggested, the percolation process may result in better considered rules of law than would a policy of blind adherence to the first holding.

Of course, the lower courts do not always engage in a meticulous or particularly thoughtful consideration of the legal issue even when confronted with the possibility of intercircuit conflict. In line with our managerial model, we would urge the Supreme Court to encourage the courts of appeals and state courts to take more seriously their duty to identify, discuss, and reconcile areas of intercourt disagreement. But even when lower court consideration is cursory, the Court at least has the benefit of seeing how a particular rule "writes," of examining a range of verbal formulations for a rule, and of exploring the operation of a rule against a range of factual settings.

Some situations do call for the Court's immediate intervention even though the issues have not been fully percolated, because the desirability of percolation is overridden by the need for a quick, definitive resolution. Such cases typically involve considerations of vertical federalism (where federal courts have invalidated state statutory programs or where state courts have invalidated federal programs) or of respect for coordinate branches of government (where federal courts have invalidated federal statutes or executive orders). Here, the imperative to resolve a profound clash in the federal system argues for a dispositive declaration of federal law even though the Court may well have to write on a clean slate. But for the more routine instances of federal-state tensions (such as federal habeas corpus review) or interbranch disputes (such as federal review of administrative action), there is no comparable imperative calling for the Court's involvement in advance of percolation.

We do not mean to imply that when, in other situations, the Court intervenes in cases of first impression or in the absence of a conflict it always acts improperly. In such situations, however, the Court's intervention is not essential, and it may properly stay its hand if it desires the benefit of further percolation of the issues.

Defining the Court's Docket

The Priority Docket

The Court's principal, overriding responsibility is to act in situations in which definitive resolution of an issue is immediately needed, when the usual managerial presumption in favor of allowing the percolation process to continue is overcome by the need for an authoritative, nationally binding ruling.

The priority docket consists of the set of cases that the Supreme Court should hear without awaiting further percolation. It is termed *priority* because the circumstances press for immediate Supreme Court review, not because the substantive issue involved is necessarily more important than in other cases. The case itself, rather than the legal issue involved (which itself might benefit from percolation), requires an immediate national resolution. Thus, when the division of powers among the branches of the federal government, between federal and state governments, or between states is threatened by a lower court ruling, the Court's role as arbiter—its unique ability to render a decisive resolution—is called into play. Similarly, when intercourt conflicts persist after substantial percolation, the Court must step in to ensure the unity of federal law. Lastly, when lower courts disregard the Supreme Court's holdings, the Court's position as the highest legal authority must be upheld.

The priority docket represents the minimum set of cases that *must* be heard in a given year in order for the Supreme Court to fulfill its essential responsibilities. It is, therefore, the relevant docket to examine in testing the overload argument for an ICT. Only after providing for the priority cases should the Court set about the job of directing doctrinal development and correcting errors of general significance (tasks assigned to the discretionary docket). If decisional capacity remains after providing for the priority cases, the Court may well go on to decide many cases falling outside the priority docket; one cannot, however, say a priori that such cases must be heard in advance of lower court percolation.

In speaking of priority cases, we are not urging that the Court must take action on each such case, as is presently the practice with mandatory appeals.[23] We have used categories that are somewhat overinclusive, and the Court may wish to exclude cases that fall within these categories but are of minor importance to the federal system. For example, our structural approach may indicate priority status in some situations in which the law is quite clear, such as invalidation of a federal or state statute on well-established constitutional principles. In such circumstances the Court may properly provide a summary disposition or decline to grant certiorari.

RESOLUTION OF INTOLERABLE INTERCOURT CONFLICTS. We regard the resolution of conflicts between two or more courts—whether state or federal and whether the issue is one of federal constitutional, statutory, or common law—as one of the Court's principal tasks. A managerial conception of the Court's role works only if the Court is prepared to take seriously its responsibility to resolve conflicts. Otherwise the system will generate, without purpose, continued uncertainty and incoherence in the law.

The threshold question of what constitutes a "conflict" triggering the Court's oversight role requires definition. A conflict, for present purposes, occurs when two or more courts—federal courts of appeals or state courts of last resort—take contrary positions on the same legal issue. We term this a *square conflict*. A conflict presses for Supreme Court review only when courts in a given jurisdiction (federal circuit or state) are bound to follow a legal rule contrary to the rule that must be followed in another jurisdiction. The ruling of a federal district court or state intermediate court of appeals would not give rise to a conflict warranting review, because a definitive position has not yet been taken by the particular jurisdiction.

When an appellate court summarily affirms or reverses a trial court, we normally cannot be certain of the precise grounds for the disposition and cannot say with confidence that the circuit or state has taken a definitive position on the question. Although Supreme Court review of such summary dispositions may be justified on other grounds, it cannot be justified on a conflict rationale.

Nor does a square conflict exist when a federal court of appeals or a state supreme court has stated its opposition to another court on a question of federal law in dicta (language in the opinion not necessary to reach the ruling) or as part of an alternative ground for the judgment.[24] Legal positions stated in dicta or in alternative holdings normally need not be followed by the lower courts within the jurisdiction, and may not be the product of the same thorough deliberation that normally attends holdings that are the sole basis for a court's decision. The full advantages of percolation have not been achieved in such circumstances; the court in question might, upon further consideration in a later case, reassess its position so as to eliminate any conflict. The federal courts of appeals and state supreme courts should be permitted—indeed, encouraged—to reconsider dicta or alternative holdings in light of conflicting signals from other courts. This not only relieves the Supreme Court of the burden of resolving conflicts that can be resolved below, but also emphasizes the responsibility of the lower courts to reconcile differences where possible, preserving their contrary positions only in cases truly calling for Supreme Court intervention. Realignment already occurs with some regularity, and the Supreme Court should encourage it further by prudent invocation of its certiorari jurisdiction.[25]

One should keep separate the situation in which a court presents alternative grounds for its ruling, leaving ambiguous whether either ground would be sufficient standing alone, from the situation in which the court makes clear that it is embracing a contrary legal rule as its governing rationale while also pointing to factual differences between the case before it and the case in the other jurisdiction. We count the latter situation as a conflict: the court has made clear its position on the rule in question, binding itself and lower courts accordingly; it is exceedingly unlikely that the attempt to distinguish the contrary ruling in the other jurisdiction presents a realistic opportunity for intercircuit realignment in a subsequent case.

Cases in which courts purport to apply the same legal standard but reach contrary results are also not square conflicts. It is inherently difficult to tell whether such contrary outcomes reflect the sub rosa application of a different legal standard rather than simply variation in the facts. (Given the presumption of regularity, it should not be lightly assumed that the lower courts are trying to evade Supreme Court review by manipulating facts while paying only lip service to the doctrine ostensibly employed.) Such decisions do not contribute to the percolation process in the way that an opinion expressly and intentionally adopting a contrary legal position would. We think, however, that when a particular court reaches results contrary to those obtainable in another court over a range of cases, despite the ostensible application of the same legal standard, the Court may wish to grant review as part of its discretionary docket.

A conflict would be present where there is disagreement over whether a particular legal doctrine extends to a set of recurring paradigmatic facts. An example would be the question whether the Supreme Court's holding permitting, under the First Amendment, patronage dismissals of public employees with policymaking duties extends to assistant district attorneys or public defenders. Similarly, the Court's conflict-resolution role is called into play where two or more courts have issued conflicting rulings as to whether an "agreement" under the antitrust laws is present when retailers complain to manufacturers that other retailers are cutting prices and manufacturers then respond by terminating dealings with the price-cutters. By contrast, the Court should not intervene on conflict-resolution grounds if the petition claims only that the lower courts are exhibiting different attitudes in applying the same legal test to determine how much of a showing plaintiffs have to make to get their cases to a jury. Although the latter situation may argue for a discretionary grant in some circumstances, it does not present a conflict over legal doctrine.[26]

Petitions seeking review from judgments of federal habeas courts are particularly difficult to characterize. Outside of the habeas area, we would certainly view as intolerable a conflict between a state court of last resort and the federal court of appeals with responsibility for that state. In the context of federal habeas review, however, Congress may be said to have made a deliberate decision to empower the federal court with oversight responsibility for the adjudication of federal rights in state criminal proceedings. As Cover and Aleinikoff observe,[27] federal habeas review presents the opportunity for a dialectic between state and federal courts, a process the Court should encourage by not intervening in habeas cases simply because they produce a conflict. We can expect significant realignment over time as a result of this dialogue. If, however, the state-federal conflict persists, or a conflict with another jurisdiction develops, or the case presents a vehicle for a major advance in the development of federal law, the Court may grant review in its consideration of the discretionary docket.

The existence of a conflict is a necessary but not sufficient condition for the Court's intervention on conflict-resolution grounds. Not all square conflicts between two or more courts present compelling cases for review and inclusion on the priority docket. The Court should halt the percolation process only when the benefits to be derived from definitive resolution of the conflict outweigh the benefits of further percolation. At that point, the intercourt conflict becomes intolerable and should be resolved.

In our view, an intolerable conflict would occur when litigants are able to exploit conflicts affirmatively through forum shopping or when planning is thwarted by the absence of a nationally binding rule. Disuniformity in the law becomes intolerable when litigants are able to bring themselves under radically different legal regimes through forum choice or are unable readily to adjust their affairs to the law's divergent commands.

In the tax area, for example, considerations of forum shopping and planning by multicircuit actors often rise to the fore. The Court should not, however, assume that they are always present. Much will depend on the nature of the issue and whether or not the appellate courts within the taxpayer's choice of venue have taken a position on the issue. The mere fact that taxpayers always have some venue choice (at least the choice between the Claims Court, the Tax Court, or the taxpayer's home district court) does not argue for assigning all tax cases to the priority docket, for the courts within the venue choice may not have taken a position on the issue. The Tax Court, although a specialized tribunal with national responsibility, operates subject to review by the courts of appeals, and, by internal acquiescence policy, will follow the law of the taxpayer's home circuit.[28] For these reasons, a Tax Court ruling is not counted as a decision of an appellate court for conflict purposes. Similarly, the Claims Court is a trial court, and only the decisions of the newly created Court of Appeals for the Federal Circuit (to which appeals from the Claims Court lie) will be counted.

Many square conflicts, however, are not accompanied by forum shopping or planning problems. In these cases, the Court may properly stay its hand and await further percolation of the issue. There comes a point, however, when the marginal costs of continued disuniformity in the legal standard exceed the marginal benefits of additional percolation. The percolation process is, after all, a tool meant to produce better legal decisions, and should be halted when it is not likely appreciably to improve decisionmaking. No hard and fast measure is available, however, for fixing that point; it is up to the Court to assess whether the ultimate resolution of a particular issue would be improved by allowing further percolation.

Given the difficulty in assessing the costs and benefits of allowing further percolation of particular issues, we have developed some rather conservative rules of thumb that permit an objective assessment of the unresolved-conflicts claim for a new national court, yet recognize that not every conflict merits the immediate attention of the Court. Square conflicts that present forum shopping or planning concerns are priority cases. When no forum shopping or planning concerns are present, we consider the conflict intolerable when at least three courts have passed on the question. Two-court conflicts unaccompanied by forum shopping or planning problems are not considered priority cases on a conflict rationale.[29]

This three-court rule is admittedly overinclusive. Appropriate percolation often requires consideration by more than three courts. For example, three courts' decisions may not be enough evidence of a trend, or the one circuit out of line with the trend may have been the first to pass on the matter, and may not have had the opportunity to consider realignment, or may have decided its case before intervening events, such as a pertinent Supreme Court ruling. There may be situations in which the Court would wish to encourage circuit-by-circuit experimentation, as in matters of trial procedure, where the primary conduct of litigants is not affected, and the law's development will benefit from knowledge of the practical effects of varying legal rules.[30] There may also be cases presenting conflicts over issues that many, including the Justices, deem too trivial to warrant the attention of a national tribunal. We do not attempt to establish a standard for the importance of issues. The Justices, however, should have some leeway to decline to review conflict cases involving plainly insignificant legal issues.

There may also be issues that the Court is simply not ready to resolve, even after virtually every circuit has taken a position. For example, until recently the Court was apparently unwilling to try to resolve the fully percolated question of the appropriate standard for judging the incompetence of defense counsel under the Sixth Amendment.[31] "Defensive denials" similarly occur when for strategic reasons particular Justices vote to deny certiorari even though the issue is fully percolated and merits review. Thus, although our full study in the *New York University Law Review* counts as improperly denied every three-court conflict the Court declined to resolve during the 1982 Term, there may be defensible bases for discounting particular conflicts.

As is developed more fully in chapter 11, we also urge the Court to adopt procedures in conflict cases that encourage litigants and lower courts to act as responsible agents in the process of development of national law. For example, the Court should not grant review at the behest of a petitioner alleging an intercircuit conflict who has not brought the existence of the conflict to the attention of the court from whose judgment review is being sought. If the district court's ruling were in conflict with another circuit's position, we would expect the presence of such a conflict to have been noted in the original set of briefs to the court of appeals. If the conflict appears only as a result of the appellate court's ruling, that court would normally refer to the conflict in its decision. If such reference is lacking, the would-be petitioner for Supreme Court review ought to be required to alert the court of appeals to the existence of a conflict by way of petition for rehearing or reconsideration en banc. It should not be a terribly onerous requirement to have the court of appeals panel, were it to deny rehearing, state in a one-paragraph opinion whether it regards itself to be in conflict with another circuit or, if not, why it believes the case before it to be distinguishable from the case in the other circuit.

CONFLICT WITH SUPREME COURT PRECEDENT. The Supreme Court should hear cases in which a lower court has disregarded authoritative Supreme Court precedent squarely on point. Care must be taken, however, to distinguish claims that a lower court has improperly declined to extend doctrine to a situation not squarely controlled by precedent. Such cases ordinarily should await the percolation process.

Most extensions of Supreme Court holdings or refusals to recognize extensions can plausibly be viewed as implicitly conflicting with at least some part of the rationale of a prior Supreme Court ruling, yet they are an inevitable, legitimate feature of case-by-case adjudication. Such dispositions do not threaten the Court's supremacy and are best viewed as "next cases" appropriately subject to the percolation process, not as cases in conflict with Supreme Court precedent.[32]

RESOLUTION OF PROFOUND VERTICAL FEDERALISM DISPUTES. Although we assume for purposes of our study the abolition of the Court's obligatory appeals jurisdiction, some of the categories of cases presently treated as appeals should remain on the Court's priority docket.

Federal Court Invalidation of State or Local Statutes. When a federal court explicitly[33] invalidates a state or local statute,[34] it normally creates a profound vertical federalism dispute that requires the Court's immediate consideration even in the absence of a fully percolated conflict. This category includes rulings declaring a state statute to be facially invalid (and thus incapable of any legitimate application). It does not extend to cases where the Court has already sustained the invalidation of similar statutes, and the lower courts are simply engaged in the process of applying such rulings to equivalent measures (the "cleanup" function). Nor does it include all rulings that void, on the facts of a particular case, the application of an otherwise valid state statute. This type of "as applied" ruling does not normally involve a significant interference with state activities; the statute remains capable of application to other cases. Of course, when a ruling of "as applied" invalidity effectively drains the statute of much of its force and effect, the case may be appropriately considered part of the Court's priority docket.

This category also does not include federal invalidation of nonstatutory state action on the assumption that whereas invalidation of a statute almost always represents a profound interference with state operations, invalidation of most nonstatutory actions does not. Where this assumption does not hold true, the case may be taken up as part of the Court's discretionary docket.[35]

State Court Invalidation of Federal Action. A state court's invalidation of a federal statute or treaty[36] calls for the Supreme Court's immediate intervention. We also include in this category the relatively infrequent occurrence of a state court's invalidation of federal nonstatutory action, even though this introduces an element of asymmetry, in recognition of the subordinate position that the states occupy with respect to the federal government and the Government's need to administer programs on a nationwide basis.

RESOLUTION OF INTERBRANCH DISPUTES. A federal court's invalidation of a federal statute[37] or executive order presents a profound interbranch dispute that requires a prompt, authoritative resolution by the Supreme Court.[38] Other interbranch disputes of a like order of magnitude, such as *United States v. Nixon,*[39] also belong on the Court's priority docket, even though they technically do not involve invalidation of a statute or executive order.

In all of these cases, the confrontation between governmental branches undermines or disrupts the workings of a government committed to principles of separation of powers. If the lower court's ruling is obeyed, then the executive or legislative branch may be disabled from acting. The cost of error in this situation is extraordinarily high. If the court's ruling is not adhered to, the result would pose a serious threat to the system of checks and balances. Such considerations override the value of percolation.

Rulings framed as interpretations of a statute, even those allegedly involving distortions of the statute in the service of perceived constitutional values, do not present the kind of confrontation with a coordinate branch that requires immediate intervention by the Court. They should be treated as discretionary cases (although the Court's receptivity to the distortion claim will no doubt strongly influence its exercise of discretion). By the same token, cases in which a federal court invalidates nonstatutory federal action typically present only a question of statutory construction. Finally, for similar reasons, we do not adopt the suggestion that review should always be granted "[w]here the court below, over the opposition of the Government, has declared invalid a federal administrative regulation of general application . . . and the Government has announced its intention of adhering to its prior position and makes a persuasive showing that the public interest requires an early resolution of the issue."[40] Such cases belong on the Court's discretionary docket.

RESOLUTION OF INTERSTATE DISPUTES. Certain interstate disputes, such as those presently falling within the Court's constitutionally mandated original and exclusive jurisdiction[41] or those arising out of the administration of interstate compacts[42] should be viewed as priority cases because they call for the Court's unique capacity to provide a forum for sovereigns of equal dignity.[43]

The Discretionary Docket

The discretionary docket consists of cases that the Supreme Court may appropriately review. Unlike the cases on the priority docket, however, they do not press for immediate resolution. The Court's first obligation is to decide the cases on its priority docket; only then should it turn to those on the discretionary docket.

Discretionary review need not be arbitrary; there are particular types of cases that the Court may properly hear, in keeping with the concept of the Court as manager of the federal judicial system. We offer the following guidelines as a basis for suggesting that not all of the nonpriority cases that the Court decides to review reflect an appropriate exercise of discretion.

SUSPICION OF THE FORUM'S CONSIDERATION OF A FEDERAL QUESTION. The Court may properly grant review when a state court sustains the validity of state action, statutory or otherwise, in the face of a federal constitutional or statutory challenge,[44] on the theory that there is reason in the structure of the situation to be suspicious of the state court's receptivity to the claim. This structural basis for suspicion of the forum's resolution is not, however, a sufficient reason for intervention in advance of full percolation. The Court should hear such cases (even as a discretionary matter) only where there appears to have been a major departure from Supreme Court precedent or a plainly erroneous extension of doctrine, and where there is reason to believe that further percolation will offer little illumination. Although we are reluctant to count cases arguably falling within this structural suspicion category as improvident grants, the Court generally should await the development of at least a two-court conflict.[45]

CONSIDERATIONS OF VERTICAL FEDERALISM PRESS FOR SUPREME COURT REVIEW. Because of considerations of vertical federalism, the Court may properly grant review when a federal court invalidates nonstatutory state action on federal constitutional or statutory grounds (excluding federal habeas). Here, too, the Court should intervene only in cases involving a major departure from Supreme Court precedent or a plainly erroneous extension of doctrine and even then only if there is reason to believe that further percolation would not prove useful.

A SIGNIFICANT INTERFERENCE WITH FEDERAL EXECUTIVE RESPONSIBILITY. Even though a federal statute or executive order may not be implicated, so that a priority case does not arise, there may be situations in which federal court rulings threaten to interfere significantly with an important federal statutory program or nonstatutory federal action. For example, a statute's reach might be significantly truncated in order to avoid collision with a perceived constitutional interest. Or the Government might announce a policy of not acquiescing in a lower court's invalidation of a federal administrative regulation of general application. Not every ruling that hinders the activities of a federal agency or that is the subject of a petition by the Solicitor General merits a grant under this category. Only if a decision necessarily has nationwide scope, as with invalidation of a federal regulation, or in some other way prevents the Government from localizing its compliance, should the Court intervene without awaiting a conflict. Although we count all cases falling within this category as proper discretionary grants, ordinarily

the Court should stay its hand until at least two courts have
addressed the issue or unless the lower court ruling involves a
major departure from established Supreme Court precedent.
The Supreme Court has acknowledged the benefits of percolation even in this context.[46]

EXERCISE OF THE COURT'S EXTRAORDINARY POWER OF SUPERVISION.
The Court's supervisory authority comes into play, according to
Hart and Wechsler, in the following situations:

> [w]here a federal court has so far departed from the ac-
> cepted and usual course of judicial proceedings in a matter
> affecting not only the correctness of its decision but the
> public interest in the process by which justice is adminis-
> tered, or has so far sanctioned such a departure by a lower
> court, as to call for an extraordinary exercise of [the Su-
> preme Court's power of supervision].[47]

The Court should not grant cases solely to correct error as it
affects the individual litigants. As manager, it should intervene
strategically to maximize the impact of occasional review of
egregious error in order to ensure responsible actions by lower
courts. We would not expect many cases to fall into this category.

RESOLUTION OF A NATIONAL EMERGENCY. There may be pressing
national emergencies that do not fall within any of the preceding categories. *Dames & Moore v. Regan*,[48] although it involved
the validity of executive orders, and thus would be on the priority docket for that reason alone, is also illustrative of this emergency category. The case involved the validity of executive
orders nullifying certain attachments and liens on Iranian assets
in the United States, subjecting all litigation on such claims
against Iran to arbitration. President Carter issued the orders as
part of an agreement between the United States and Iran that
provided for the release of United States citizens who had been
taken hostage in Tehran. The resolution of this dispute required
prompt review and legitimation that only Supreme Court approval could provide. We do not wish to suggest, however, that
all cases involving disputes with other countries belong on the
discretionary docket. Typically, the United States as a sover-

eign is not directly involved, and there is no pressing need for nationally binding resolution of the issue.

In particular circumstances, litigation over the constitutional amendment process or election campaigns might also pose an emergency requiring the Court's intervention. This category should not be viewed in expansive terms, and would not embrace cases that simply present important national controversies—such as affirmative action or abortion—absent sufficient percolation.

VEHICLES FOR ADVANCES IN THE DEVELOPMENT OF FEDERAL LAW. A managerial conception of the Court's role justifies strategic intervention for the purpose of announcing new doctrine, overruling precedent, or trying to bring coherence to an area of law. The Court may wish to seize on a particular case as a vehicle without awaiting the development of a conflict, although it should rarely issue an authoritative ruling in the absence of lower court percolation.

We are not suggesting a handy catch-all for cases that the Court wishes to hear merely because it is interested in a particular issue. Rather, the vehicle category presents a strategic opportunity for the Court to advance and clarify the law without waiting for a conflict to develop, in contexts in which the percolation process cannot be counted to yield square conflicts or sufficiently crystallized lower court consideration. Vehicle cases fall into the following subcategories.

Prior reservation of the issue or prior fractionated ruling. A grant may be justified if a previous Court ruling reserved judgment as to the precise reach of its holding[49] or a divided Court has produced considerable uncertainty as to the precise reach of a prior holding.[50] Although we believe that the Court should ordinarily await the development of a fully percolated conflict, we recognize that it might feel a special responsibility to clarify questions that it had itself raised to a level of national prominence by a reference that could distort lower court consideration and spawn unforeseen areas of litigation if not clarified early on. Prior reservation of the issue in question is not, however, a sufficient condition for a proper vehicle: the petitioner must also show that the reservation has provoked unintended doctrinal developments that threaten to proliferate unless the Court intervenes in advance of a conflict—in short, grounds for halting the percolation process.

Doctrinal incoherence. A grant is also justified if a petition demonstrates a level of doctrinal incoherence in the lower courts calling for authoritative Supreme Court guidance despite the absence of a conflict between two or more courts. *Incoherence,* as used here, describes a situation in which varying legal standards are applied by different courts to closely analogous situations. No square conflict emerges; either there is some way of distinguishing the holdings, or the legal standards can be placed along a spectrum so that cases can be plausibly distinguished on their facts. Nonetheless, the law remains fundamentally opaque, thwarting compliance or planning by the federal government or other multicircuit actors. An example would be the question of the extent of market share that constitutes monopoly power under the Sherman Act:[51] square conflicts may never occur because the lower court resolutions will tend to be fact-specific. Normally, a conflict will ultimately develop, and the Court should stay its hand until then. It may also be the case that the Court's intervention will prove fruitless because the particular issue cannot be harnessed by a new doctrinal synthesis. Nevertheless, where extensive lower court consideration has occurred, if the Court determines that the benefits of further percolation are outweighed by the need for definitive guidance, it may appropriately take a case to attempt to impart coherence to the area.

Other sources of doctrinal incoherence warranting review under this rubric include a fractionated Supreme Court ruling or the existence of two or more fairly established lines of Supreme Court precedent that appear to be in tension or conflict. In such circumstances, although some percolation will certainly be useful, the lower courts are unlikely to be able to resolve the controversy decisively; the Court may properly intervene in advance of a conflict. Sometimes the perceived tension is not between two (or more) established lines of doctrine, but rather comes from a recent Supreme Court ruling arguably casting doubt on well-established precedent.[52] These are "next case" situations that should await percolation.

Overruling precedent. We count as proper discretionary grants those cases in which the lower court applied Supreme Court precedent that the Court now wishes to reconsider.[53] Obviously, the lower courts cannot, without ample hints from the Supreme Court, be counted on to reexamine established precedent. It is, however, generally unwise for the Court to remake law in wholesale fashion without the benefit of lower court consideration of the issue. The Court would be better advised to announce in a suitable case that it is prepared to consider overruling a prior decision or to break new doctrinal ground. It might then remand to the lower court for reconsideration. The Court can also signal its predisposition to reconsider prior law in other ways, such as suggestive footnotes in decisions in related areas.[54]

Although the objection might be made that we are urging the Court to render advisory opinions beyond its authority under article III of the Constitution, we do not see any justiciability bar to granting review for the limited purpose of signaling a predisposition to reconsider precedent, and then remanding for the lower court's view. We do not require a conflict in such situations because the Court's invitation to reexamine precedent creates destabilizing consequences for the policy of stare decisis, which should be minimized.

Review of cases related to cases on priority or discretionary dockets. A managerial conception of the Court would also justify a decision to grant review of cases that raise issues related to those in other cases presently under review—given the obvious efficiencies and the likelihood that there will have been sufficient percolation of the cluster of issues prior to Supreme Court resolution.[55] The granting of cases under this category depends, of course, on the Justices' judgment whether it would be better to settle the related issues by granting review or whether better law would be made by awaiting further percolation.

Review of a court of exclusive jurisdiction. Where review is sought from a court of exclusive jurisdiction for certain subject matter, such as the Court of Appeals for the Federal Circuit[56] or the Court of Appeals for the District of Columbia Circuit,[57] the Court might wish to grant certiorari in particular circumstances as an exercise of its supervisory authority. Because of the lower court's exclusive jurisdiction over the subject, the Supreme Court cannot usually expect conflicts to develop.

This category of the discretionary docket raises serious questions about the effectiveness of an ICT for reducing the Court's workload. Should an ICT be established, the Court might well feel compelled to review cases with some regularity, on an analogous rationale.

Application of settled Supreme Court precedent to situations presenting a risk of serious dislocation. A declaration by the Court that a statute or government action is invalid often leaves some questions open, such as the retroactive effect of the holding, where the standards have been amply ventilated in prior rulings and what is called for is a prompt decision by the Court. For the lower courts to attempt to resolve this question on their own may result in serious disruption of settled proceedings, yet there is little to be gained from their consideration of the matter. The Court may act without awaiting additional percolation of this type of issue.

Categories not included. Some may argue that the Court can properly grant review simply in order to forestall serious economic dislocation from a possibly erroneous lower court ruling. We do not endorse this ground for a discretionary grant because it is inconsistent with our vision of the Court's role. Whatever the consequences to the parties, the Court does not sit merely to correct error; definitive declarations of law should normally await completion of the percolation process.

It has also been suggested that, for a narrow category of cases presenting challenges to federal or state election procedures, the benefits of percolation may be dispensed with because delay in securing a definitive judicial resolution may lead to irrevocable loss of the federal claim or invite the uncertainty, disruption, and expense of a new election. Again, we are reluctant to lend support to any case of special pleading. Erroneous judicial rulings are no more (or less) disruptive in the election context than in other areas. Our criteria provide for a discretionary grant when a state court sustains a state or local election procedure against federal challenge, when a federal court invalidates a state or local election, or when the Attorney General can demonstrate a significant interference with executive responsibility in enforcing, say, the Voting Rights Act. By contrast, a federal court's sustaining the validity of state or local election rules does not generally justify a discretionary grant.

With some disquiet, we also reject as a species of special pleading a discretionary category for cases challenging the imposition of the death penalty and presenting a substantial federal question. Although we understand the peculiar finality of such decisions, once the Court has clearly sustained the validity vel non of the death penalty, the principal justification for special treatment disappears. Of course, in particular circumstances, a priority or discretionary grant may be justified under our criteria.

The Improvident Grant Segment

We have tried to identify the types of cases in which the Court should or might grant review based on what we believe to be a principled view of the Court's role in the adjudicatory system. The categories comprising the priority and discretionary dockets outlined above are exhaustive and generous. If cases are granted that cannot be fitted into any of these categories, we can only conclude that they are improvidently granted.

We offer a few general criteria for identifying improvident grants. First, intercourt conflicts between only two courts that do not present problems of forum shopping or planning by multicircuit actors should not be heard in the absence of some other basis for priority or discretionary review. Second, the Court should not review a federal court's resolution of an issue of nonconstitutional law in the absence of an intolerable conflict or of one of the other grounds for a priority or discretionary grant. The availability of appeal to the legislative process and the absence of vertical federalism difficulties argue against a grant. Third, the Court should never grant review to decide questions of state law, but should permit the state courts to rectify any erroneous readings of state law made by the federal courts.

Finally, the Court should not hear cases in which a state court has invalidated state action on a federal ground in the absence of a conflict or a decision to treat the case as a vehicle for a major pronouncement of federal law. Without further percolation, there is ordinarily little reason to believe that the issue is one of recurring national significance. Moreover, unlike a federal court's invalidation of state action, here a structural justification for intervention is generally missing, given the absence of vertical federalism difficulties and the built-in assurance that state courts functioning under significant political constraints are not likely to invalidate state action lightly, even on federal grounds.[58] Indeed, it was not until the latter part of the nineteenth century that the Supreme Court even had appellate jurisdiction to hear such cases. We recognize that a state court ruling premised on the Constitution would be immune from correction by ordinary political processes, and certainly if there is reason to believe that a particular state supreme court is systematically disregarding the Supreme Court's decisions or setting itself against the general tenor of its rulings, the Court could intervene under a supervisory or vehicle rationale. It should not grant, however, merely to correct perceived error, even regarding a matter of constitutional law.

The term *improvident grant* is not intended to be pejorative; in a process that requires nine Justices to review over 5000 petitions per Term (over 2000 in the "paid" docket), some inappropriate grants are bound to occur. Nonetheless, the presence of a significant number of such cases would suggest that the Court's resources could be better used. In particular, a demonstration that the number of improvident grants exceeds the number of cases in which review was improperly denied (assuming that the cases present fairly equivalent claims on the Court's decisional resources) should place in question both the overload and unresolved-conflicts arguments for an ICT, impose a burden on ICT proponents to specify and prove their incoherence claim, and at the very least impel a consideration of changes in the Court's procedures for considering certiorari petitions.

Chapter 7

Probable Criticisms
of the Criteria

The goal of our study is to alter the terms of the debate over the overload problem—to shift attention away from generalities and to focus on the proper role of the Supreme Court, and on whether the Court can fulfill that role without the creation of a new appellate court. But, to a large extent, one's view of the Court's role colors one's analysis of the alleged overload problem. For this reason we have carefully laid out our arguments and assumptions and have tried to be both principled and overinclusive in our categories, yet responsive to widely shared conceptions of the Court's responsibilities. Given the central importance of the criteria to our study, we anticipate that they will be scrutinized closely and criticized. Although we cannot anticipate the full extent of this criticism, in this chapter we address some of the arguments that we expect to be raised.

One possible criticism is that our managerial model is fundamentally at odds with the view that courts are obligatory decisionmakers who do not "manage" dockets but render justice in all cases properly before them, so that open avowal of the Court's managerial discretion is likely to exacerbate doubts about the legitimacy of its judicial review function. In the context of the Supreme Court, however, this general approach seems misguided. The Court ceased long ago to be a court of mandatory jurisdiction, and we think it better for the Court to state forthrightly that, whereas it lacks the capacity to hear all cases in a given year—even all cases raising significant federal issues—its inaction does not connote approval of a lower court's resolution; rather, it reflects a judgment that finalization of the process of doctrinal development on the point at issue is likely to be premature.

Another criticism is that we have understated the importance of uniformity of federal law. One premise of our study is that the system is not in fact committed to immediate achievement of uniformity on all points of federal law. We have tried in our delineation of the priority docket to identify the types of situations that do call for uniformity irrespective of the possible utility of further percolation. We admit that there might be areas of federal law in which certainty and predictability are particularly important and for which specialized national courts might be appropriate. Our study is, however, an evaluation of the case for an ICT of general subject-matter jurisdiction.

A third objection maintains that our definition of the priority docket is underinclusive. Most powerfully, it is urged that many common conceptions of the Supreme Court emphasize its role in defining and vindicating constitutional rights.[1] In this view, a Supreme Court properly discharging its responsibilities should hear cases in which a litigant is deprived of a substantial constitutional right; yet our priority docket does not contain such a category.

We would indeed be delinquent if we did not provide for cases in which constitutional rights are implicated. However, there is ample room on the priority docket for many constitutional cases. Whenever a lower federal court invalidates a state or federal statute on constitutional grounds, or whenever a state court invalidates a federal program on constitutional grounds, the case is placed on the priority docket. In addition, whenever a constitutional issue results in an intolerable intercourt conflict, or conflicts with Supreme Court precedent, the case should be accorded priority treatment. The only cases presenting constitutional issues that are not on the priority docket are those in which (1) a state court has invalidated state action on federal constitutional grounds, (2) a federal court has invalidated nonstatutory federal, state, or local action on federal constitutional grounds, or (3) a state or lower federal court has denied a constitutional claim, without creating an intolerable intercourt conflict or conflict with Supreme Court precedent. Those who would say that our theory ignores litigants deprived of constitutional rights would presumably have little problem with a failure to review cases in the first two categories. As to cases in which courts have rejected constitutional claims, unless they fall within the discretionary docket, we find no compelling need to disturb the presumption of regularity simply because a constitutional question is involved. In the context of defining the Court's responsibilities, which embrace all questions of federal law, we reject the notion that constitutional cases are necessarily more important than other kinds of cases.

The discretionary docket does contain, moreover, several categories in which these constitutional cases might fall. For example, there might be a structural basis for suspicion of the lower court's determination of the issue, or the case might be an appropriate vehicle. If, however, the case does not fit into one of the discretionary categories, we believe that it would be improvident for the Court to hear it even if it deals with a constitutional issue.

A fourth charge is that we have overstated the benefits of percolation—that the Supreme Court does not really learn very much more from lower court consideration of conflicts than from the lawyers' briefs when the issue first appears, so that all we have done is elevate to the plane of principle the sacrifice of individual justice to administrative convenience. Even if, for the sake of argument, our positive claims for percolation are deemed misguided, the alternative proposal would be not Supreme Court consideration but review by some new national court. The choice is not between having the Supreme Court hear all cases or only some, but between creation of new layers of courts and adherence to the present structure. Given the limited resources of the Supreme Court, we think that opting for further percolation in situations not plainly calling for a prompt national decision is both justified and preferable to the establishment of new courts. No one has demonstrated why a national ruling by a court of necessarily limited authority such as an ICT should be preferred to the flexibility and potential for informed reconciliation that inheres in lower court percolation under the Supreme Court's overall managerial superintendence.

A fifth general criticism is that our improvident grant category is hopelessly presumptuous. If four Justices believe that an issue is important for the development of law, who are we to say that the grant was improvident? The Court certainly has the power to deem any case properly before it to be worthy of review, and we would strongly oppose legislation seeking to constrict the Court's discretion. However, we show no disrespect in questioning, as have some of the Justices, whether the criteria for case selection should remain wholly indeterminate—not only encouraging a spate of clearly meritless petitions that hope to come up lucky but, more important, fueling the perception that the Court is incapable of deciding all of the apparently significant cases on its docket. Whether or not new courts are created, it would be better for the Court and all affected by its work if the Justices began to elucidate a meaningful set of criteria for determining which cases merit review.

It has also been suggested that our criteria, even if widely accepted, would be too difficult to implement, or unlikely to be implemented, by a necessarily politicized Supreme Court. This argument dooms most proposals for reform, for it raises the question whether the Court's referrals to a new national court would really consist of cases that need authoritative national resolution or merely of cases appearing on the political agenda of the four or five Justices whose votes would be necessary for referral. Even if one thinks an ICT is warranted, one needs to specify a set of criteria for referral to that court. Moreover, acknowledging that the Court occasionally reviews cases to enforce a political view, we still think there is room enough in the discretionary docket for the differing political agendas of the individual Justices.

Ultimately, we hope to spark debate—to shift the focus of analysis from impressions and abstractions to a systematic evaluation of the Court's role, to criteria, and to data. The burden is on proponents of change—advocates of an ICT—to demonstrate the case for new national courts.

We view our criteria as a tool for understanding the Court's role in our society and for exploring the claims for an ICT. Though we recognize that our specific categories may not be concurred in by all, the development of a principled conception of the Court's role is essential to analysis of the claims for an ICT. The only constructive way to criticize our criteria is, we submit, to develop alternative ones. We invite others into the thicket.

Chapter 8

The Criteria Applied

Study Design

The NYU Supreme Court Project provides a concrete empirical examination of the Court's workload using the criteria developed in the previous chapter. It examines all of the cases that the Supreme Court agreed to hear (201) and all of the "paid" cases that the Court refused to hear (1860) during the 1982 Term. The 201 cases the Court agreed to hear include those cases in which review was granted with oral argument (169) and those in which the judgment was summarily affirmed (24) or reversed (8). Counting petitions or jurisdictional statements arising from a lower court decision as one case, we examined a total of 164 cases accepted for review. We have not considered cases in which judgment was vacated and the matter remanded for lower court consideration, as these cannot be considered decisions on the merits. We chose to study the cases the Court agreed to hear during the Term, rather than the cases it actually heard, because we wanted to replicate as nearly as possible the case selection process that occurs during a particular Term. The 1860 paid cases the Court refused to hear refer to petitions for certiorari denied review and jurisdictional statements filed on appeal and dismissed by the Court. Appeals that were summarily affirmed or reversed are treated as cases in which review was granted. The study does not consider other types of petitions acted upon by the Court, such as petitions for writs of mandamus or prohibition, or applications for stays of execution. Nor have we included the in forma pauperis petitions denied review during the 1982 Term. We are not aware of any claim that a significant number of these cases is being improperly denied review because of the Court's workload.

Ours is not a study of trends in the Court's workload. We focus on one year only, but we chose the 1982 Term advisedly. First, during that Term several Justices expressed concern about the workload problem. It is reasonable to assume, therefore, that in the 1982 Term the Justices were sensitive to the size of the workload and, consequently, were especially cautious in granting review. Moreover, during the 1982 Term the Court agreed to hear only 169 cases with oral argument—a sharp reduction from 203 in the previous Term. Because the Court presumably was exercising greater care in the case selection process and greater parsimony with its resources than in previous years, this period provides an ideal test for our hypothesis. If the Court's increased workload is forcing it to deny review in cases that it should hear, the problem of improper denials should be especially acute in a year in which relatively few cases have been granted.

Have we picked a period in which the Court may have gone out of its way to hear intercourt conflicts, and in more normal times is the incidence of unresolved conflicts likely to be higher? We think not, for there is no reason to suppose that the Court was particularly concerned with resolving conflicts during this Term; the findings reported here are quite consistent with those of Casper and Posner, and even with the figures in Feeney's study (after redaction to conform to our case selection criteria). But even assuming, for argument's sake, that we have chosen a period producing an artificially low number of unresolved conflicts, this is a virtue rather than a flaw. Such a result would tend to prove our primary point: greater care in case selection will minimize the incidence of unresolved conflicts. Proponents of a new national appellate court must still prove that the Court's supposed attention to conflicts during this Term prevented it from performing other essential functions.

We recognize the hazards of a study limited to a single year.

Aside from the inability to predict future trends or control for the impact of case selections of prior years, the year studied may be atypical for unanticipated reasons. We invite efforts at verification by scholars who would apply our criteria to the dockets of earlier or later Terms.

Using the criteria derived from our view of the Supreme Court's role, we have examined each of the granted cases to determine whether it was a priority case, a discretionary case, or an improvident grant. We examined the 201 granted cases ourselves. Each one is discussed in the project as reported in the *NYU Law Review*. Twenty-two *Law Review* editors and four research assistants examined the 1860 cases denied review. The students determined whether the denied cases presented an intercourt conflict or clash with Supreme Court precedent. The students did not, however, try to determine whether the cases denied review were within other categories of the priority docket or the discretionary docket. The students' findings are presented in the *Review,* and cases having the strongest claims to a place on the priority docket or otherwise presenting inter-esting insights into the workload problem are discussed at length in the student Notes published as part of the project. Our position on each of the granted cases and the student's position on each of the denied cases—2061 in all—are summarized either in a textual discussion or in an appendix entry in that journal.

In examining the 2061 cases, we worked with a complete library of the certiorari petitions and responses, provided through the courtesy of Chief Justice Warren E. Burger and the Law Library of Columbia University. We also examined the lower court opinions and, where a conflict was alleged, the opinions alleged to be in conflict. In evaluating the granted cases, we did *not* consider the opinions eventually issued by the Supreme Court. We attempted, as far as possible, to assess the cases *ex ante*—as the Justices are forced to do. We did, how-ever, examine the opinions, if available, to determine whether any apparently improvident grants were in fact vehicles for ad-vances in the development of federal law.

One final point. We have rejected on grounds of practicability certain controls of the sort found in some social science investigations. We are aware of the existence of social science literature on rater bias.[1] This literature identifies several kinds of biases potentially applicable here. For example, a hindsight assimilation bias might occur because information provided to the rater in advance (e.g., that a given case was granted or denied review) might predispose the rater to a particular result (confirming the grant or denial). Or, for another example, a motivation bias might occur because the rater has a conscious or subconscious incentive to obtain a particular result. Although we welcome further studies by social scientists applying our case selection criteria under conditions that would control for such purported biases, we do not believe that such controls were necessary to our study, for the following reasons.

First, and foremost, we were not engaged in a survey of the preferences or perceptions of the raters (the two law professors and two dozen students). The study we were engaged in involved a conventional exercise for legally trained professionals: application of legal principles (our criteria) to a set of cases (the cases granted and denied review in the 1982 Term).

Since our study provides a comprehensive explanation of the legal principles employed, and a full exposition, in terms understandable and verifiable by other legally trained professionals, of the application of those principles to *every* case, errors or biases, if any, would appear on the record. One does not have to believe that all legal decisionmaking is neutral to believe that legal discourse is largely bounded by principle and that one legal professional, if properly trained, can evaluate the application by another of principle to fact. In designing our study, moreover, we adopted special measures to ensure that the criteria would be applied consistently and accurately to the cases— for example, each application of the criteria by the students was reviewed anew by two other student editors.

Second, in our study the possible assimilation and motivation biases tended to work at cross-purposes with each other and arguably tended to cancel each other out. The student authors, while they may have been laboring under an assimilation bias to find proper denials of review (consistent with our hypothesis), were also independently motivated to find *improper* denials of review (inconsistent with our hypothesis) for discussion in their Notes. And, though the law professors had a subconscious incentive to find improvidently granted cases (consistent with our hypothesis), we may also have been operating under an assimilation bias that would have caused us to second what the Court had done and view the cases as having been *properly* granted (inconsistent with our hypothesis). Powerful corroborative evidence for our belief that these alleged biases tended to cancel each other out is found in the striking parallel between the students' findings and those of Casper and Posner and even Feeney (after appropriate adjustments for differences in criteria). Neither of these studies—the former disputing the unresolved-conflicts claim, the latter supporting it—controlled for rater bias.

Third, we observe that the case for the ICT has been built on a series of impressionistic studies and assertions that enjoy none of the safeguards and self-validating qualities of our study, let alone social science "controls". Even the social science literature—including the major "cue" studies—does not uniformly apply controls for rater bias.[2] Cue studies inquire whether there is a correlation between cases granted review and several cues, such as the existence of a disagreement in the lower courts, the existence of a civil liberty issue, or the presence of the Government as a party. Typically, the cues are not self-defining; indeed, there is a general failure in this literature to develop baseline definitions. Both the terms employed as cues and their application to particular cases are subject to rater biases of the types discussed above. For example, there appears to be considerable confusion in the cue studies over what is meant by disagreement among the lower courts.[3] Unlike the cue studies, our project used trained researchers conducting evaluations that can be verified by other trained professionals and students of the Court.

Analysis of the 1982 Term

The Court granted review in 164 cases during the 1982 Term.[4] As table 1 indicates, 48 percent (seventy-eight) were on the priority docket, 28 percent (forty-seven) were on the discretion-

Table 1. Breakdown of Docket, 1982 Term

	Number	Percentage
Priority	78	48
Discretionary	47	28
Improvident	39	24
Total	164	100

ary docket, and 24 percent (thirty-nine) were improvident grants.

Tables 2 through 4 show that the relative size of the three categories changes only slightly if one excludes summary dispositions, appeals, or cases that most likely would not have been reviewed had the Court's obligatory jurisdiction been abolished. Assuming that the 1982 Term is representative, nearly one-half of the cases the Court hears are cases it must hear in a given year (the priority docket); over one-quarter are other cases it properly may but need not hear (the discretionary docket); and about one-quarter are cases that it should not hear (improvident grants).

As table 5 shows, of the thirty-four appeals heard on the merits and not dismissed during the 1982 Term, almost one-half belonged on the priority docket, and only 21 percent (seven) were improvident grants under the criteria of this study. If the Court's obligatory jurisdiction had been abolished, however, the Court would not have heard three of the priority grants and two of the discretionary grants, in addition to the seven improvidently granted cases, so that the Court's docket would have been reduced by 7 percent (twelve cases). Aside from these modest gains, repeal of obligatory jurisdiction would also have freed the Court from the burden of having to act on each of the appeals and from the dilemma of creating binding precedent by summary disposition.

The Priority Docket

The priority docket is summarized in table 6:

Of the seventy-eight cases on the priority docket, 73 percent (fifty-seven) involved intercourt conflicts. Only nine cases in-

Table 2. Plenary Docket, 1982 Term
(excludes summary dispositions)

	Number	Percentage
Priority	69	48
Discretionary	42	29
Improvident	32	22
Total	143	99

Table 3. Certiorari Docket, 1982 Term
(excludes appeals)

	Number	Percentage
Priority	62	47
Discretionary	36	27
Improvident	33	25
Total	131	99

volved federal decisions invalidating state statutes, and seven cases involved federal decisions invalidating federal statutes. Three were appeals involving the invalidation of statutes, but the courts in these cases did not clearly invalidate the statutes;[5] these grants are more convincingly grounded on a conflict rationale.

The incidence of intercourt conflict is summarized in table 7. The high proportion of conflict cases on the Court's docket— 42 percent of the cases the Court heard during the Term— suggests that the Court does take seriously its conflict-resolution responsibility.

Of the fifty-seven conflict cases on the priority docket, fifty-two presented conflicts involving three or more courts. Of the five that presented two-court conflicts, four were in the tax, labor, and civil rights areas, and were placed on the priority docket because of their significant potential for forum shopping or impact on planning by multicircuit actors.[6]

Five cases—6 percent of the priority docket—presented conflicts with Supreme Court precedent. Of course, virtually every case heard by the Court could plausibly be viewed as conflicting with the Court's past rulings. The law develops through dialectical evolution; cases appear on the scene to extend or contract

Table 4. Breakdown of Docket, 1982 Term
(excludes obligatory jurisdiction)[a]

	Number	Percentage
Priority	78	50
Discretionary	47	30
Improvident	32	20
Total	157	100

[a]Excluding cases that the Court most likely would not have heard had obligatory jurisdiction been abolished.

Table 5. Appellate Docket, 1982 Term
(excludes petitions for certiorari)

	Number	Percentage
Priority	16[a]	47
Discretionary	11[b]	32
Improvident	7[c]	21
Total	34	100

[a]Nos. 81–2302, 81–2385, and 82–857 involved the application of settled principles and in all likelihood would not have been heard had obligatory jurisdiction been abolished.
[b]No. 81–2008 et al. involved the application of settled principles and in all likelihood would not have been heard had obligatory jurisdiction been abolished. No. 82–874 involved an issue pertaining to the Court's obligatory jurisdiction.
[c]Nos. 82–284, 82–952 et al., 82–39, 82–360, 82–1080, 82–1141, and 82–1408 involved the application of settled principles and in all likelihood would not have been heard had obligatory jurisdiction been abolished.

existing doctrine. Generally, this process should take place at the lower court level until full percolation of the issues has occurred. Nevertheless, the Court should not tolerate lower court rulings that make bald or thinly disguised attempts to circumvent controlling principles.[7] Such cases are relatively rare; the inconsistency is usually somewhat less direct and obvious.

There are situations in which percolation has occurred and the Court may properly intervene to review a decision plainly at odds with its past rulings. An obvious example would be a case presenting both a two-court conflict and a substantial claim of conflict with Supreme Court precedent. A case in point is *Muel-*

Table 6. Analysis of Priority Docket, 1982 Term

	Number	Percentage
Intercourt conflicts	57[a]	73
Resolutions of interbranch disputes	7[b]	9
Federal invalidations of state statutes	9[c]	12
Conflicts with Supreme Court precedent	5	6
Total	78	100

[a]Two-court conflicts in Nos. 81–1985, 82–411, 82–599, and 82–774 merited priority treatment because of the potential for forum shopping; No. 81–2147 et al. involved a two-court conflict in which further doctrinal development was unlikely. All other cases involved at least three-court conflicts.
   Although petitions in some cases did not allege conflicts, they were counted as grants on a conflict rationale if they raised the same issue as petitions demonstrating at least three-court conflicts.
[b]Six of these cases involved federal invalidation of federal statutes. No. 82–1186 et al. sought review of a Second Circuit decision that in effect invalidated the Warsaw Convention.
[c]Nos. 82–695 and 82–1085 involved successful "as applied" challenges to state statutes. However, these grants are more convincingly founded on an intercourt conflict rationale.

ler v. Allen,[8] in which the Eighth Circuit upheld a Minnesota statute that provided taxpayers with a deduction for the tuition, textbook, and transportation expenses of students enrolled in elementary and high schools, whether public or parochial. The appeals court acknowledged the contrary ruling of the First Circuit[9] and the problematical status of the Minnesota statute under *Committee for Public Education & Religious Liberty v. Nyquist.*[10] Nevertheless, *Nyquist* was distinguishable, in the Eighth Circuit's view, because the Minnesota statute applied to parents of public school children as well as parochial school children, and offered a benefit tied to actual school-related expenditures.[11] Given the two-court conflict, the similarity between the Minnesota statute and the statute invalidated by the Court in *Nyquist,* and the questionable line drawn by the Eighth Circuit, a priority grant here was plainly indicated.

   Dirks v. Securities & Exchange Commission[12] is another ex-

Table 7. Intercourt Conflicts, 1982 Term

		Number	Percentage (base = 164)
Three-court (or more) conflicts		52	32
Priority	52		
Discretionary	0		
Improvident	0		
Two-court conflicts		17	10
Priority	5		
Discretionary	7[a]		
Improvident	5[b]		
Total cases presenting multiple court conflicts		69	42
Cases not involving conflicts		95	58

[a]See Nos. 81–2125, 81–2149, 81–2337 et al., 82–23, 82–500, 82–849, and 82–1474.
[b]See Nos. 81–2169, 82–472, 82–1041, 82–1330, and 82–1453 et al.

ample; here, the District of Columbia Circuit's ruling was exceedingly difficult to reconcile with the Court's reluctance, in *Chiarella v. United States,*[13] to recognize a general duty on the part of noncorporate insiders to forego market transactions because of the possession of material, nonpublic information. Given the likelihood that the District of Columbia Circuit would be the principal forum for SEC enforcement litigation, and the impact of *Dirks* on planning by multicircuit securities analysts operating in a necessarily national market, the Court was justified in granting review to determine whether *Dirks* could stand in the wake of *Chiarella.*

The Discretionary Docket

Table 8 offers an analysis of the discretionary docket.

VEHICLES FOR MAJOR ADVANCES IN THE DEVELOPMENT OF FEDERAL LAW. Fourteen cases (30 percent) presented vehicles for advances in the development of federal law. Under the criteria of

Table 8. Analysis of Discretionary Docket, 1982 Term

	Number	Percentage
Structural suspicion[a]	8	17
Vertical federalism[b]	5	10.5
Significant interference with federal executive, responsibility[c]	13	27.5
Vehicles for advances in the development of federal law[d]	14	30
Miscellaneous	7	15
Ruling from a court of exclusive jurisdiction[e]	(1)	
Serious risk of dislocation[f]	(1)	
Supervisory power[g]	(1)	
Ruling implicating Supreme Court's jurisdiction[h]	(2)	
Ruling related to recently decided cases[i]	(2)	
Total (excludes miscellaneous)	47	100

[a] See Nos. 81–2110, 81–2394, 82–11, 82–500, 82–556, 82–585 et al., 82–708, 82–1127, and 82–1565

[b] See Nos. 81–2159, 81–2257, 82–401, 82–1127, and 82–1253.

[c] See Nos. 81–984 (foreign policy concerns), 81–1889 et al., 81–2125, 81–2337 et al., 81–2399 et al., 82–29, 82–34 et al., 82–282, 82–354 et al., 82–432, 82–524 et al., 82–1005 et al., and 82–1371.

[d] See Nos. 81–757 et al., 81–2386 et al., 82–23, 82–65, 82–485, 82–675, 82–849, 82–1031, 82–1150, 82–1260, 82–1367, 82–1401, 82–1474, and 82–1666.

[e] See No. 82–1071.

[f] See No. 81–2149.

[g] See No. 82–91.

[h] See Nos. 82–874 and 82–1448.

[i] See No. 81–2000 et al. and 82–935 et al.

this study, it is not sufficient that the Court wishes to consider a particular issue, even if that issue has been previously identified and reserved for decision. Appropriate vehicles arise when (1) prior reservation of an issue has generated unexpected and undesired doctrinal development to which only the Court can put a stop; (2) lower court rulings on an issue display a level of doctrinal incoherence and disarray falling short of an outright conflict yet providing sufficient percolation to permit Supreme Court intervention; (3) the Court wishes to reconsider a well-established principle and, after identifying its willingness to re-evaluate prior doctrine, sets the law on a new path; or (4) in the interest of efficiency and to benefit from comparative evalua-tion of an issue, the Court hears a case because it raises issues related to a case already properly granted review.

Examples of each situation can be found among the fourteen discretionary vehicle grants. In *DelCostello v. International Brotherhood of Teamsters*[14] and *United Steelworkers of America v. Flowers*,[15] the Court was presented with an opportunity to decide which statute of limitations should govern an employee's fair representation suit against his union. In *United Parcel Service, Inc. v. Mitchell*,[16] the Court had endorsed the application of state statutes of limitations for vacating arbitration awards in employee-employer disputes. However, the *Mitchell* decision never reached, and can be said to have reserved decision on,[17] the question of which statute of limitations should govern an employee's claim against his union. Although a square post-*Mitchell* conflict had yet to surface over which limitations pe-riod should apply—the state statute of limitations or the six-month period provided by section 10(b) of the National Labor Relations Act[18]—the prior decisions in this area had produced considerable doctrinal incoherence.[19] Most of this incoherence was directly attributable to *Mitchell,* which created the anoma-lous possibility that different limitations periods would govern an employee's suits against his union and against his employer, though both suits arose out of the same discharge. Only the Supreme Court could decisively clarify the intended reach of *Mitchell. DelCostello* and *Flowers* provided the Court with an opportunity to do so. Similarly, in *Roadway Express, Inc. v. Warren*,[20] the Court appropriately granted review to attempt again to develop a majority position, found to be elusive in *Thomas v. Washington Gas & Light Co.*,[21] on a full-faith-and-credit issue of recurring significance.

Allen v. Wright[22] is an example of the second type of vehicle grant. There the Court granted review to determine which of two seemingly conflicting lines of Supreme Court decisions would govern standing to compel federal agency enforcement of antidiscrimination laws. Similarly, before *Copperweld Corp. v. Independence Tube Corp.*,[23] the lower courts had staked out a variety of positions on the appropriate treatment under the federal antitrust laws of a conspiracy between a parent corporation and its wholly owned subsidiary. There had been extensive lower court percolation, which commentators unanimously maintained left the law in a state of hopeless disarray and confusion.[24]

Where the percolation process has resulted in doctrinal incoherence, the Court need not await a square conflict to review a ruling that is difficult to reconcile with Supreme Court doctrine. In *Local No. 82, Furniture & Piano Moving v. Crowley*,[25] the First Circuit continued twenty years of judicial effort to clarify *Calhoon v. Harvey*[26] and to reconcile the private right of action for violations of Title I of the Labor-Management Reporting and Disclosure Act of 1959 (LMRDA)[27] with the Secretary of Labor's exclusive enforcement authority over violations of the union election safeguards set out in Title IV of the LMRDA.[28] The First Circuit ruled that the district court retained authority to remedy Title I violations occurring during a union election until the ballots were actually counted. In light of the confusion remaining after extensive lower court consideration of the appropriate judicial role in cases presenting arguable violations of both Title I and Title IV, and the problems created by the unstable line drawn by the First Circuit, which made jurisdiction turn on whether a party could sue before the ballots were counted, a discretionary grant was justified in *Crowley*.

Marsh v. Chambers[29] illustrates the third type of vehicle grant. The case involved the constitutionality of a state legislature's retention of a sectarian minister to open its legislative sessions. Apparently, the Court granted review to reconsider the standards for establishment clause scrutiny set out in *Lemon v. Kurtzman*.[30] Similarly, the decision rendered in *Copperweld* indicated that the Court was prepared to reconsider its prior decisions and recognize that a corporation and its wholly owned subsidiaries are incapable of conspiring with each other for the purposes of antitrust law.[31]

Keeton v. Hustler Magazine, Inc.[32] is an example of the fourth type of vehicle grant. Although *Keeton* standing alone might have been an improvident grant, it raised issues related to *Calder v. Jones.*[33] *Calder* was a proper discretionary grant to resolve doctrinal incoherence in the lower courts. The Court appropriately considered *Keeton* along with *Calder* in an effort to clarify the assertion of *in personam* jurisdiction over writers, editors, and publishers of multistate publications charged with libel or defamation and arguably suable in every state of publication.[34]

SIGNIFICANT INTERFERENCE WITH FEDERAL EXECUTIVE RESPONSIBILITY. The second largest category of the discretionary docket, 27.5 percent (thirteen cases), involved cases presenting a significant interference with executive responsibility. A number of these involved invalidation of federal agency regulations of national applicability.[35] An equal number fell short of invalidating national regulations, but involved rulings posing serious threats of interference with executive responsibility. In the latter cases, either significant percolation of the underlying issue had occurred or the federal government could not readily confine its compliance to the particular jurisdiction. For example, in *Metropolitan Edison Co. v. People Against Nuclear Energy,*[36] the District of Columbia Circuit addressed whether post-traumatic anxieties following nuclear disasters (such as those associated with Three Mile Island) need be considered in environmental impact statements. Although not squarely in conflict with the rulings of the other circuit courts that had rejected mandatory consideration of general psychological effects, the District of Columbia Circuit's novel, dubious reading of the environmental law threatened to impose a significant burden on the federal licensing of nuclear reactors, and there had been ample intercircuit exploration of the underlying issue. Similarly, in *Heckler v. Day,*[37] the Second Circuit considered an issue previously addressed by a number of other circuit courts—the appropriate judicial role in controlling delay in the administration of the Social Security Act's disability program. The Second Circuit's imposition of deadlines in disability adjudication was bound to affect other jurisdictions, not only as a matter of precedent, but

also because of the need to reallocate scarce adjudicative resources, perhaps from cases in other circuits, to effect compliance with the Second Circuit's deadlines.

STRUCTURAL SUSPICION. The next largest category—eight cases
(17 percent)—involved state court rulings sustaining state action against federal challenges. In this context, there is a structural basis for suspicion of the forum's receptivity to the federal
claim. In the interest of preserving the supremacy of federal
law, the Court may act in advance of a conflict or significant
lower court percolation.

Typically, the structural suspicion factor does not stand
alone. For example, in *Southland Corp. v. Keating*,[38] a two-
court conflict provided additional justification for a grant to
review the California Supreme Court's refusal to find the Federal Arbitration Act preemptive of a state regulatory statute's
anti-arbitration policy. Occasionally, a serious claim of conflict
with Supreme Court precedent is present in a state decision
rejecting a federal claim. For example, in *Mennonite Board of
Missions v. Adams*,[39] the Indiana intermediate appellate court's
holding that due process required no more than notice by publication to mortgagees of a pending tax sale did not sit well with
the Supreme Court's strictures against such constructive notice
in *Mullane v. Central Hanover Bank & Trust Co.*[40] and its progeny. In other cases, a state court sustained plainly protectionist
legislation, as in *Bacchus Imports, Ltd. v. Freitas*.[41] In sum, the
Court may act to uphold the supremacy of federal norms even
though the occasion may not otherwise be ideal for a definitive
declaration of federal law.

VERTICAL FEDERALISM. Five cases (10.5 percent) contained
claims involving considerations of vertical federalism, in which
a federal court has invalidated state action. As with the structural suspicion category, the vertical federalism element also
tends not to stand alone. Thus, in *Solem v. Helm*,[42] there had
been considerable lower court percolation, though no square
conflict. The Eighth Circuit's ruling, voiding the life sentence
without parole eligibility of a habitual offender who had
pleaded guilty to a felony charge of uttering a "no account"

check for $100, clashed with the Court's recent Eighth Amendment jurisprudence in *Rummel v. Estelle*[43] and *Hutto v. Davis.*[44] Several cases involved federal rulings finding federal preemption of areas of significant state regulatory involvement, as in *Silkwood v. Kerr-McGee Corp.*[45] and *Bill Johnson's Restaurants, Inc. v. NLRB.*[46]

In criminal proceedings, as previously noted, the mere fact that a federal court voids a state conviction on federal habeas corpus review does not justify a discretionary grant, for Congress specifically contemplated such "dialectical federalism" as a fairly regular feature of our criminal justice system.[47] It is only when the state court persists in its view after the initial federal habeas reversal that the occasion may arise for a discretionary grant.[48]

MISCELLANEOUS DISCRETIONARY GRANTS. No one theme unites the remaining seven cases (15 percent of the discretionary docket). We were surprised to find only one case in which a grant was justified solely on the ground that the decision was issued by a court of exclusive jurisdiction.[49] Only one case appears to have been premised principally on the supervisory authority rationale: the Court granted review in *INS v. Phinpathya,*[50] apparently to undo the Ninth Circuit's persistent efforts to dilute the "continuous physical presence" requirement for suspension of deportation. One case fell in the discretionary category for decisions involving the application of settled Supreme Court precedent to situations involving a risk of serious dislocation: in *Solem v. Stumes,*[51] the Court granted review to decide the question of the retroactive application of *Edwards v. Arizona.*[52] Two grants were premised on lower court rulings implicating the Court's appellate jurisdiction.[53] Finally, one case[54] was apparently held over as a case related to *INS v. Chadha,*[55] which had been decided the previous Term.[56]

The Improvident Grants

The improvident grants are analyzed in table 9.

Out of 164 cases, there were thirty-nine improvident grants, or 24 percent of the total. If one looks only at the 143 cases receiving plenary review, table 2 indicates that there were

Table 9. Analysis of Improvident Grants, 1982 Term

Extent of Overgranting	Number	Percentage
Total improvident grants	39	24 (base = 164)
Excluding summary dispositions	32	22 (base = 143)
Discounting influence of obligatory jurisdiction	32	20 (base = 157)

Extent of Reversal[a]			
Affirmed	16	(42)	41 (33)
Reversed (includes affirmed in part and reversed in part)	21	(75)	54 (59)
Vacated (includes affirmed in part and vacated in part)	1	(10)	2.5 (8)
Dismissed	1	(0)	2.5 (0)

Extent of reversal excluding Appeals (6)			
Affirmed	10	(42)	30 (33)
Reversed	21	(75)	64 (59)
Vacated	1	(10)	3 (8)
Dismissed	1	(0)	3 (0)

Categories of Improvident Grants[b]			
Civil	23	(129)	59 (80)
Criminal (including habeas corpus cases)	16	(33)	41 (0)
State	7	(29)	18 (18)
Federal	32	(133)	82 (82)

Origins of Improvident Grants (from federal courts)	
3-judge district court	5
1st Circuit	3
2d Circuit	2
3d Circuit	1
4th Circuit	3
5th Circuit	4
6th Circuit	2
7th Circuit	1
8th Circuit	0
9th Circuit	4
10th Circuit	1
11th Circuit	2
D.C. Circuit	4

Table 9 (cont.)

Causes of Overgranting	Number	Percentage
Obligatory jurisdiction[c]	6	15
State court invalidation of state action[d]	6	15
Deference to Solicitor General[e]	4	10
Inappropriate vehicle[f]	4	10
Two-court conflicts[g]	4	10
False conflicts[h]	5	13
Premature reconsideration of Supreme Court precedent in light of recent Supreme Court rulings[i]	2	5
Error Correction	8	21
Unusual rulings[j]	3	
Expansive ruling[k]	1	
Fact-specific error correction[l]	4	

[a]*Harvard Law Review*'s statistics for disposition of cases reviewed on writ of certiorari and decided by full opinion, 97 Harv. L. Rev. 299 (1983), in parentheses.
[b]*Harvard Law Review*'s breakdown for dispositions with full opinions, 97 Harv. L. Rev. 302 (1983), in parentheses.
[c]See Nos. 82–39, 82–284, 82–360, 82–952, 82–1080, and 82–1141.
[d]See Nos. 81–1843, 81–1857, 81–1859, 81–1893, 81–2318, and 82–357.
[e]See Nos. 81–1891, 82–215, 82–242, and 82–1326 et al.
[f]See Nos. 82–52, 82–738, 82–1095, and 82–1135.
[g]See Nos. 81–2169, 82–472, 82–1041, and 82–1453 et al.
[h]See Nos. 81–1374, 82–63, 82–271, 82–372, and 82–1330.
[i]See Nos. 82–1246 and 82–1479.
[j]See Nos. 82–940, 82–945, and 82–1432.
[k]See No. 81–2332.
[l]See Nos. 81–2066, 82–958, 82–1408, and 82–1496.

thirty-two improvident grants, or 22 percent of the total. And if one excludes all cases that the Court would most likely not have heard were its obligatory jurisdiction abolished, table 4 reveals that there were thirty-two improvident grants, or 20% of the total of 157. However the data are analyzed, nearly one out of every four or five cases that the Court agreed to hear should not have been reviewed under the criteria of this study.

An analysis of the thirty-nine improvident grants by subject matter reveals that twenty-three involved civil claims and sixteen criminal prosecutions (including habeas review). Compared to the *Harvard Law Review*'s breakdown for dispositions with full opinions during the 1982 Term (129 civil and 33 criminal and habeas cases),[57] it is clear that a disproportionate number of improvident grants arose out of criminal prosecutions or federal habeas review. To some extent, this can be attributed to the criteria of this study, which emphasize the importance of intercourt conflicts for placement on the priority docket, discount the state-federal disagreement in particular habeas cases, and reject a state court's invalidation of state action on federal grounds, standing alone, as an appropriate occasion for discretionary review. The reader who agrees with these criteria, cannot escape the conclusion that the Court is too quick to grant review in criminal cases.

Table 9 indicates that federal courts were the principal source of "overgranting." No one federal circuit appears to stand out, although the Fifth, Ninth, and District of Columbia Circuits each accounted for four improvident grants, for a total of twelve (31 percent).

In appendix A we provide a brief discussion of each of the improvident grants for the reader who would like to see our reasoning on every one of the thirty-nine cases. The discussion here (and in appendix A) is necessarily summary; interested readers are encouraged to consult the appendix entries, which are found in the full study as reproduced in the *New York University Law Review*.

ILLUSTRATIVE IMPROVIDENT GRANTS. In *Hishon v. King & Spalding*[58] petitioner claimed that respondent, a large law firm that operated as a general partnership, violated Title VII of the Civil Rights Act of 1964[59] by refusing to invite her to join the partnership although she had been an employee of respondent for six years and had performed satisfactory work. This, she alleged, was due to discrimination on account of her sex in violation of Title VII. The district court dismissed the complaint, holding

Title VII to be inapplicable to partnership decisions, and the Eleventh Circuit affirmed.

At one level, an argument could be made that this is an ideal case for Supreme Court review. The issue posed—whether Title VII applies to partnership decisions—is surely one of national significance, and the decision below was, in our view, palpably incorrect. Ultimately, the Supreme Court unanimously reversed the decision of the Eleventh Circuit.

Under our criteria, however, this was an improvident grant. The Court should not intervene simply to undo error below. There was a conflict alleged in the petition, but the single case conflicting with the Eleventh Circuit's opinion was a district court decision in the Second Circuit that had never been appealed; a definitive position had not yet been taken by another court of appeals. None of the other criteria that would make this case a priority or discretionary grant were present.

Hishon, even if wrongly decided, should not have been taken up by the Court until further percolation had occurred. It is entirely possible that other circuits might have disagreed with the Eleventh Circuit and that the Eleventh Circuit itself would eventually have reversed or modified its position without any action by the Court. Further lower court percolation would have generated a more complete account of the range of possible factual settings and, hopefully, a more precise analytical framework to govern adjudication of partnership-denial claims. These inputs would have been available to the Court and might have influenced its rationale in ruling on the issue of Title VII coverage. The advantages of percolation are lost if the Court prematurely decides to resolve "notorious" cases such as *Hishon.* In addition, if the Court reaches out to correct error in cases like *Hishon,* it fuels the perception that a denial of discretionary review connotes agreement in some sense with the ruling below, which, in turn, tightens pressure on the Justices not to let error below go uncorrected in other cases.

California v. Ramos[60] involved a challenge to a California statute that required the judge presiding at the penalty phase of a capital case to inform the jury that a sentence of life without possibility of parole may be commuted or modified by the governor. The California Supreme Court held that this instruction (known as the "Briggs instruction") violated the defendant's rights under the Eighth and Fourteenth Amendments. The court reasoned that the instruction improperly invited the jury to consider the speculative possibility of future commutation rather than the character of the defendant and the circumstances of the crime. It also found the instruction misleading on the ground that it incorrectly implied that a sentence of death could not be commuted, leading the jurors to believe that only by imposing the death sentence could they ensure that the defendant would never be released from custody.

Ramos is a classic case of state invalidation of state action—a type of case that does not belong on either priority or discretionary docket in the absence of a fully percolated conflict. There was no federal-state conflict presented, and the decision of the court below would have had precedential effect in only one state. It was alleged that the ruling of the California Supreme Court conflicted "in principle" with several cases in other jurisdictions and with a previous decision of the United States Supreme Court, but we found no conflict at all. Nor was this an appropriate vehicle grant, since there was no doctrinal incoherence in the lower courts calling for authoritative Supreme Court guidance. Even if one were to accept the notion that death penalty cases should be given special consideration in the case selection process—a view we do not endorse—here the court below had reversed the death sentence. That a majority of the Court perceived that the lower court decision was in error cannot justify its decision to grant review.

In *McKaskle v. Wiggins*,[61] respondent—who was charged in state court with armed robbery—requested permission to conduct his own defense. This request was granted, but the trial court also appointed two attorneys as standby counsel. During the trial, one of the standby attorneys began to take an active role, sometimes against the wishes of respondent, who protested against the lawyer's behavior. The court refused to instruct counsel to remain on the sidelines; instead, it told the respondent that he was going to receive counsel's aid whether he wanted it or not. Respondent was convicted and sentenced to life imprisonment as a recidivist. After exhausting his appellate and state habeas remedies, respondent filed a petition for federal habeas relief. The district court denied the petition, but the Fifth Circuit reversed, holding that the conduct of the standby counsel and the trial court's tolerance of that conduct deprived respondent of his right to conduct his own defense, guaranteed by *Faretta v. California.*[62]

Although petitioner argued that Supreme Court review was justified because of a conflict, we found none. Nor can the decision to review this case be justified on the ground that it presented a vehicle to advance the development of the law in this area. It is true that the Court dropped a footnote in *Faretta* to the effect that "a State may—even over objection by the accused—appoint a 'standby counsel' to aid the accused if and when the accused requests help." But this footnote does not allude to the problems resulting from an intrusively aggressive standby counsel. In any event, there was no demonstration of doctrinal incoherence or of sufficient percolation to justify a vehicle grant to establish guidelines for the participation of standby counsel. The Court's disagreement with the result below (it reversed by a six-to-three vote) and desire to make a pronouncement on the law in this area does not justify a grant.

Finally, in *Bose Corp. v. Consumers Union of United States, Inc.*[63] petitioner, a manufacturer of a stereo loudspeaker system, sued respondent, the publisher of a magazine that contained an article evaluating stereo systems, for product disparagement under the Lanham Act. The district court found that petitioner had met its burden of proving that respondent's statements were disparaging and that one of its statements was false, and that petitioner had shown that respondent's statements were made with knowledge of their falsity or with reckless disregard for their truth or falsity, as required by *New York Times v. Sullivan.*[64] On appeal, however, the First Circuit reversed, holding that petitioner's proof on the issue of malice did not satisfy the "clear and convincing proof" test established by *Gertz v. Robert Welch, Inc.*[65] The court did not hold the findings of the court below to be "clearly erroneous"—the standard for reversal of trial court findings under Federal Rule of Civil Procedure 52(a); rather, it undertook its own *de novo* review of the record in making its determination on the issue of malice.

Petitioner alleged that the decision below conflicted with a Ninth Circuit case, but the Ninth Circuit (just like the First Circuit in *Bose*) had conducted a *de novo* review, so that there was no conflict on that question. Petitioner also alleged that the First Circuit's decision conflicted with two recent Supreme Court decisions interpreting Rule 52(a), *Inwood Laboratories, Inc. v. Ives Laboratories, Inc.*,[66] and *Pullman-Standard v. Swint*.[67] But these cases—while stating that Rule 52(a) "does not make exceptions or purport to exclude certain categories of factual findings from the obligation of a court of appeals to accept a district court's findings unless clearly erroneous"— were *not* libel cases. The Court's repeated references to the "clear and convincing" standard of review in *Gertz* and earlier decisions and the Court's own seemingly *de novo* review of "constitutional fact" determinations in libel cases governed by *Sullivan* make it difficult to argue that the decision of the First Circuit was plainly in conflict with Supreme Court precedent. Indeed, the Court ultimately affirmed by a vote of six to three. *Bose* involved the claim that recent Supreme Court rulings (*Inwood* and *Swint*) had implicitly overturned well-established precedent (post-*Sullivan* practice)—analytically a "next case" situation that should have undergone percolation.

Patterns of Overgranting

ERROR CORRECTION. We initially believed that much of the overgranting phenomenon could be attributed to the Court's supposed penchant to grant review even without structural justification whenever four or more Justices simply do not like the result below. This might explain eight (21 percent) of the thirty-nine improvident grants (including the three summary reversals). For example, the grant in *Hishon v. King & Spalding*[68] may have turned solely on the Court's perception that an error had been committed. Similarly, *California v. Ramos*[69] is an example in which the Supreme Court decided to review a case involving a state court's expansion of a federal constitutional right beyond the limits that the Court felt were justified. In our view, the

Court should not grant review simply to ward off the possibility that the uninformed public will feel the Court is validating the result below by declining discretionary review. Grants like *Hishon* and *Ramos* fuel rather than stem such expectations.

It is not clear, however, that the error-correction thesis fully explains the extent of overgranting. A comparison of the *Harvard Law Review*'s statistics for disposition of cases reviewed on certiorari and disposed of by full opinion with the extent of reversal in the improvident grants studied here[70] reveals that these improvident grants were reversed no more frequently than the overall certiorari docket. Admittedly, if the six summary affirmances that came to the Court as appeals are excluded, a divergence does appear, with a 64 percent reversal rate for the improvident grants as compared to 54 percent for the overall certiorari docket. We doubt, however, whether this difference, whatever its statistical significance, proves the error-correction thesis.

We suspect that simply focusing on the actual disposition of the case understates the role that disagreement with the result below plays in the case selection process. Although four Justices may vote to grant review to correct error, they may be unable to form a Court majority for reversal. Moreover, we expect (and would hope) that even Justices initially inclined to reverse (and voting to grant certiorari on that basis) may modify their views in light of the briefs and arguments in a given case.

It is difficult to say anything conclusive about the error-correction thesis from this type of gross numerical comparison. We now turn to some of the other factors which, in combination with visceral reaction to error, may have increased the likelihood of a grant of certiorari in these thirty-nine cases.

STATE COURT INVALIDATION OF STATE ACTION. Along with the six obligatory appeals, the largest category of improvident grants after "error correction" involved state court rulings invalidating state action. This statistic confirms a trend identified by Justices Brennan[71] and Stevens[72] and our colleague Lawrence Sager:[73] the Court is increasingly concerned with state court activism in the name of the Constitution. We agree that the Court may properly grant review to resolve intercourt conflicts in such

situations. However, there is no structural justification for issuing definitive declarations of federal law—here, constitutional
law—in advance of sufficient lower court percolation.[74]

DEFERENCE TO THE SOLICITOR GENERAL. The Court's deference to
the Solicitor General's views is a third factor warranting consideration. In the 1981 Term, 96 percent of the petitions receiving
the amicus support of the Solicitor General were granted
review.[75] Where the Government is the petitioner, the Court
may be even more deferential. For want of any other justification, three of the improvident grants may be attributed principally to the Government's affirmative recommendations. All
three involved appellate decisions of first impression.[76] A fourth
case[77] under this category involved an alleged two-court conflict
that, in our view, does not withstand analysis, and ultimately
led to unanimous affirmance by the Court.

TREATMENT OF CONFLICTS. Nine of the improvident grants may
be attributed to the Court's treatment of allegations of intercourt conflict. In three of these cases—*Blum v. Stenson*,[78] *Chardon v. Soto*,[79] and *Federal Trade Commission v. Grolier,
Inc.*[80]—the Court apparently perceived conflicts that we could
not find. *United States v. Whiting Pools*[81] can also be added to
this list. The other five cases, *Haring v. Prosise*,[82] *Russello v.
United States*,[83] *Thigpen v. Roberts*,[84] *Dickman v. Commissioner*,[85] and *Badaracco v. Commissioner*,[86] involved two-court conflicts that we found were tolerable under the criteria of this
study. In *Haring*, the conflict was with a ten-year-old circuit
ruling, and the Fourth Circuit's approach in the case granted
review was the one most consistent with traditional collateral
estoppel doctrine; the Court unanimously affirmed the judgment in that case. In *Russello*, there was reason to believe that
the contrary position of the Ninth Circuit was in a state of flux,
and basis for doubt that the forfeiture rule in question would
animate forum choice, even if available; the Court affirmed
here as well. In *Thigpen*, the alleged conflict predated the
Court's changes in double jeopardy doctrine in *Illinois v.
Vitale*.[87] *Dickman* and *Badaracco* involved two-court conflicts
without significant potential for forum shopping or implications
for planning by multicircuit actors.

INAPPROPRIATE VEHICLES. At least three of the improvident grants—*Arizona Governing Committee for Tax Deferred Annuity and Deferred Compensation v. Norris,*[88] *Migra v. Warren City School District Board of Education,*[89] and *McKaskle v. Wiggins*[90]—may have been due to a perception on the Justices' part that a case is certworthy merely because it deals with an issue on which the Court had previously reserved decision. Prior reservations of issues occurred in *Norris, Migra,* and *Wiggins.* Prior reservation is not, however, sufficient; a discretionary grant for vehicle purposes requires some showing that the process of lower court percolation cannot confidently be relied upon to work as it should.

Pulley v. Harris[91] did not even present an issue that the Court had previously reserved. There, the Court acted prematurely in rejecting mandatory proportionality review (comparison of the prisoner's sentence to the punishment meted out in similar cases)—an issue on which the Justices could not agree in *Gregg v. Georgia,*[92] *Proffitt v. Florida,*[93] and *Jurek v. Texas,*[94] and which might have benefited from further percolation.

RECONSIDERATION IN LIGHT OF RECENT SUPREME COURT RULINGS WITHOUT AWAITING PERCOLATION. At least two of the improvident grants, *Bose Corp. v. Consumers Union of United States, Inc.*[95] and *Justices of Boston Municipal Court v. Lydon,*[96] stemmed from the Court's desire to resolve alleged conflicts with Supreme Court precedent that arose from lower court efforts to reconcile earlier Supreme Court rulings with more recent ones. These, too, were "next case" issues that should have been permitted to percolate.

In conclusion, we readily concede that much of what we have said rests on a numerically small base. We believe that we have chosen a year in which the Court took great care in selecting cases for review. If the reader disagrees with our judgment in a given case, it should be noted that our list of improvident grants understates the overgranting phenomenon, for at least a half-dozen cases were assigned to the discretionary docket in the interest of maintaining as conservative a statement of our results as would be consistent with our criteria.[97]

If our criteria are accepted, there is reason to believe that significant additional capacity is presently available to the Court for resolution of other cases, for devoting more time to the process of case selection, or for greater deliberation in the process of reaching judgment and writing opinions. This assumes, of course, that the Court is not failing to hear a significant number of cases that should be heard.

Cases Denied Review during the 1982 Term

The *New York University Law Review* examined all of the paid cases denied review during the 1982 Term: 1860 petitions and jurisdictional statements. This figure includes petitions for certiorari denied review and jurisdictional statements dismissed between October 5, 1982 and June 28, 1983. The *Review* examined the denied cases for unresolved intercourt conflicts and conflicts with Supreme Court precedent. The *Review* did not, however, examine the denied cases for any of the other priority docket categories, because the other priority cases generally would arise as obligatory appeals (already considered among the cases granted review). With this exception, then, the *Review* directly investigated whether the Court's workload prevented it from hearing cases that ought to have been heard.[98]

Out of the 1860 petitions examined, the *Review* found thirteen petitions presenting twelve intolerable conflicts that should have been heard under the criteria of the study. The *Review* determined, however, that seven of these petitions were properly denied review for other reasons. Therefore, according to the *Review*'s findings, only five petitions were improperly denied review. All but one of the thirteen petitions involved three-court conflicts. In addition, the *Review* found seven petitions raising two-court conflicts that did not present any significant potential for forum shopping or burden on multi-circuit actors. Table 10 summarizes these findings.

Thus the *Review* found nineteen intercourt conflicts—comprising 1.02 percent of the cases denied review—that the Court failed to resolve during the 1982 Term. These findings are strikingly consistent with those of the Casper and Posner study, which found that only 1.3 percent of the cases studied

Table 10. Cases Denied Review, 1982 Term

	Number	Percentage (base = 1860)
Intolerable conflicts	12[a]	.65
3-court conflicts	11	.59
2-court conflicts	1	.05
Intolerable conflicts that should have been heard during the 1982 term	5	.27
Tolerable 2-court conflicts	7	.38
Conflicts with Supreme Court precedent	0	0

[a]Although thirteen petitions—Nos. 81–2240, 81–2273, 81–2343, 82–72, 82–194, 82–949, 82–1161, 82–1322, 82–1531, 82–1838, and 82–1801—presented intolerable conflicts, two of these petitions—Nos. 82–949 and 82–1838—involved the same conflict.

during the 1971–73 Terms presented conflicts that the Court declined to review. The *Review*'s findings are also consistent with the reanalysis of Feeney's study undertaken in one of the Notes.[99] That reanalysis suggests that, under the criteria of our study, there were only eight or nine intolerable conflicts left unresolved by the Court during the 1972 Term studied by Feeney[100]—as compared with twelve unresolved conflicts (only five of which the *Review* categorized as improperly denied) during the 1982 Term.

Because (disregarding the students' own discounting) at most twelve intolerable, unresolved conflicts were denied review during the 1982 Term—a mere one-third of the thirty-nine improvident grants of the 1982 Term—we may safely conclude that the Court had the capacity to reach the improper denials. Although not all cases burden the Court's decisional resources equally, there is no reason to assume that the conflicts denied review were three times more difficult than the improvident grants. At the very least, these numbers undermine the claim that docket incapacity prevents the Court from resolving conflicts among the circuits. A discussion of the *Review*'s findings is presented in appendix B.

Chapter 9

The Avoidable Causes
of Overgranting

Our study of the Court's docket during the 1982 Term demonstrates that the Court granted review in a significant number of cases that did not merit review under our criteria and denied review in only a small number of cases involving fully percolated conflicts. Clearly, the Court is presently overgranting.[1]

The Court's tendency to overgrant is in part the product of a tension between individual Justices' interests and doctrinal agendas and the Court's institutional role. Because this tension is inevitable, some overgranting may be unavoidable. A significant amount of overgranting, however, is attributable to other, avoidable factors ranging from matters of principle—such as the Justices' reluctance to abandon completely a responsibility for error correction—to matters of detail such as the mechanics of the case selection process. One of the principal avoidable causes of overgranting, in our view, is the Court's own internal procedures. To the extent that the Court can change those procedures to address the problem of overgranting, it will reduce the need for major structural changes such as an NCA or ICT.

The Case Selection Process

The Justices' private group meeting—the "conference"—is the linchpin of the case selection process. The first conference of each Term is held near the end of September, when the Justices meet to study all requests for review filed with the

Court since the end of the previous Term and to decide which cases will receive plenary consideration. The Justices reassemble throughout the Term, usually weekly, to consider petitions listed by the Clerk of the Court since the previous conference and to determine which cases will be added to the plenary docket.

A case is set down for plenary review if four or more Justices vote, at conference, to hear it. This procedure is known as the "Rule of Four."[2] If fewer than four Justices want to hear a case, any of those who *do* want to hear it may relist it for further consideration. A case might be relisted repeatedly before it gains four votes—or before the persistent Justice (or Justices) acquiesces. Occasionally when a case is denied review, one or more of the Justices who believe that certiorari should have been granted will publish a dissent.[3] If an order issues granting review, the case is not reexamined until it is considered on the merits.[4]

Over the years the Justices have reduced markedly the personal attention they give to petitions for review. In 1925, when the Judges' Bill was enacted, the Justices themselves did most of the preparation for the conference. First, each Justice received a copy of the briefs and of the printed record in every case filed with the Court. Second, each Justice studied these papers and produced a memorandum on the case. Third, the Justices discussed every case at conference. Because only 350 to 400 cases were filed with the Court each term in the 1920s— about seven to eight per week—the Court had no trouble allocating sufficient resources to each petition.[5] By 1947, however, the Justices no longer discussed every petition submitted. Instead, the Chief Justice circulated a "dead list" identifying cases he deemed unworthy of discussion at the weekly conference. Any Justice could remove cases from the dead list and have them discussed at conference, but petitions not rescued were denied without further discussion.[6]

Today, the "discuss list" has replaced the dead list. The Chief Justice now circulates a list, to which other Justices may add, of cases he deems worthy of discussion at the conference. Cases omitted from the discuss list are denied review without discussion.[7] In an average week, only ten to twenty cases out of the approximately one hundred listed are discussed at conference.

Until about fifteen years ago, almost every Justice continued to receive a memorandum, prepared by his law clerks, on each case. In recent years, however, six Justices—Chief Justice Burger and Justices White, Blackmun, Powell, Rehnquist, and O'Connor—have collaborated in a "cert pool" where the Justices pool their law clerks to review appeals and petitions for certiorari. The weekly load of petitions is divided among the twenty-three or so law clerks of the participating Justices, with each assigned about five petitions a week. Each law clerk must produce a detailed memorandum on the assigned cases, which is then circulated to the participating Justices.

Lack of Criteria as a Cause

Supreme Court Rule 17 embodies the Court's only official public definition of the salient characteristics of a Supreme Court case. As we have seen, it is hopelessly indeterminate and unilluminating. Rule 17 leads inevitably to overgranting because it fails to articulate manageable yet principled criteria for case selection. As a result, the case selection process invariably turns into a subjective search for "significant" cases from among a seemingly enormous pool of candidates. This lack of detailed criteria exacerbates the tendency of other factors, such as the Justices' personal agendas, to move cases onto the plenary docket.

This open-ended search for significant cases, reflected in the absence of guiding criteria, admits of no principle and yields no basis to appraise and resolve differing perceptions of significance other than by force of the Rule of Four. Not surprisingly, the Court exhibits an ambivalence, unwillingness, or inability to define with any clarity what its role should be.

It has been accepted at least since the 1925 Judges' Bill that the Court cannot and should not sit as a court of error. Yet some of the cases granted review in the 1982 Term appear to have been selected solely to correct lower court error. Given the vagueness of the selection criteria, however, a Justice may with complete sincerity and fidelity to Rule 17 premise a vote to grant on a desire to correct what is perceived to be a serious error below. Such arguments apparently abound in the criminal law area, where many improvident grants were found.[8]

The lack of case selection criteria not only muddles the Court's role but also aggravates the ever-present inclination of the Justices to conceive of the case selection process in political terms. Each Justice develops an individual agenda of issues and becomes interested in pressing for plenary consideration of the cases that present those issues favorably. When the governing norm is simply the "importance" of the case—the clear message of Rule 17—and when there is no effort to develop guiding principles through a shared vision of the Court's overall role, the search for certworthy cases is predestined to generate a plenary docket reflecting the particular agendas of shifting coalitions of four or more Justices.

In the absence of case selection criteria, even a Justice without an interest in a particular case might vote for review. Although efforts to identify coalition behavior in the certiorari process are hardly conclusive at this point,[9] the literature suggests that, depending on the personality of the Justice[10] or the nature of the case, some Justices might "join three" to vote for review simply because the other three Justices feel that the case is worthy of review.[11] The Chief Justices often have been willing to provide the needed fourth vote "to build social stability on the Court [and] to increase overall good feelings on the Court."[12] The willingness of any Justice to join three is reinforced by the lack of meaningful case selection criteria.

Other factors help produce a predisposition to grant review simply to undo perceived error. For example, the lack of a common or dominant judicial philosophy on the Court can be expected to accentuate the Justices' individual interests or their tendency to join three. Or the Court might be more inclined to grant review in order to correct error when its judicial philosophy is at variance with the philosophy prevailing in the lower courts.[13]

Because the Court sometimes grants review simply to correct perceived error, a denial of review may be viewed as an approval in some sense of the lower court ruling. Even though the denial has no precedential effect, litigants often read traces of the Court's substantive views from its willingness or unwillingness to grant review and tend to perceive certiorari denials as agreement with the result below.[14] This perception puts the Court in a quandary when the court below has rejected an attractive, novel theory. On the one hand, the Court might feel compelled to grant review, even though adequate percolation has not yet occurred, in order to avoid sending the false signal that the court below was correct in disapproving the advance in doctrine. On the other hand, if the Court denies review, it might stifle further development of the law by prematurely curtailing argument and percolation. A similar dilemma is present when the lower court accepts a novel extension of prior law.

It may be argued that even were the Justices wholeheartedly to endorse our criteria, nine Justices operating on a Rule of Four are bound to produce an application of the criteria at variance with the results of our study. This point is not entirely without force, but should not be overstated.

First, the point of our study was not to replicate the political process by which Justices select cases. If trained professionals agree with our criteria and their application to the cases granted review in the 1982 Term, our finding of thirty-nine improvident grants is not effectively impeached by the argument that the "political reality" at the Court will produce a different result. Ultimately, this point sweeps too broadly, impeaching even the Court's referral decisions to the proposed ICT, and indeed all reform efforts. The application of legal principles (like our criteria) to cases is a bounded exercise—an exercise in principled decisionmaking with respect to which broad consensus can be expected and forged. Moreover, in identifying the thirty-nine improvident grants, we attempted to isolate those cases in which application of our criteria produced clear, fairly indisputable results. We did not "model" the Court's decisionmaking processes in the sense that we did not have nine decisionmakers; nonetheless, we feel confident that, were our criteria the norm governing case selection, fewer than four of nine legal professional decisionmakers would vote to grant review in the thirty-nine cases identified.

Second, nothwithstanding the possibility of some residual overgranting in any event, adoption of our criteria (or other criteria of comparable specificity) would be a vast improvement over the present state of affairs. At present *no* salient vision of the Court's role guides the case selection process. To our knowledge, the Justices have not addressed the issue. We know from our own experience that the law clerks, who play an important role in the case selection process, are given little guidance other than the vague provisions of Rule 17 and a sense of the individual Justice's concerns. And we know that, other than some general appreciation that intercircuit conflicts are important, the Supreme Court bar does not perceive any normative set of principles guiding case selection (and hence does not frame argument within any such context). Therefore, even if some overgranting would remain after adoption of detailed criteria, the Court's case selection burden would be lightened and its case selection performance substantially improved.

The Court's Screening Procedures as a Cause

Although the absence of case selection criteria is perhaps the most important factor in overgranting, another contributing cause may be the Court's procedures for processing review applications. The Justices presently vote on requests for review as part of their weekly conferences. Consequently, most of the cases the Court selects come from relatively small and unrepresentative samples of the annual pool of filed cases. During these weekly conferences, case selection is conducted without any real sense of how the docket is evolving. By contrast, the Justices' major conference each September, at which they have before them approximately one-fifth of the cases filed in a year, provides a striking lesson in how case selection might differ if the weekly conference were dropped in favor of less frequent deliberations. Presumably the cases at the September conference are representative of those filed throughout the year. Yet, over the last four Terms, the ratio of cases granted certiorari to petitions considered at the September conference has been significantly lower than that for the rest of the year. During the

1979 Term, for example, the ratio of grants to petitions considered at the September conference was only 1 in 20 (22 of 391), whereas for the rest of the year it was 1 in 12 (110 of 1385). During the 1980 Term, the ratio was 1 in 23 at the September conference (21 of 458), but 1 in 11 for the rest of the year (146 of 1541). During the 1981 Term, the ratio was 1 in 14 at the September conference (26 of 373) and 1 in 10 for the rest of the year (177 of 1727). During the 1982 Term, the ratio was 1 in 24 at the September conference (16 of 412), and 1 in 10 for the rest of the year (153 of 1480).[15]

It also has long been the Court's practice that once an order has issued granting review, the case is not reexamined until it is considered on the merits. There is no second look at cases slated for plenary consideration to probe their appropriateness for Supreme Court review. Because the Court's preconference consideration is necessarily both cursory and individual, some inappropriate cases inevitably pass through the screen.

Chapter 10

Unsuitable Remedies: The Proposals for a New Appellate Court

The Chief Justice's 1983 ICT proposal, our paradigm for presenting the essential elements of the present ICT plans, does not deal with the absence of detailed criteria to guide case selection—in our view, the major cause of overgranting. Moreover, a new tier of courts would not prevent the Justices from pursuing their individual agendas, or diminish the willingness of some Justices to join three. And even after the creation of an intermediate court, the Justices still would select the cases in weekly conferences without providing for a second look at the appropriateness of the grants. In short, the new court would not address *any* of the causes of overgranting identified in the previous chapter and would in fact aggravate existing problems and may well create new ones.

THE STRUCTURAL RELATIONSHIP BETWEEN THE ICT AND THE SUPREME COURT WOULD EXACERBATE THE COURT'S SCREENING BURDEN. There is a serious constitutional question whether Supreme Court review of ICT decisions can be precluded,[1] and not surprisingly, the current proposals preserve an appeal to the Supreme Court. The availability of Supreme Court review is a serious structural problem for any ICT proposal, suggesting that an ICT may well worsen the Court's workload problem.

The ICT's very creation would probably spur growth in the number of petitions for review filed with the Court. Because an ICT would increase, at least in the short run, our judicial system's intermediate appellate capacity, it would also be viewed as improving the odds of obtaining review beyond the circuit courts; an ICT would encourage disappointed litigants to take another shot at a favorable decision.[2] If petitions for review beyond the circuit court level become more frequent and routine, corresponding pressure will be placed on the Supreme Court to refer cases to the ICT and, later on, to review the ICT's work.

In addition, an ICT would further complicate the Supreme Court's screening decisions. The Justices would have to determine not only whether a case warranted review but also whether they should retain it for themselves or refer it to the ICT (which might decline to accept it), or refer it with directions that it be heard. Decisions as to referral would themselves be freighted with a significance greater than that associated with the denial of a certiorari petition.

INTERPOSING AN ICT BETWEEN THE COURTS OF APPEALS AND THE SUPREME COURT WOULD CONTRIBUTE TO INSTABILITY AND INCOHERENCE. Contrary to its proponents' claims, the ICT would be unlikely to promote greater coherence in the law. Adding another round of review above the present courts of appeals would devalue their rulings. This devaluation would reflect an accurate perception of the change in status of the courts of appeals in the judicial hierarchy. By dramatically increasing the odds in favor of obtaining review of a circuit court decision, an ICT would diminish the weight accorded circuit opinions, destabilizing the law by encouraging additional appeals and thereby exacerbating incoherence.

The ICT itself would be unlikely to be able to render decisions with sufficient authoritativeness not only to compensate for the courts of appeals' loss of influence but also to improve upon the stability and coherence of federal law. Moreover, disappointed litigants would still have a chance of obtaining Supreme Court review in cases involving controversial issues over which the circuits have split. Even if the Court intervened only rarely, a disappointed litigant would be likely to pursue the remote chance of review; truly authoritative resolution would not come about until the Court decided the issue. Thus any benefits the ICT would provide through additional appellate capacity would probably be outweighed by the instability and delay it would generate.

THE ICT WOULD EXPAND THE SUPREME COURT'S MANDATORY CASE-LOAD. Proponents of a new court unjustifiably assume that the Supreme Court would rarely intervene to review ICT rulings. Admittedly, the Supreme Court is unlikely to review decisions frequently from a court with exclusive jurisdiction over certain narrowly defined areas, such as tax and patents, in which the issues are not likely to generate wide controversy and the affected communities may well place a higher premium on getting a definitive answer than on getting the right answer. The history of the relationship between the Court of Appeals for the District of Columbia Circuit (the exclusive or alternative venue in many regulatory cases) and the Supreme Court suggests, however, that the Court has more reason to review cases from a court with exclusive appellate jurisdiction over controversial areas of federal law. This is especially true when the judges of the appeals court enjoying exclusive jurisdiction have a different jurisprudential or ideological perspective from that of a majority of the Justices on the Supreme Court.

In the 1980–83 Terms, the Supreme Court reviewed decisions of the D.C. Circuit nearly three times as often as it reviewed those of any other circuit.[3] Moreover, the Court's affirmance rate for the D.C. Circuit was only about 25 percent of the affirmance rate for the other circuits.[4] Although the lower affirmance rate appears to be due primarily to ideological disagreement between the two courts[5]—a point also relevant to evaluation of the success of an ICT—sixteen of the forty-eight D.C. Circuit cases reviewed during this period involved either the exclusive jurisdiction or the alternative venue of the D.C. Circuit.[6] When an appeals court enjoys such jurisdiction over areas of general interest, it necessarily has a certain prominence or visibility that makes a special claim on the Supreme Court's attention. Moreover, because a court of exclusive jurisdiction can bind the nation in a given category of cases, the Supreme

Court cannot rely on the percolation process and understandably is less willing to tolerate error.

An ICT would operate much like a court of exclusive, general jurisdiction. Although ICT proponents envision a court that is merely an adjunct of the Supreme Court to alleviate its workload, such modesty will not reflect reality. Because ICT decisions would bind the nation, the Supreme Court would be forced to examine closely the ICT's work. Suspected ICT errors would be likely candidates for review. Indeed, Supreme Court review simply for purposes of error correction might well prove unavoidable in many cases. Even dicta in ICT rulings would acquire special significance and would command the Court's attention during case selection.[7] If an ICT were established, the Supreme Court would have the added burden of carefully overseeing the new court's decisions.

ICT advocates evision an ICT working easily with the Supreme Court and populated by judges congenial—jurisprudentially and ideologically—to the Justices of the Supreme Court. There would certainly be times, however, when the ICT would be at loggerheads with the Supreme Court. At such times, the Court would simply be making more work for itself by referring cases to the ICT. But if the Court declined to refer cases to the ICT because of incompatibility, it would sacrifice any advantages of such a court. If the ICT's jurisdiction were not based on Court referrals, its rulings—should the ICT and the Court diverge in jurisprudential or ideological outlook—would be irresistible candidates for plenary review by the Supreme Court.

Recent ICT proposals have offered only a temporary "experimental" ICT. The obvious virtue of an experimental ICT is that it could be dismantled with relatively little institutional cost. For the reasons just noted, however, any such "experiment" would be seriously flawed because it would artificially suppress the risk of disagreement that might occur between the ICT and the Supreme Court after an ICT developed an institutional identity of its own.

ROTATING MEMBERSHIP ON THE ICT WOULD CONTRIBUTE TO INSTABILITY AND INCOHERENCE. Under the Chief Justice's 1983 proposal, the ICT would draw its judges on a rotating basis from those now sitting on the courts of appeals.[8] Unfortunately, the practice of rotating judges could produce major doctrinal shifts when judges are replaced. The appointment process is often the critical vehicle for remaking constitutional law. Under current arrangements, we have a gradual process that requires substantial maturation before the development of constitutional doctrine is significantly altered.[8] The rotation of judges on the ICT, however, would dramatically accelerate such doctrinal shifts, possibly compromising the authoritative guidance ICT proponents claim their court would provide.

Even if judges on rotating ICT panels shared the same jurisprudential and political veiws, the court would be unlikely to produce doctrinal coherence. A court consisting of shifting panels of seven judges drawn from a pool of twenty-six or twenty-eight would be unlikely to develop the institutional identity and habits of collegiality necessary to the production of a relatively stable, coherent body of federal law. The changing membership of the panels, the geographical separation of the judges, and the press of other judicial duties would combine to prevent ICT judges from forging a carefully reasoned and coherent body of federal law on subjects that have generated conflicts in the courts of appeals.[10] An ICT with rotating panels, issuing rulings purportedly speaking for the nation, would suffer from infirmities that might well produce additional incoherence and instability in the law.

Chapter 11

Tailoring the Remedy
to the Problem

Even if the Supreme Court is presently overburdened,[1] there is no need for a major structural change such as the proposed ICT. The remedy should be tailored to the problem, which, in our view, stems largely from deficiencies in the Court's case selection process. If these deficiencies are addressed, radical solutions to possibly nonexistent problems need not be hazarded.

We propose instead changes in the case selection process designed to minimize the overgranting phenomenon by enhancing the Court's ability to identify cases on the priority and discretionary dockets. Such modest reforms would permit a sounder use of the Court's scarce decisional resources and ease substantially whatever problem of docket overload may exist, while avoiding unnecessary structural alteration of the federal judiciary. We also assess certain other proposals that do not require creation of a new layer of appellate review.

Most of the reforms we propose could be effected by the Justices themselves; one or two would require congressional action. Each would enable the Court to perform its managerial functions better and to fulfill its role as articulator of authoritative and uniform federal law.

We do not consider proposals that, although seemingly procedural in nature, have a latent substantive purpose. For example, recent proposals to strip the Supreme Court of jurisdiction over various kinds of cases have been couched in terms suggesting that they are intended to alleviate the Court's burden by removing troublesome classes of cases from its docket.[2] These political attempts to manage the Court's docket[3] raise serious questions of constitutionality,[4] and are unlikely to pass into law. In any event, they offer no real lasting improvements in the administration of the Court's business. We also avoid the debate over the length and quality of the Supreme Court's opinions,[5] for that debate does not touch directly on our primary concern—the impact of the case selection process on the workload problem.

Recommendations

Abolish Mandatory Appellate Jurisdiction

All the Justices and virtually all commentators endorse the proposal to abolish mandatory jurisdiction. The Court's mandatory appellate docket normally accounts for somewhere between 20 and 30 percent of the Court's caseload (21 percent in the 1982 Term).[6] In our view, commentators have overstated the significance of abolition, as most appeals (other than state rulings of statutory validity) would still be assigned to the priority docket.[7] Nevertheless, an appreciable number of cases—in our study, 12 of 164, or 7 percent of the overall docket—would not merit the Court's attention if obligatory jurisdiction were abolished. More important, abolition would relieve the Court of the burden of acting on all cases denominated as appeals, and thus would also eliminate the nettlesome question of the precedential effect of summary dispositions in such cases. Where summary dispositions present hurdles to a desired outcome, the Court often attempts to deprecate their precedential effect.[8] Yet even dismissals of appeals, though not fully deliberated,[9] are deemed judgments on the merits.[10] The confusion thus created requires the Court to grant review on occasion principally to dispel the supposed precedential effect of a prior dismissal.[11]

The mandatory appellate docket is a remnant of the outdated view that the Court ought to hear any case a disappointed litigant has the resources and determination to carry to the highest level of review. Abolition of mandatory appellate jurisdiction would give the Court full control over its docket and endow it with the flexibility necessary to carry out its managerial responsibilities.[12]

Formulate Specific Criteria for Case Selection

The lack of meaningful criteria contributes to overgranting and overpetitioning because litigants can never be certain whether their cases merit review.[13] Although the criteria in this study are not the final word, our model indicates the kind of inquiry the Justices ought to pursue in the effort to formulate (with the assistance of the legal community) coherent, workable guidelines for managing the Court's docket.

A principled set of case selection criteria would send clearer signals to the bar. Definite criteria for certworthiness would enable practitioners to refrain from filing petitions that, while presently satisfying Supreme Court Rule 17, clearly do not merit review.[14] Moreover, the tendency to construe a denial of review as approval of the result below would be significantly diminished.

Linking Requests for Review to the Court's Enunciated Criteria

The rules governing petitions for certiorari should require petitioners to file a short supplemental statement—possibly on a checklist form developed by the Court—setting forth procedural information to facilitate the Court's evaluation of the certworthiness of each petition. This statement should indicate whether the petition is from a final judgment of the court below and should explicitly link the petitioner's request for review to the Court's articulated criteria. When the basis of the request for review is an alleged conflict among the circuits, the statement should provide three additional pieces of information. First, the petitioner should identify the precise issue on which a conflict is alleged. Second, the petitioner should cite, say, at least three, but no more than six, cases presenting the conflict. Third, the petitioner should aver that the alleged conflict was brought to the attention of the court below. The entire statement should require no more than a few marks on a checklist coupled with a paragraph or two of case citations for allegations of intercourt conflicts. Many petitions would not survive a prima facie examination. For others, the checklist would highlight the purported basis for requesting the Court's intervention. In all cases, the Court would no longer need to wade through prolix petitions and string cites; litigants would be compelled to focus their arguments for Supreme Court review.

In order to promote intercircuit reconciliation, we recommend that a petitioner who alleges a conflict be required to demonstrate that the conflict was considered by the lower court. The petitioner should be required to bring the conflict to the attention of the court of appeals. If the lower court does not acknowledge the existence of the alleged conflict in its opinion, the petitioner must again raise the issue in the petition for rehearing or suggestion for rehearing en banc. In the rare case in which a conflict arises after the petition for rehearing is filed, but before the last date for filing with the Supreme Court, the petitioner should be permitted—indeed, encouraged—to return to the court of appeals for reconsideration based on the allegedly conflicting decision.

Certifying that the Case Merits Supreme Court Review

The Supreme Court, on the model of Rule 11 of the Federal Rules of Civil Procedure, should require certification by the petitioner that the request for review is not frivolous under the Court's criteria. Costs or other sanctions should be imposed on attorneys who file frivolous petitions. Certification could take various forms. Kurland and Hutchinson tentatively suggest that the Court publish separately certiorari denials that do not merit discussion, list the names of counsel who file meritless petitions, and impose substantial costs for such filings.[15] Milton Handler proposes that the court of appeals itself certify that a particular decision presents an issue meriting the Court's review. If a litigant seeks review of an uncertified case and the petition is unanimously denied, Handler suggests, the full costs of the respondent should be imposed on the petitioner or its attorney.[16]

We favor the adoption of a version of Federal Rule 11 modified to fit the special conditions of Supreme Court practice. An attorney would certify that he has examined the case selection criteria articulated by the Court and that he has in good faith a reasonable basis for urging Supreme Court review in a particular case. The Court could then impose sanctions (costs and attorney's fees involved in opposing the petition) if, under the Court's criteria, the attorney filed a frivolous petition.

This approach would achieve its intended goal with less risk of undesirable and unintended consequences than the above proposals. Kurland and Hutchinson concede that they have not fully worked out their proposal.[17] Handler's suggestion would require the lower court judges to reevaluate decisions they have already rendered, this time as a screen for the Supreme Court. Our certification proposal would not require the courts of appeals to second-guess themselves and would keep the decision to seek Court review within the discretion of the litigants.

A "Second Look" Mechanism

Under present procedures, once four Justices vote to hear a case, review is granted. Usually the announcement is made by the Court on the Monday following the conference. The case is not studied again until the Court considers it on the merits.

Occasionally the Justices dismiss a writ of certiorari as improvidently granted. As recently illustrated by *Gillette Co. v. Miner*,[18] *Westinghouse Electric Corp. v. Vaughn*,[19] and *Illinois v. Gates*,[20] this practice wastes scarce judicial resources and damages the Court's credibility. Moreover, we suspect that the incidence of overt dismissals understates the Court's own tally of its improvident grants, because the Court tends to decide a case once certiorari has been granted.

Relatively modest procedural changes could reduce the number of improvident grants. The Justices at the initial conference should vote on each petition to grant or deny review, as they do now. However, the results of that vote should not be announced. Instead, petitions that receive at least four votes should be submitted to an independent staff of the caliber of Justices' clerks, headed by a leading member of the Supreme Court bar who would serve for a term of years. The staff would evaluate each proposed grant under the Court's criteria to determine whether the case merited review. They would also inquire whether there were any procedural obstacles to consideration of the merits, such as the absence of a final judgment, and evaluate the state of the record to determine whether the case provided a suitable vehicle for review. Then the petitions, accompanied by the staff reports, would be returned to the Justices for reconsideration and a final vote at a second conference. If the case still received at least four votes, review would be granted and the result announced.

We recognize that some critics will view this suggestion as a further step toward "bureaucratic justice," whereby the Justices do not make legal decisions themselves but merely manage a bureaucratic machine.[21] But our proposal is not such a step, because the function of our proposed staff is purely advisory; its members simply would highlight difficulties with the tentatively granted petition in light of the Court's criteria, the state of the record, and the suitability of case as a proposed vehicle. The Justices would receive and act on the staff's recommendations, but they would not be bound by them in any way.

The screening process should include another preliminary step when a petition is to be granted as a possible vehicle for announcing a major doctrinal shift or innovation. There is no point in a vehicle grant that will yield only a plurality opinion and a splintered Court. As former Secretary of Transportation William T. Coleman recently suggested, fragmented opinions encourage later litigants to seek review on the chance that a plurality or concurring opinion might presage a shift in the Court's position.[22] Therefore, to identify suitable vehicles better, the Justices should take a straw vote or in some other way determine whether they will be able to unite on an opinion that authoritatively sets forth clear and easily applied rules and legal principles. Naturally, this straw vote would not (and should not) preclude a change of mind after briefs and argument. But if the Justices' straw vote indicates that there is no consensus on the structure or substance of an eventual Court opinion, then the Justices will have had advance notice that the case may prove to be an unsuitable vehicle. This proposal creates some tension with the Rule of Four, but we intend here only an educational device for the Justices and not a justification for suspending the rule.

Less Frequent Conferences and Screening by Fewer Justices

The Justices presently vote on requests for review as part of their weekly conference. As noted above, this procedure often reveals only a fragmentary and unrepresentative view of the annual docket. If, however, the Justices were to review petitions on a monthly basis, they could gain a more accurate overview of the developing docket and the work of the lower courts. By locating each decision to grant or deny review in the context of a larger sample of the docket, monthly review would help reduce the incidence of improvident grants.

Further Research through Increased Data Collection

The Court should facilitate empirical research by publishing the Justices' votes on decisions to grant or deny review. Publication need not be simultaneous with the actual vote; records on votes to grant or deny review could be made available several years after the actual vote. Such information would be extraordinarily useful in discussion of proposals for reform. For example, it would provide a data base for assessing the operation of the Rule of Four, and for evaluating proposals for a Rule of Five. Similarly, publication of these votes would permit students of the Court to evaluate the contribution, if any, of the cert pool practice to the overgranting phenomenon.

We do not suggest that the clerks' bench memoranda on each case be published or otherwise made available.[23] These memoranda are not final decisions or even well-considered resolutions. They are written solely to familiarize individual Justices with the issues presented by the petitions, and should not be used for any other purpose. There is also no need to give disappointed litigants possible grounds for urging reconsideration by publicizing a clerk's necessarily preliminary recommendations.

Use Transfer and Venue Rules to Avoid Forum Shopping

That two circuits are in conflict presents no pressing reason for Supreme Court intervention unless a party can take advantage of the conflict by forum shopping or the conflict stymies the planning of multicircuit actors. Much can be done, however, to minimize these undesirable features of conflicts while preserving the benefits of percolation and reducing significantly the number of conflict cases on the Supreme Court's priority docket.

The most promising approach, in our view, would be for Congress generally to restrict federal venue to the district or circuit where the claim or cause of action arose.[24] Under a restrictive venue regime, parties would know with certainty the law that would govern their affairs, and they would be unable to bring themselves under a different set of legal rules by forum choice. We recognize that this approach raises difficult questions, such as the assignment of a situs to multidistrict or multi-circuit transactions. Special rules would also be needed for cases involving challenges to government regulations or to decisions of national applicability; for example, venue could be restricted to the District of Columbia Circuit or to the principal place of business or the residence of the challenger. For actions originating at the district court level, provision for transfer of venue for reasons of litigation convenience would be necessary, but, by analogy to the rules governing transfer in federal diversity cases,[25] the law of the transferor circuit would apply.[26]

A second approach is to preserve existing venue rules, which maximize considerations of convenience of litigation, but to stipulate choice of law rules either by legislation or by Supreme Court rulemaking.[27] We would prefer, however, the venue approach to the choice of law alternative, because it would be easier to apply.

Less Desirable Possibilities

In our view, the proposals that follow should be adopted only as a last resort before the creation of a new intermediate appellate court. These cures pose difficulties or undermine important values and practices, yet in our view are distinctly preferable to creation of an ICT.

Modification of the Rule of Four

Several commentators and at least one Justice have suggested that the Rule of Four may have to be replaced by a Rule of

Five.[28] This proposal's drawback is that it would enable an entrenched majority to foreclose even threshold consideration of issues of concern to a significant minority of Justices. Our principal objection is that a Rule of Five is ill-designed to meet the problem of overgranting. Although a Rule of Five might increase the reversal rate for cases on the certiorari docket or reduce the aggregate number of grants per Term, adoption of the proposal would provide no additional assurance of appropriate case selection.

Giving Nationally Binding Effect to En Banc Circuit Decisions

Justice White and several commentators have proposed a novel way of addressing intercircuit conflicts. If, after a panel of one circuit decides a legal issue, a panel of a second circuit decides the same issue differently, the second circuit court must convene en banc to reconsider the issue. The resulting en banc decision would become a nationally binding rule that could be overturned only by the Supreme Court.[29]

Although this proposal appears at first glance to be an attractive way to dispose of intercircuit conflicts, we do not support it for several reasons. First, it does not give sufficient weight to the value of percolation. Legal issues are susceptible of more than two polar resolutions; the Court should have the benefit of intermediate approaches. Second, this proposal would permit a circuit with little experience and knowledge in an area of law to overrule a circuit with widely acknowledged expertise in that area (for example, the Second Circuit on securities regulation law or the District of Columbia Circuit on administrative law). Third, this proposal shares some of the difficulties that would beset an ICT. Because the en banc decision would purport to bind the nation yet be authoritative only if not overturned by the Supreme Court, litigants still would have incentive to press their claims, and the Court would be under considerable pressure to review the en banc ruling.

In any event, adoption of this proposal would be premature at this point. It would be wiser to implement less radical reforms and see whether they work. Still, whatever its faults, the binding en banc decision remedy does not involve the severe systemic problems and destabilizing effects that would result from the creation of a new tier of appellate review.

Another proposal for resolving intercircuit conflicts is set forth in a recent article by former Secretary of Transportation Coleman.[30] It calls for special panels to rehear cases in which a circuit court has rendered a decision that conflicts with the law of another circuit. Each special panel would be composed of three judges from each of the two conflicting circuits and a seventh judge from another circuit, assigned by the Chief Justice. This panel's decision would be binding on all circuits, subject only to discretionary Supreme Court review. However, "[s]hould a third circuit fail to follow the precedent established by the inter-circuit en banc hearing, the petitioner [in the third case] could request an en banc hearing by seven judges, two from each of the three circuits that had addressed the issue and one assigned by the Chief Justice."[31] Presumably the seventh judge would be from a fourth circuit, and this new panel's decision would have nationally binding effect subject only to Supreme Court review.

Aside from obvious problems of unwieldiness, the unacceptable extent to which serendipity would control which judges served on each proposed intercircuit en banc panel is bound to frustrate hopes for coherence in national law. Further, it is not clear how designation of judges from conflicting circuits would necessarily produce decisive conflict resolution. Especially in cases that provoke dissents from the original circuit decisions, it is far from certain that the intercircuit panel would be able to provide an authoritative final judgment. As long as there was an opportunity to appeal, disappointed litigants would continue to seek a truly authoritative resolution of the conflict from the Supreme Court irrespective of the number of intervening en banc intercircuit panel decisions. Surely the binding en banc decision rule proposed by Justice White is preferable to this proposal.

Referring "Trivial" Conflicts to Disinterested Circuits

Two variants of the binding en banc decision proposal deserve further discussion. Some commentators contend that many of the conflicts the Court hears involve relatively narrow issues of statutory construction in areas of federal law that are not of general interest and are too insignificant to merit the Court's attention.[32] There are, of course, reasons to be skeptical of this contention. A conflict among three or more circuit courts or state courts of last resort suggests that the issue is at least difficult and recurring. Assuming, for the sake of argument, the existence of trivial conflicts, a statute authorizing the Court to refer them to a randomly chosen circuit court is still preferable to the ICT proposals. Such a statute might authorize the circuit court to issue a nationally binding resolution reviewable at the discretion of the Supreme Court, freeing up docket capacity without sacrificing the benefits of lower court percolation or creating a new tribunal whose only ostensible task would be handling parochial, relatively insignificant cases.

Instead of creating new courts, Congress might consider proposals to establish a National Law Revision Commission designed to identify on a continuing basis conflicts on statutory questions for legislative resolution.[33] The National Law Revision proposal has the advantage of involving Congress in the clarification of statutory law while liberating docket capacity.

Significant number of trivial conflicts or no, any referral function makes the case selection process more complex and time-consuming. We doubt that the Justices will agree readily on which conflicts are trivial. Moreover, trivial conflicts can quickly be decided without substantial expenditure of the Court's decisional resources, and the Court may well benefit institutionally from the occasional easy case in which the Justices can reach agreement without a proliferation of separate opinions or rancor.[34]

Specialized Appellate Courts

Some commentators have suggested the creation of specialized appellate courts, on the model of the Court of Appeals for the Federal Circuit.[35] These courts would eliminate the possibility of intercircuit conflicts about issues over which they had exclusive jurisdiction. A specialized court for tax appeals is the most

frequently aired proposal.[36] Those who oppose this suggest that
a judge familiar with the full range of legal questions potentially
implicated in a federal case will decide cases more soundly and
creatively than a specialist judge, and that a court that deals
exclusively with a governmental agency might become too deferential to the views of either the agency or a specialized segment of the bar.[37] We doubt that specialized appellate courts
can effectively reduce the Court's caseload. Such courts would
sacrifice the benefits of percolation, are vulnerable to capture
by special interests, and if given responsibility over controversial subjects would require active Supreme Court supervision.

Courts of exclusive jurisdiction, if established, should be confined to areas that are not likely to generate wide controversy,
to areas in which certainty and predictability in the law are
paramount. Patent litigation is one such area,[38] and assignment
of patent cases to the Court of Appeals for the Federal Circuit
was appropriate.[39] We do not expect litigants in patent cases to
seek Supreme Court review regularly, or the Justices to feel any
strong temptation to intervene. Tax litigation might be another
such area.[40] To avoid the "captive court" problem, tax cases
should also be assigned to the Court of Appeals for the Federal
Circuit. This practice would expand the subject-matter responsibilities of that court, and, correspondingly, the breadth of
perspective of its judges.

We do not at present urge the creation of additional specialized tribunals. Even in the tax area, the case has yet to be made
with convincing clarity that such a change is needed. Forum
shopping in tax cases could be eliminated by restricting the role
of the Claims Court and codifying the policy by which the Tax
Court follows the law of the circuit in which the dispute arises.
Moreover, our study does not identify any significant number of
conflicts in the tax area that are left unresolved by the Court
(only one two-court conflict was found).[41] It is true that, in the
tax area, planning by the parties may be imperiled as much by
incoherence in the law as by conflicts. If that is the case, however, assignment of tax cases to the Court of Appeals for the
Federal Circuit might be the answer.

Chapter 12

Implications and Conclusions

In these concluding remarks, we step aside from the immediate controversy that inspired this book—the various proposals for a new national appeals court—to consider some of the broader implications of our managerial model of the Supreme Court's responsibilities. In our view, the time has come for a fundamental rethinking of the Court's role in our legal system— a forthright disavowal of the vaguely comforting yet ultimately unavailing notion that the Court is potentially available to correct error in all federal cases. In its place we suggest an open embrace of a vision that looks to the Court as the manager of a process of national lawmaking in an increasingly federalized society served by a multilayered, regionally diverse system of federal and state courts. A principled elaboration of this model should permit the Court to make optimal use of its limited decisional resources and promote an atmosphere in which the lower federal and state courts take seriously their own responsibilities in the national lawmaking process.

The implications of the managerial model radiate well beyond the ICT controversy. The model has a radicalizing potential for altering our basic conceptions about the Court's relationship to the federal lawmaking process, the nature of practice before the Court (quite apart from the selection of cases), and the roles of other actors in the system. In the paragraphs that follow, we offer some preliminary suggestions along these lines.

Recasting the *Marbury v. Madison* Model

As students learn early on in law school, the legitimacy of the Court's decisionmaking, particularly on constitutional questions but in other areas as well, hinges on what might be called the "*Marbury v. Madison* model," or what our colleague Lawrence Sager felicitiously terms the "bleeding plaintiff model." Thus, as John Marshall observed in the *Marbury* ruling, the Supreme Court, just like any other court, makes law—constitutional or otherwise—only in the course of resolving actual disputes, in the course of binding the wounds of real, live "bleeding" litigants.[1] The "bleeding plaintiff" imagery implies to some that, like any ordinary court, the Court must be ever available to correct error in the system. Even after the 1925 Judges' Bill and its avowed recognition of the Court's largely discretionary jurisdiction, the perception persists that if the Court is not potentially available for all federal cases, then in some fundamental sense it has been cut loose from the tethers of its legitimacy.

We agree that the Court's legitimacy is ultimately traceable to its role in deciding actual controversies—and for reasons more fundamental than the formal notion that the "judicial power" granted by Article III extends only to "cases and controversies." It does not follow, however, that such legitimacy is impaired when the Court relies on federal and state appellate courts for error correction and reserves its limited decisional capacity for strategic, managerial intervention along the lines suggested in this book.

Even in its first century the Court did not and could not sit as a true court of errors, for the system was largely dependent on the state judiciary for vindication of federal claims, and the Justices, pressed by their circuit-riding responsibilities and limited institutional resources, could offer at best sporadic oversight. For the better part of the of the nineteenth century, moreover, major areas of federal law—most federal criminal cases[2] and state court rulings sustaining federal claims[3]—were not even assigned to the Supreme Court's appellate jurisdiction.

When one turns to the radically different conditions of this century, with its explosive proliferation of federal law and development of an expansive network of federal courts of appeals and state tribunals, it is evident that the 1925 Judges' Bill merely ratified what was then already evident: the Court was not, and could not be, principally an appeals court. Its responsibility was to safeguard the federal lawmaking process.

The Constitution has never been read to require a right to more than one layer of appeal.[4] Moreover, the fact that the court intervenes strategically—not at the behest of claims of error—is fully consistent with the proposition that it may legitimately make law only in cases presenting actual controversies. In short, we believe that the claimed linkage between the *Marbury v. Madison* model and the insistence on universal availability is not supported by history, constitutional requirements, or logic.

A severing of the false connection between legitimacy and universal availability would liberate the Court from the distorting influences of an unrealistic set of responsibilities on the case selection process and free the Justices from the inevitable, paralyzing frustration that must seize them if they take seriously their obligation to satisfy the current level of expectations.

We recognize the concern that panels of federal courts of appeals, often manned in part by district judges and judges sitting by designation, may provide a less than optimal appeal as of right, and perhaps there are steps (some suggested below) that Congress and the Court can take to ensure greater intracircuit uniformity. These and other concerns should be addressed directly, not by saddling the Court with a vision of its responsibilities that it cannot satisfy under any circumstances.

Redesigning Practice before the Court

An open acknowledgment by the Court that its principal responsibility is to the federal lawmaking process rather than to the correction of error, that it does not sit simply as an ordinary court atop the judicial hierarchy, should not only facilitate a more self-conscious case selection process but also encourage the Court to experiment with departures from the tradition of party control of the process that may be better suited to the job of rendering nationally binding law. Under current practice, with few exceptions, the Court deals with the certiorari petition as the parties have crafted it, and learns about the facts and the law from the briefing and argument of the parties and self-appointed amici (with some assistance from the Justices' law clerks). The *Marbury* model does not, however, require unyielding adherence to this tradition. Without impairing its legitimacy in the slightest, the Court can take some practical steps to expand substantially the informational base upon which national law is made.

In the course of considering petitions for review, particularly in cases serving as potential vehicles for advances in federal law, the Court should not be hesitant to invoke its "limited grant" practice as well as occasionally to reformulate the questions presented by the petition in order to ensure that its decisional resources will be expended only in the service of issues truly warranting attention. In addition to the "second look" and preliminary vote procedures suggested in chapter 11 for vehicle cases, the Court should consider inviting the views not only of the Solicitor General but also of organizations with particular interest in the subject matter (e.g., the ACLU, the AFL-CIO, groups of attorneys general or district atorneys), and academic experts on the suitability of the petition as proposed vehicle.

Once the case has been set for argument and briefing, the Court also need not tolerate a state of affairs in which counsel for the parties are, as Chief Justice Burger has often lamented, poorly equipped for the assignment. In appropriate cases, the Court would benefit from soliciting the views of selected amici targeted to issues of particular salience to the Justices. Such invitations could elicit perspectives not represented among amici likely to come forward on their own (or the case might not have come to the attention of particular organizations that regularly file amici briefs), and targeted briefs may well prove of greater assistance to the Court than amici submissions that simply repeat what the parties are saying in their principal briefs. In addition, argument time can be expanded or a portion of the available hour reserved for focused presentations by selected amici. There is here a vast informational resource available to the Court that is now only partially tapped.

Even during the decisionmaking process the Court can avail itself of the expertise of interested amici and scholars. Under current arrangements, the Justices fend for themselves at this stage with whatever assistance they can muster from their chambers.[5] But law clerks, however talented they may be, are recent law school graduates whose appreciation of the practical realities upon which the law operates is necessarily limited. In addition, academic commentary rarely keeps pace with the Court's agenda and too often comes to light only after the fact; insightful postmortem is still only postmortem. One means by which the Justices can tap the expertise of the outside world in time to improve the product of their deliberations would be to borrow a leaf from the federal administrative process and issue tentative opinions in the hope of eliciting written comments from affected organizations and academic experts. We mean no disrespect to the Court in suggesting that often its efforts at grand synthesis—for example, the reformulation of the rules governing *in personam* jurisdiction in *Shaffer v. Heitner*[6] or the reappraisal of the bargaining obligations of companies planning major entrepreneurial decisions in *First National Maintenance Corp. v. NLRB*[7]—leave in their wake at least as much confusion and incoherence as preceded the Court's opinion. Admittedly, the comments will not always be helpful, and our suggestion will certainly create more paper for the Justices to sift through, but even if the comments only occasionally encourage the Court to limit the reach of its ruling or recognize an exception grounded in practical realities that may have eluded the Justices and their clerks, the process will have been worth the price of the venture.

Rethinking the Role of Federal and State Appellate Courts

The presumption of regularity accorded to the decisions of federal and state appellate courts is a mainstay of our managerial model. To warrant this presumption, however, these courts must live up to their responsibilities. In this regard, there is much that the Court can do, in the exercise of its supervisory authority, without having to render decisions on the merits in particular cases.

For example, in the preceding chapter we suggested procedures by which the circuits can be alerted to the existence of conflicts and encouraged to express their views on the disputed proposition of law.[8] Such procedures may in some cases eliminate conflicts or promote intercircuit reconciliation, and at the very least will give the Court the benefit of explicit circuit consideration of the issue in conflict.

Intercircuit conflicts are, however, only one of the reasons why thoughtful students of the federal courts have urged creation of enhanced national appellate capacity. Another pressing cause of discontent—one likely to persist even after the incidence of intercircuit conflict is reduced—is *intracircuit* dissonance. It is claimed that because of the burgeoning growth of federal law, the "limited publication" rules of the various circuits that dispense with written opinions in many appeals[9] and the utilization of senior judges, district judges, and judges of other circuits sitting by designation,[10] the law in a circuit is often in disarray.[11] Although petitions for rehearing en banc are potentially available to resolve such conflicts, the argument runs, because of the geographical dispersion of judges in many of the circuits, the size of some of the circuits, and the limited capacity of the appeals courts, such petitions are so rarely granted that this avenue of redress is for all practical purposes nonexistent.[12]

Although we are not certain that the problem of intracircuit conflict is as prevalent as is claimed, and seriously question whether an ICT is an appropriate remedy for a management problem *within* the circuit, there are means available to the Court as manager substantially to reduce the incidence of intracircuit conflict without the necessity of direct intervention. One approach might be for the Court to promulgate rules curtailing the limited publications practice by requiring that at least a per curiam opinion issue whenever a party seeks rehearing upon a plausible assertion of lack of fidelity to circuit law, or that such a case be set for rehearing before a different panel.[13]

Even in the absence of intercircuit or intracircuit dissonance, there may still be legitimate concern that the appeals courts are not doing enough to correct error at the district court level, or that too much rides at present on the happenstantial composition of circuit court panels. A new national appellate court or more frequent intervention by the Supreme Court is not, however, an appropriate or measured response to this problem, if it indeed exists to the extent suggested by ICT proponents. In our view, the Court as manager has ample means available to it to encourage the adoption of procedures at the circuit court level to minimize the occurrence of error and to facilitate error correction at that level.

For example, the Court could order that, at least in cases where there is an objective warning signal that the circuit panel is in error, petitions for rehearing be directed not to the panel that decided the case, but to another panel of that court. A fundamental problem with the petition for rehearing as presently constituted is that the petition is directed to the panel that decided the case, and it requires no excess of skepticism to anticipate no special penchant for self-criticism.[14] The Court might promulgate a rule that when a circuit panel reverses a district court or when there is a dissent from the panel opinion, a petition for rehearing be directed to the then sitting motions panel of the circuit court (substituting a judge where a member of the original panel happens to be sitting on motions at the time). If this second panel grants the rehearing petition, the case could be assigned for rehearing by either the judges on the motions panel or an entirely new panel. This procedure does require some investment of judicial resources, because the motions panel must make a preliminary assessment of the case and decision rendered, but the investment would be significantly less than that required for rehearing en banc, and would provide the meaningful review that can come only from a panel with no preconceptions about the case. If the second panel to hear the case reaches a different result from the first, a strong case for rehearing en banc would be present. Conversely, if the second panel reaches the same result as the first, en banc review would presumably not occur—yet a contribution would have been made to the development of a circuit-wide consensus on the legal issue involved.

Either independently of this suggestion or in conjunction with it, the Court could order that, at least in cases where the circuit court intends to reverse the district court, the panel should circulate a draft opinion to the parties for comment. This procedure, used with some success in the D.C. Circuit,[15] engages the court in a dialogue with the parties during the decisionmaking process—a dialogue designed to avoid and correct error without higher court intervention.

With respect to the state courts, the Court's authority to fashion procedures not mandated by the Constitution or federal statue is less clear.[16] Even here, however, the Court has found means, illustrated by its *Krivda* remand practice,[17] to ensure that the state court judgment indeed rests on an adequate, independent state ground. Often, the Court is also not sure that the state high court has spoken on the question presented for review, because the only opinion rendered is that of the state intermediate appellate court, and the state supreme court has declined discretionary review. In such cases, by analogy to the *Krivda* remand, the Court should send the case back to the state high court to elicit its view as to whether the ruling below indeed represents the law of that state and, where an intercourt conflict is alleged, that the state high court was aware of the opposing view when it declined discretionary review.

The suggestions we have offered in this chapter, undoubtedly in need of further refinement, are intended to be no more than illustrative of the means available to the Court as manager to improve the informational base on which it renders national law, as well to enhance the sense of responsibility of state and federal appellate courts in the process.

These administrative reforms aside, our essential message is that, for its own sake, the Supreme Court must be demythologized. We no longer have a national court of errors ready to right any wrong committed by a lower court in a federal case, and we are not going to undo this reality by creating new courts. It is not the Supreme Court's job to ensure justice in the particular case. Its special responsibility, which it alone can shoulder, is to oversee a system of federal and state courts—and to intervene strategically—so as to maximize the system's ability to produce sound law and just results. What is needed is a systematic, hard-headed appraisal of how the Court can best employ its scarce decisional resources to perform its essential function. We have made such an attempt here. We invite others to join in the enterprise.

The Improvident Grants

For a fuller discussion of these cases, the reader is directed to the appendix entries of the NYU Supreme Court Project, 59 N.Y.U. L. Rev. at 1003 (1984).

(1) Blum v. Stenson.[1] The Court granted review to consider the appropriate standard for awarding attorney's fees to prevailing plaintiffs represented by nonprofit legal organizations in civil rights litigation. Although a two-court conflict on the permissibility of a "bonus" award to compensate attorneys for especially difficult litigation was alleged, we did not find a square conflict. Another alleged conflict, concerning the applicability of a "market rate" standard for nonprofit lawyers, was similarly unsubstantiated. The Court might have granted review on a "vehicle" rationale, but the petitioners' unfocused suggestion of lower court disarray was wholly undocumented.

On March 21, 1984, Justice Powell, writing for a unanimous Court, affirmed on the legal standard (recognizing both the market rate standard and the legitimacy of bonus awards), but reversed as to its application to the facts. Nothing in the Court's opinion suggests, however, that this case was regarded as a vehicle.

(2) Illinois v. Andreas.[2] In this case, the Illinois intermediate appeals court invalidated the search of a large, locked metal container that had been unlawfully opened by customs inspec-

tors, delivered to the respondent by undercover police officers, and left in the respondent's possession for thirty minutes before being seized and opened by the officers without a search warrant. The court rejected the rationale behind the "controlled delivery" cases on the ground that the officers, by relinquishing control of the respondent's property, had renewed the respondent's legitimate expectation of privacy. Although the state alleged several conflicts, these cases were distinguishable on the basis asserted by the Illinois appellate court. Even if one assumes, arguendo, that the ruling of the intermediate state court below could be counted for purposes of evaluating the alleged conflict between two or more courts, there was no conflict in principle over the controlled delivery cases—only a fact-specific dispute over the application of an agreed-upon standard. The grant was especially inappropriate because here a state court had invalidated state action, albeit on federal grounds. On July 5, 1983, the Supreme Court reversed (6–3).

(3) Oregon v. Bradshaw.[3] As in the preceding entry, this case involved an intermediate state court's invalidation of a search, this time on Fifth Amendment grounds. Here, the respondent requested an attorney after being informed of his right to counsel as required by *Miranda v. Arizona.*[4] Respondent then asked, "What is going to happen to me now?" Although the *Miranda* warnings were repeated, an incriminating conversation ensued. The state court found that the respondent had not "initiated" the conversation within the meaning of *Edwards v. Arizona.*[5] The petitioner alleged no conflicts, merely a disagreement over whether *Edwards* had been applied properly. None of the preconditions for a vehicle grant was present here, inasmuch as *Edwards* had been decided only the previous year. On June 23, 1983, the Court reversed in a plurality opinion, finding on the facts a knowing waiver of a previously asserted right to counsel.

(4) Illinois v. Lafayette.[6] This case involved yet another intermediate state decision invalidating, on Fourth Amendment grounds, a search of the respondent's purse as part of a normal booking procedure incident to arrest. The state alleged a misapplication of *United States v. Chadwick,*[7] an inappropriate con-

traction of the scope of an inventory search, and intercourt conflicts. However, even if the position of the Illinois Supreme Court could be regarded as fixed by the intermediate appellate decision, there was no square conflict between two or more courts. The Court should not grant certiorari simply to review a factual variant on its inventory search cases or to correct possible errors. Even if the Court were prepared to promulgate a broad rule for inventory searches, none of the preconditions for a vehicle grant was present here. On June 20, 1983, the Court reversed, holding that it is reasonable for police to search the personal effects of a person under lawful arrest as part of routine booking procedure.

(5) Morrison-Knudsen Construction Co. v. Director, Office of Workers' Compensation Programs.[8] At the behest of the Solicitor General, and even though appeals before two other circuits were pending when this petition was filed, the Court agreed to review the first appellate decision on whether employer contributions to pension funds constitute "wages" under the Longshoremen's and Harbor Workers' Compensation Act.[9] No interference with a significant executive responsibility was present here. Deference to the Goverment's wishes— the only fathomable explanation for a grant in this case—is not a sufficient basis for review. On May 24, 1983, the Court reversed (8–1).

(6) California v. Ramos.[10] Relying on *Witherspoon v. Illinois*,[11] the California Supreme Court struck down a statute requiring the presiding judge at the penalty phase of a capital case to inform the jury that a sentence of life without parole may be commuted. There was no clear conflict with Supreme Court doctrine, for the ruling could readily be reconciled with the teaching of *Jurek v. Texas*,[12] which permitted jury consideration of future dangerousness. Even if, contrary to the criteria of this study, one recognizes a special category for decisions sustaining a death sentence, *Ramos* would not fit such a category. Moreover, this case is yet another instance of state court invalidation of state action—a situation that rarely presents a compelling reason for Court review in the absence of a fully percolated conflict. On July 6, 1983, the Court reversed (5–4).

(7) Anderson v. Harless.[13] The Court summarily reversed a federal habeas ruling overturning a conviction under *Sandstrom v. Montana*[14] because of a garbled jury instruction on malice. The only question considered by the Court was whether the prisoner's claim of error accompanied by invocation of a state decision "fairly presented" his *Sandstrom* claim to the state court—a fact-specific issue not meriting the Court's attention under any circumstances.

(8) Haring v. Prosise.[15] The Fourth Circuit rejected arguments that a guilty plea should preclude a subsequent section 1983[16] action challenging the propriety of a police search of the respondent's apartment. The case presented at best a two-court conflict with a 1970 decision in the Tenth Circuit,[17] and forum shopping is unlikely in a context necessarily involving localized controversies. The decision below was consistent with general collateral estoppel law; although a guilty plea may have an issue-preclusive effect regarding the substantive elements of the offense, it does not ordinarily embrace questions regarding police conduct.[18] On June 13, 1983, the Court unanimously affirmed.

(9) Florida v. Casal.[19] This case presented yet another state decision overturning a state conviction on federal grounds. Here, police officers boarded a fishing boat when the respondents could not produce the boat's registration, and searched the boat's hold when the respondents admitted that the hold contained marijuana. The state's argument that the Florida Supreme Court misapplied the search-incident-to-arrest and investigatory search exceptions to the Fourth Amendment's warrant requirement did not present a serious claim of conflict with Supreme Court precedent. The petitioner identified no intercourt conflicts. Moreover, there was reason to believe that the Florida decision was based principally on state law.[20] On June 17, 1983, the Court dismissed the petition as improvidently granted.

(10) Norfolk Redevelopment & Housing Authority v. Chesapeake & Potomac Telephone Co.[21] The Fourth Circuit held that the Uniform Relocation Assistance and Real Property Acquisi-

tion Policies Act of 1970[22] extended beyond interests recognized
at common law to embrace the respondent utility's relocation
costs occasioned by federally aided redevelopment projects.
The petitioner's claim of conflict lacked merit, and the Solicitor
General opposed the petition. On November 1, 1983, the Court
unanimously reversed the Fourth Circuit.

*(11) Hispanic Coalition on Reapportionment v. Legislative Re-
apportionment Commission.*[23] Appellants urged that the district
court should have overturned Pennsylvania's redistricting of a
single legislative district on grounds of intentional racial discrimination. The Court summarily affirmed. Had the Court's
obligatory jurisdiction been abolished, this case would not have
been reviewed.

*(12) Arizona Governing Committee for Tax Deferred Annuity
& Deferred Compensation v. Norris.*[24] The Ninth Circuit held
that *Los Angeles Department of Water & Power v. Manhart*[25]
extended to Arizona's deferred compensation program, which
selected the companies with which the employee must contract
for a life annuity. All the companies selected by Arizona used
gender-based actuarial tables in computing monthly benefit
payments. The petitioners alleged no conflicts, but asserted that
Manhart did not disturb benefit plans that simply mirrored benefit options available on the open market. Even though this
"open market" issue had been reserved in *Manhart*, prior reservation of an issue is not sufficient to justify a vehicle grant. This
was a "next case" that should have been subjected to further
percolation before Supreme Court intervention. Moreover, a
vertical federalism rationale for a discretionary grant was un-
available because the state here was sued as employer rather
than as sovereign. In any event, the Ninth Circuit's ruling was
not an unwarranted extension of *Manhart*. On July 6, 1983, a
divided Court affirmed on liability, but reversed on the question of retrospective application (an issue not among the questions presented in the petition for certiorari).

(13) City of Revere v. Massachusetts General Hospital.[26] In
this case, the Massachusetts Supreme Judicial Court, relying on

Estelle v. Gamble,[27] held that Eighth Amendment principles required the city to reimburse respondent for medical care extended to a pretrial detainee while under its custody. Although the petitioner alleged a number of intercourt conflicts, the decision was consistent with prior lower court rulings. The petitioner also alleged a conflict with the Supreme Court's rulings in *Bell v. Wolfish*[28] and *Ingraham v. Wright*,[29] which, taken together, hold the Eighth Amendment inapplicable to pretrial detainees. Although the Massachusetts high court may have been mistaken in its reliance on *Estelle*, which preceded *Wolfish* and *Ingraham*, the city plainly had a due process obligation to provide for the medical care of the pretrial detainee. The question of who should pay for the medical care was simply not passed on by the Supreme Court in any prior ruling, and is analytically best viewed as a matter of state law. This case ultimately involved an intramural dispute between a municipality and a public hospital, which a state court, perhaps mistakenly, resolved on federal grounds. On June 27, 1983, the Court reversed.

(14) United States v. Whiting Pools, Inc.[30] At the Government's request, the Supreme Court granted certiorari to resolve an alleged two-court conflict over whether taxes levied on property before the filing of a reorganization petition were subject to the bankruptcy court's "turnover" authority. Although the Second Circuit acknowledged a conflict with the Fourth Circuit, our analysis indicated that the two decisions were reconcilable. Moreover, even a two-court divergence among the circuits over the effect of a prepetition levy does not justify a grant when the opportunity for forum shopping is limited and government planning would not be thwarted. Nor could the grant be justified on the ground of interference with executive responsibility, because no nationally applicable regulation had been disturbed and because the Second Circuit had insisted on assurance of "adequate protection" of the Government's interest.[31] On June 8, 1983, the Court unanimously affirmed.

(15) Ruckelshaus v. Sierra Club.[32] The District of Columbia Circuit held that attorney's fees could be awarded to a nonprevailing party under the Clean Air Act[33] when the party had

made a contribution to the quality of judicial decisionmaking. The Government did not identify any lower court conflicts; it merely contended that the court had misconstrued the statute and violated principles of sovereign immunity by not insisting on unmistakable legislative authorization for such payments out of the national fisc. On July 1, 1983, the Court reversed (5–4).

(16) Chardon v. Soto.[34] The First Circuit held that the filing of a section 1983[35] class action tolled the applicable statute of limitations and renewed the full limitations period—by virtue of section 1988's[36] reference to state tolling rules—once class certification had been denied. The petitioners' assertion of intercourt conflict was without merit because other rulings had not reached the renewal issue. Moreover, the rulings cited by the petitioner predated *Board of Regents v. Tomanio*,[37] which underscored the relevance of state law. The Court's decision in *American Pipe & Construction Co. v. Utah*[38] did not purport to announce, and indeed disclaimed any intention of announcing, uniform rules for all federal causes of action. There the Court had relied specifically on the tolling provision of section 5(b) of the Clayton Act.[39] On June 20, 1983, the Court affirmed.

(17) International Association of Machinists v. Federal Election Commission.[40] This case was an appeal under the special certification procedure for constitutional challenges under the Federal Election Campaign Act.[41] Appellants attacked the statute's alleged failure to maintain a balance between corporate and union speech, and to protect dissenting corporate employees and shareholders. As the Court's summary affirmance on November 8, 1982, indicates, the appeals court's rejection of these rather marginal constitutional arguments would not have warranted Supreme Court review had the Court's obligatory jurisdiction been abolished. Under the criteria of this study, a federal decision sustaining the validity of federal action does not merit a discretionary grant in the absence of intercourt conflict. No such conflict was alleged here.

(18) Michigan v. Clifford.[42] The Michigan intermediate appeals court reversed a conviction because the Detroit Fire De-

partment's search was unlawful under *Michigan v. Tyler*.[43] The fire department's investigation had not begun until several hours after the fire had been extinguished and the firefighters had left the scene. The state argued that under *Tyler* the search was a continuation of the original entry by the firefighters and that the investigators had acted in good faith. This was an improvident grant because (1) *Tyler* was distinguishable in that the fire department there had not relinquished control of the premises before the search commenced; (2) orderly development of a "good faith" exception to the Fourth Amendment would have the Court first establish the exception in a defective-warrant case, and then allow lower court percolation of more controversial applications bordering on a "mistake of law" defense; and (3) a state court had invalidated state action. On January 11, 1984, the Court affirmed in part and reversed in part (5–4).

(19) Burton v. Hobbie.[44] Appellants challenged the district court's interim authorization of voting changes that had not been cleared in advance by the Attorney General under section 5 of the Voting Rights Act.[45] Were the Court's obligatory jurisdiction abolished, this case would in all likelihood not have been reviewed, because the federal court sustained state action on grounds not clearly at odds with established Supreme Court doctrine. The issue was highly fact-specific, which further militated against a grant unless the Court was prepared to hold that interim authorization is never permissible. On November 1, 1982, the Court summarily affirmed.

(20) Federal Trade Commission v. Grolier, Inc.[46] The District of Columbia Circuit held that exemption 5 of the Freedom of Information Act (FOIA)[47] did not extend to the work product of terminated litigation absent the existence of related actual or potential litigation. This was the first appellate decision to consider whether the FOIA requires a temporal limitation on nondisclosure of work product. The other appellate decisions cited by the petitioner arose in a civil discovery context, in which an FOIA-based presumption in favor of disclosure was not present. The Court, though recognizing the close relationship between exemption 5 and civil discovery privileges, had never

ruled that they were coextensive in coverage. Although the Court in *Federal Open Market Committee of the Federal Reserve System v. Merrill*[48] held that exemption 5 incorporates a qualified privilege for government-generated commercial information, *Merrill* itself expressly questioned whether exemption 5 incorporates all civil discovery privileges.[49] The Court may have granted certiorari because it perceived a close relation between this case and *United States v. Weber Aircraft Corp.*,[50] which involved a fully percolated conflict over FOIA treatment of the civil privilege for witness statements made to air crash safety investigators. In our view, such linkage would have been inappropriate because no resolution of the issue in *Weber* would have shed much light on the temporal limitation question. On June 6, 1983, the Court unanimously reversed in *Grolier*.

(21) Russello v. United States.[51] The Fifth Circuit held that the forfeiture provisions of the Racketeer Influenced and Corrupt Organizations Act[52] extended to income or profits derived from a pattern of racketeering activity, and were not limited to interests in the enterprise itself. We doubt that there was a two-court conflict, because the position of one of the circuits was in flux.[53] Even though in some multistate conspiracies the Government may be able to forum shop, we doubt whether the scope of the forfeiture remedy would significantly influence forum choice. On November 1, 1983, the Court unanimously affirmed.

(22) Migra v. Warren City School District Board of Education.[54] The Sixth Circuit held that federal preclusion principles in section 1983[55] cases extended to claim preclusion as well as issue preclusion. Although issue preclusion was authorized by *Allen v. McCurry*,[56] claim preclusion arguably involved a far more significant restriction of the section 1983 plaintiff's access to federal court. There was no post-*Allen* conflict on the issue; indeed, all of the post-*Allen* decisions were in accord with the Sixth Circuit. Although the issue had been reserved in *Allen*,[57] prior reservation is not sufficient to justify a vehicle grant. Here, the reservation in *Allen* had not generated any unintended offshoot rulings; the courts were apparently uninfluenced by the reservation and construed *Allen* broadly. This was

a "next case" situation that did not warrant Supreme Court attention until a conflict developed. On January 23, 1984, the Court unanimously vacated and remanded for a determination of state preclusion law, while agreeing with the Sixth Circuit that no section 1983 based policy would override a state rule of claim preclusion.

(23) Hishon v. King & Spalding.[58] The Eleventh Circuit held that Title VII of the Civil Rights Act[59] did not apply to partnership promotion decisions. There was no circuit conflict in this case, only a contrary district court opinion that was never appealed. The case was in all likelihood wrongly decided, inasmuch as Title VII purports to reach promotion decisions in all employment contexts, but error correction is not a sufficient basis for a discretionary grant. Moreover, adequate percolation might well have enhanced resolution of the Title VII coverage issue by unearthing the range of potential factual variants and possibly by generating alternative analytic frameworks for adjudication of partnership-denial claims. We disagree with the suggestion that the Court should selectively grant review in notorious cases such as *Hishon* to avoid the appearance of approving the result. In our view, the lower courts are perfectly capable of accurately interpreting a denial of certiorari. Indeed, were the Court routinely to engage in error correction, a denial of certiorari might well be construed as tacit approval of a lower court's decision. Such expectations would make it increasingly difficult for the Court to manage its docket. On May 22, 1984, the Court unanimously reversed.

(24) Sure-Tan, Inc. v. NLRB.[60] The Seventh Circuit ruled that the National Labor Relations Board (NLRB) could mandate reinstatement of undocumented alien workers who had been discharged for union activity, but modified the Board's order to require that the reinstatement offers be kept open for four years in order to permit the workers to take steps to reenter the country legally. There was no circuit conflict in this case. Nor was there any significant interference with federal executive responsibility. The NLRB had not challenged the court's modification of its order, and the Immigration and Naturalization Service,

which had not participated in any stage of the proceedings, interposed no objection to the Board's actions. On June 25, 1984, the Court affirmed on the issue of coverage of illegal aliens but reversed the modification of the Board's order.

(25) Maryland v. United States.[61] These appeals grew out of the district court's approval of a settlement modifying a 1956 consent decree and terminating the Government's antitrust suit against American Telephone & Telegraph Company. The appellants objected to the court's provision authorizing newly organized local operating companies to commence new services or to abandon existing services without securing the approval of state public service commissions. As the Court's summary affirmance indicates, well-established federal preemption principles governed the issue. This case would not have been reviewed had the Court's obligatory jurisdiction been abolished.

(26) McDonough Power Equipment, Inc. v. Greenwood.[62] The Tenth Circuit reversed a jury verdict in this product liability case because during voir dire the jury foreman had not disclosed that his son had suffered an injury similar to plaintiff's. This case involves a fact-specific question about the proper application of an undisputed juror misconduct standard in a diversity suit. Absent a showing of persistent misapplication of that standard by the Tenth Circuit, triggering the Court's supervisory responsibility, this localized dispute did not belong on the discretionary docket. On January 18, 1984, the Court unanimously reversed.

(27) Simon v. Davis.[63] The district court sustained a state's redistricting plan, rejecting the appellant's invitation to place constitutional limits on political gerrymandering. This case involved the application of well-settled principles, and the Court would not have granted review were its obligatory jurisdiction abolished. On July 6, 1983, the Court affirmed summarily. Justices Brennan, Marshall, and Stevens would have set the case for oral argument.

(28) Dickman v. Commissioner.[64] The Eleventh Circuit overturned a Tax Court ruling that intrafamily, interest-free loans that were payable on demand did not result in taxable gifts. The

petitioners alleged a conflict with the Seventh Circuit, which the court below had acknowledged. This case presented a two-court conflict but no significant potential for forum shopping, given the Tax Court's acquiescence policy and the fact that the Claims Court (now part of the Court of Appeals for the Federal Circuit) apparently had not taken a position on the issue. The nature of the issue suggested no significant planning difficulties for multicircuit actors. On February 22, 1984, the Court affirmed (7–2).

(29) Pulley v. Harris.[65] The Ninth Circuit reversed a state prisoner's death sentence on habeas review because the California courts had not engaged in proportionality review (comparison of the prisoner's sentence to the punishment meted out in similar cases). The petitioner alleged a conflict with the Fifth Circuit.[66] The cases, however, were not squarely in conflict; the Fifth Circuit's allegedly conflicting holding was merely dictum.[67] In any event, a two-court conflict would not suffice for such localized controversies not presenting a potential for forum shopping. Moreover, there was no conflict with any Supreme Court opinion. The Ninth Circuit's ruling drew support from the opinions of Justices Stewart, Powell, and Stevens in *Gregg v. Georgia*[68] and *Proffitt v. Florida.*[69] Although the capital punishment scheme upheld in *Jurek v. Texas*[70] did not provide for proportionality review, the Court did not squarely pass on the point. Nor does the vertical federalism rationale for a discretionary grant justify the review of an isolated instance of state-federal disagreement in the context of federal habeas review. This case involved a very important death penalty issue that had received very little percolation. On January 23, 1984, the Court reversed (7–2).

(30) McKaskle v. Wiggins.[71] The Fifth Circuit, relying on *Faretta v. California,*[72] held that the respondent's right to self-representation under *Faretta* had been abridged by court-appointed "standby" counsel's aggressive, overzealous intervention at trial. The petitioner identified no intercourt conflicts. Resolution of the issue reserved in *Faretta*—the permissibility of appointing "standby" counsel over defendant's objec-

tions[73]—would not have reached this case of overzealous representation. There was no demonstration of doctrinal incoherence or of sufficient percolation to justify a vehicle grant to establish guidelines for the participation of "standby" counsel. On January 23, 1984, the Court reversed (6–3).

(31) Common Cause v. Bolger.[74] The appellants challenged the district court's refusal to strike down a federal statute granting franking privileges to members of Congress. No conflict was alleged. The appellants' claim sought a significant extension of First Amendment doctrine. In the absence of obligatory jurisdiction, this would be an improvident grant. On May 2, 1983, the Court affirmed.

(32) Bose Corp. v. Consumers Union of United States, Inc.[75] The First Circuit engaged in *de novo* rather than "clearly erroneous" review of a jury verdict reached under the "actual malice" standard of *New York Times Co. v. Sullivan*[76] and its progeny. The petitioner argued that *de novo* review was inconsistent with the Court's insistence in *Inwood Laboratories, Inc. v. Ives Laboratories, Inc.*[77] and *Pullman-Standard v. Swint*[78] on "clearly erroneous" review under Federal Rule of Civil Procedure 52(a) even in the context of mixed questions of law and fact. The question here was whether *Inwood* and *Swint* applied to *Sullivan* libel actions. The Court had on several occasions directed the lower courts to require "clear and convincing" proof of actual malice and to engage in seemingly *de novo* review,[79] yet *Inwood* and *Swint* arguably presaged a rule of greater deference to district court fact-finding. The issue here was certainly important, but the impact of *Inwood* and *Swint* on *Sullivan* libel actions should have awaited the percolation process. On April 30, 1984, the Court affirmed (6–3).

(33) Secretary of the Interior v. California.[80] The Ninth Circuit held that an outer continental shelf lease sale that does not itself authorize any conduct having physical impact on the coast is federal activity "directly affecting the coastal zone" under the Coastal Zone Management Improvement Act of 1980.[81] Therefore, such activity must be consistent, to the maximum extent

possible, with approved state-managed programs. The Government urged review of this first appellate ruling on the subject, claiming a significant interference with federal executive responsibility, even though (1) no nationally applicable regulation was affected, and (2) no contention was made that such lease sales are restricted to the Ninth Circuit (a variant of the exclusive jurisdiction problem) or that compliance could not be confined to that jurisdiction. On January 11, 1984, the Court reversed (5–4).

(34) Thigpen v. Roberts.[82] The Fifth Circuit, on federal habeas review, overturned a Mississippi automotive manslaughter conviction on double jeopardy grounds. While the defendant, having been found guilty of misdemeanor charges, was invoking his right under state law to a trial *de novo*, he was indicted and convicted for manslaughter based on the same accident. The Fifth Circuit, relying on *Illinois v. Vitale*,[83] held that proof of the greater crime necessarily included proof of the lesser crime, so that a second prosecution was barred. The petitioner alleged a conflict with two state court decisions that predated *Vitale*, one of which was a Mississippi ruling.[84] However, this study does not count a federal-state conflict arising in the federal habeas context as meriting review unless the conflict persists after the federal court has made known its views. The Fifth Circuit also never reached the district court's alternative due process ground under *Blackledge v. Perry*[85]—a point not briefed by the parties. On June 27, 1984, the Court affirmed (6–3) on due process grounds without reaching the double jeopardy issue.

(35) Maggio v. Fulford.[86] On habeas review, the Fifth Circuit overturned a state conviction because the defendant's competence to stand trial in 1972 had not been adequately determined. Petitioner argued that the court ignored clear evidence of competency in the record, including the defendant's presentation of alibi witnesses. This fact-specific dispute was not appropriate for Supreme Court consideration, absent a showing that the Fifth Circuit systematically had failed to show appropriate deference to state court findings of fact as required by the federal habeas statute. On June 6, 1983, the Court reversed (5–4).

(36) Pulliam v. Allen.[87] The Fourth Circuit sustained an attorney's fees award against a state magistrate, holding that (1) judicial immunity did not extend to injunctive relief under the Attorneys' Fees Awards Act of 1976;[88] (2) prospective injunctive relief had been properly ordered; and (3) the attorney's fee award was reasonable. There was no intercourt conflict in this case and the claim of conflict with *Supreme Court of Virginia v. Consumers Union of the United States, Inc.*[89] was without merit. On May 14, 1984, the Court affirmed (5–4).

(37) Badaracco v. Commissioner.[90] The Third Circuit held that the filing of a nonfraudulent amended return after the filing of an original fraudulent return did not start the running of a three-year statute of limitations under section 6501(a) of the Internal Revenue Code.[91] The petitioners alleged a conflict with the Tenth Circuit and with the Second Circuit's summary affirmance of a district court ruling. As developed in chapter 6, a summary affirmance does not count as an appellate court decision for conflict purposes, for we can never be entirely certain of the precise grounds for the appeals court's judgment, and therefore the position of that court remains unfixed. Thus this case presented only a two-court conflict. Since the Tax Court follows the rulings of the Circuit Court in which the case before it arises, and the Claims Court had not ruled on the matter, there was no danger that an individual taxpayer would confront inconsistent governing regimes. Moreover, the issue involved was not likely to affect legitimate planning considerations of multicircuit actors. On January 17, 1984, the Court affirmed (8–1).

(38) Justices of Boston Municipal Court v. Lydon.[92] Under state law, a defendant could choose either a bench or jury trial. If the defendant chose the former, he had an absolute right to a trial *de novo* before a jury without need to allege error at the bench trial. The respondent here chose a bench trial, was convicted and sentenced, and then requested a *de novo* jury trial. Before the jury trial commenced, the respondent moved to dismiss the charge on the ground that no evidence of intent had been presented at the bench trial, and therefore retrial was

barred on double jeopardy grounds. Ultimately, on habeas review, the First Circuit held that under *Burks v. United States*[93] a second trial was foreclosed if the evidence against the respondent at the bench trial was insufficient, and then went on to find that there had been insufficient evidence of intent at the bench trial. Thus the question for review was whether under Massachusetts's two-tier system, which had been sustained in *Ludwig v. Massachusetts*,[94] a trial judge's ruling on evidentiary sufficiency after a bench trial should be regarded as a first-level consideration of sufficiency. In other words, the issue involved was *Burks*'s possible impact on *Ludwig*—an unpercolated issue over which there was no intercourt conflict. Furthermore, under the criteria of this study, a federal-state conflict arising in the context of federal habeas review does not merit resolution by the Court unless the conflict persists after the federal court has made its views known. On April 18, 1984, the Court unanimously (through several opinions) reversed.

(39) Cardwell v. Taylor.[95] The Ninth Circuit, on habeas review, overturned a state conviction because the respondent had been placed in custody before the police had probable cause to arrest him. The petitioner argued that the appeals court failed to accord a presumption of correctness to the state court's findings of fact as required by the federal habeas statute. This fact-specific dispute did not merit Supreme Court intervention, even if only for the summary reversal that the Court issued on May 23, 1983.

The Unresolved Conflicts
Denied Review

The Eleven "Intolerable" Three-Court Conflicts

(1) Alabama v. Mylar.[1] In *Mylar* the Eleventh Circuit aligned itself with the Fifth Circuit, holding that even when state law requires a state appellate court to review all criminal proceedings for plain error, an appellate counsel who fails to file a brief renders ineffective assistance as a per se matter.[2] This holding squarely conflicts with the Tenth Circuit's requirement that ineffective assistance of counsel must be demonstrated by actual prejudice, even where the state appellate court is required *sua sponte* to review convictions for plain error.[3] Nevertheless, the Note author concludes that review was properly denied because (1) the Tenth Circuit had rejected the per se rule ten years earlier and the Fifth and Eleventh Circuits had recently sustained the rule; (2) the newly created Eleventh Circuit had simply adopted an earlier Fifth Circuit ruling (and such wholesale adoption should not be counted) and thus there was arguably only a two-court conflict; and (3) the Court granted several effective-assistance cases diring the 1982 Term,[4] suggesting that further percolation in light of those cases was warranted.

(2) Caminita v. Louisiana.[5] *Caminita* presented a conflict between the Louisiana Supreme Court and other courts over

These summaries are distillations of the *Law Review* editors' analyses of the cases denied review during the study period; they do not necessarily reflect the views of the authors of this book.

whether the prosecution is free to withdraw an accepted plea offer if there is no evidence of detrimental reliance by the accused or of prosecutorial bad faith. Review was properly denied, the Note author finds, because (1) recent rulings had also adopted the revocability position of the Louisiana high court, suggesting that an earlier conflicting Fourth Circuit ruling[6] was aberrational; and (2) the record in this case was muddled in several crucial respects. Moreover, once the Eighth Circuit adopted the Fourth Circuit's position, in *Johnson v. Mabry*,[7] the Supreme Court did grant review during the 1983 Term.

(3) Shoemaker v. Riley.[8] The Sixth Circuit in this federal habeas case held that the state court's misapplication of standing rules deprived the respondent of the opportunity to litigate fully his Fourth Amendment claim, which must be provided to preclude federal habeas relief under *Stone v. Powell*.[9] The Sixth Circuit's holding conflicts with the Fifth Circuit's broader reading of *Stone v. Powell*,[10] as well as with the more restrictive reading of the Tenth Circuit.[11] According to the student author, this case should have been reviewed.

(4) Wilkinson v. United States.[12] *Wilkinson* presented a multicircuit conflict regarding whether the Federal Tort Claims Act's statute of limitations[13] is tolled when suit is mistakenly filed against an individual rather than his federal employer.[14] The Supreme Court had previously declined to settle this recurring issue.[15] According to the Note author, this case should have been reviewed.

(5) International Rectifier Corp. v. Cohen.[16] In this diversity action, the Eighth Circuit asserted ancillary jurisdiction over a fee dispute between a corporation and its nondiverse former attorney. The dispute arose in connection with a federal antitrust action that had been settled without an award of legal fees. The Eighth Circuit's position conflicted with that of the Fourth and Seventh Circuits.[17] Nevertheless, the Note author concludes, review was properly denied because (1) the Eighth Circuit was presented with an incomplete record inherent in this interlocutory appeal; and (2) the Eighth Circuit rendered a ten-

tative judgment, inviting reappeal of the jurisdictional issue after a final determination by the trial court.

(6) Fricke v. United States.[18] In *Fricke*, the Fifth Circuit addressed the question, which other courts had resolved in a variety of ways, whether a jury instruction that violated *Sandstrom v. Montana*[19] could ever be harmless error.[20] The court answered the question in the affirmative, and upheld the defendant's conviction.[21] The Supreme Court had previously failed to reach a majority position on this same issue in *Connecticut v. Johnson.*[22] The Note author determined that *Fricke* was an inappropriate vehicle for resolving the issue left open in *Johnson* because the Fifth Circuit's opinion suggests that the appeals court was unsure whether a burden-shifting presumption was actually conveyed to the jury. This possibility of an alternative ground blunted the opportunity for a clear-cut resolution of the *Johnson* issue. Moreover, the issue arises with sufficient frequency to justify the decision to await a better vehicle. Indeed, the Court subsequently divided on the *Johnson* issue in *Koehler v. Engle*[23] and granted certiorari to reconsider it in *Francis v. Franklin.*[24]

(7) Nieszner v. Orr.[25] This petition pointed out that the Eighth Circuit and other circuits are in conflict with the Third Circuit over the appropriate test for determining the justiciability of constitutional challenges to military regulations. According to the Note author, this case was improperly denied review.[26]

(8) Teamsters Local No. 243 v. Sears, Roebuck & Co.[27] This Sixth Circuit ruling conflicts with the decisions of at least three other circuits over the appropriate standard of judicial review of labor arbitration awards.[28] In contrast with other courts that have adopted a highly deferential "rationality" standard, the Sixth Circuit in this case insisted that arbitrators have limited authority to depart from the unambiguous language of a collective bargaining agreement.[29] Although these cases often turn on their particular facts, including the bargaining history and past practices of the parties, the Note author found a square conflict

over the appropriate standard of review and concluded that certiorari had been improperly denied in this case.

(9) Willamette Industries v. United States.[30] In *Willamette*, the Ninth Circuit aligned itself with the District of Columbia Circuit and opposite the Seventh Circuit in determining the scope of the Haskell Amendment to the Internal Revenue Code.[31] That amendment provides that the Freedom of Information Act exemption for tax return information does not apply to "data in a form which cannot be associated with, or otherwise identify, directly or indirectly, a particular taxpayer."[32] The Ninth Circuit held that the Haskell Amendment allows disclosure of documents related to specific taxpayers as long as the documents are edited sufficiently to prevent taxpayer identification, whereas the Seventh Circuit would limit disclosure to data that were "changed in form, by amalgamation with data from other taxpayers to form statistical tabulations or studies."[33] The Note author concluded that review was improperly denied here.

(10) Bank of Nova Scotia v. United States.[34] In this case the Eleventh Circuit aligned itself with other circuit courts in rejecting the Third Circuit's requirement that the government demonstrate the relevancy of documents that it requests by grand jury subpoena.[35] The Third Circuit's position was based on its supervisory authority rather than any perceived constitutional mandate.[36] Hence, the Third Circuit's approach may be proper "law of the circuit" regardless of contrary determinations, and the Court therefore properly denied review.

Bank of Nova Scotia also presents a conflict with the Seventh Circuit regarding the application of the foreign illegality defense to justify noncompliance with domestic discovery orders.[37] This conflict, however, is only between two courts; moreover, it concerns the application of a test that all circuits endorse, and it is too early to tell whether the Seventh Circuit is in practice applying a different standard.[38] Thus, with respect to both alleged conflicts, review was properly denied, according to the Note author.

(11) Michigan v. Alexander.[39] This petition presented the same issue as *Fricke v. United States.*[40] Review was properly denied, however, because the case presented the issue in a posture likely to produce the same plurality opinions that frustrated definitive resolution in a prior Supreme Court case that addressed the issue.[41]

(12) Perez v. United States.[42] In *Perez*, the Second Circuit aligned itself with the majority of the circuits and opposite the Tenth Circuit.[43] The Tenth Circuit had ruled that it was per se reversible error for a trial court to admit coconspirator hearsay before making an on-the-record finding that the elements of Federal Rule of Evidence 801(d)(2)(E) had been satisfied.[44] This conflict did not merit priority review because forum shopping is generally not a concern in criminal cases. The conflict illustrates permissible variation among the trial procedures of different circuits—a context appropriate for "law of the circuit" treatment.

The One "Intolerable" Two-Court Conflict

(1) City of Marietta v. Dills.[45] *Dills* presented a conflict between the Eleventh Circuit and the Georgia Supreme Court over whether the First Amendment voids a Georgia statute regulating the use of neon signs. Because Georgians can obviously forum shop between state and federal systems, this conflict should have been resolved by the Court, the Note author finds.

The Seven "Tolerable" Two-Court Conflicts

(1) Uncle Ben's, Inc. v. Johnson.[46] In *Texas Department of Community Affairs v. Burdine*,[47] the Supreme Court held that a plaintiff's prima facie showing of discrimination in a Title VII disparate treatment suit shifts only the burden of production to the defendant. In *Uncle Ben's*, the Fifth Circuit held that *Burdine* does not extend to disparate impact cases. The Third Circuit reached an opposite conclusion in *NAACP v. Medical Center, Inc.*[48] and *Croker v. Boeing Co.*[49] Although other cir-

cuits have continued to rule that a prima facie showing by the disparate impact plaintiff shifts the burden of persuasion to the defendant, only the Third and Fifth Circuits have considered the application of *Burdine* to this issue.[50] Thus the conflict exists between only two circuits. Although limited forum shopping is possible under Title VII's special venue provision, in the overwhelming number of cases the only proper venue will be the district of the place of employment, so this conflict is tolerable.

(2) Bath Iron Works Corp. v. Director, Office of Workers' Compensation Programs.[51] In *Calbeck v. Travelers Insurance Co.*[52] the Supreme Court extended the scope of federal compensation under the Longshoremen's and Harbor Workers' Compensation Act.[53] Twenty years later, in the case below, the First Circuit held that *Calbeck* applies retroactively to a claimant who had previously received state compensation.[54] This holding squarely conflicts with the Fifth Circuit's determination that *Calbeck* does not apply retroactively to workers who had received state awards.[55] This conflict, however, presents little danger of forum shopping.[56] Because the *Calbeck* decision is more than twenty years old, exceedingly few litigants can now be affected by its retroactive application.

(3) Treasure Isle, Inc. v. United States.[57] This case presents a conflict between the Eleventh and Fourth Circuits over whether a corporation can be both an "enterprise" and a "person" under the Racketeer Influenced and Corrupt Organizations Act (RICO).[58] An alleged conflict with an Eighth Circuit ruling in a civil RICO case is reconcilable because the Eighth Circuit drew a distinction between civil and criminal RICO cases.[59] Although forum shopping can occur under RICO—particularly in prosecutions of multiple defendants—the conflict here is not likely to influence forum choice, because the Eleventh Circuit has held that a corporation and its employees can be charged as an "association in fact" even if the corporation could not be both an "enterprise" and a "person."[60] Neither the Fourth nor the Eighth Circuits has rejected this theory; indeed, the Eighth Circuit has intimated its approval.[61]

(4) Coletta v. United States.[62] The Ninth Circuit in this case held that nonminority defendants lack standing to challenge grand jury foreperson selection procedures that allegedly discriminate against minorities.[63] The Eleventh Circuit reached an opposite conclusion in a similar case.[64] At the time *Coletta* was denied certiorari, there was only a two-court conflict, in circumstances negating any significant forum shopping potential. The denial of certiorari was therefore proper. After that denial, however, the Fifth Circuit aligned itself with the Ninth Circuit on this issue.[65]

(5) Nobel v. United States.[66] *Nobel* presented a conflict between the Second and Seventh Circuits over whether the right to disqualify a judge[67] is waived by failure to make an objection after disclosure of information suggesting bias. This conflict, however, neither affects the primary behavior of multicircuit actors nor creates a potential for forum shopping, because the issue arises only after a case has been assigned to a particular judge.[68]

(6) Goose Creek Consolidated Independent School District v. Horton.[69] *Goose Creek* presented a conflict between the Fifth and Seventh Circuits over whether the Fourth Amendment restricts general searches of public school students by the use of drug-sniffing dogs.[70] There is no potential for forum shopping in local controversies of this type. After the Court denied certiorari in *Goose Creek*, it decided *New Jersey v. T.L.O.*,[71] which also involved the Fourth Amendment rights of public school students.

(7) A v. X.Y.Z.[72] The Supreme Courts of Wyoming and Colorado rendered conflicting decisions over the constitutionality of the Uniform Parentage Act's provisions governing the standing of putative fathers to establish paternity. The conflict was deemed tolerable because (1) paternity suits do not by their nature implicate multicircuit actors; and (2) although an opportunity for forum shopping exists, it is, for all practical purposes, insignificant.[73]

Notes

Chapter 1: The Need for a New Vision of the Court

1. R. Posner, Federal Courts: Crisis and Reform 63–64 (1985).
2. 52 U.S.L.W. 3025 (July 26, 1983).
3. *Id.*
4. Taft, The Jurisdiction of the Supreme Court under the Act of February 13, 1925, 35 Yale L.J. 1, 2 (1925).
5. Address before the American Bar Association, Sept. 7, 1949, quoted in R. Stern & E. Gressman, Supreme Court Practice 258 (5th ed. 1978).
6. Griswold, The Supreme Court's Case Load: Civil Rights and Other Problems, 1973 U. Ill. L.F. 615; S. Hufstedler, The Quiet Collapse: The Crumbling of the Federal Appellate Structure 13–17 (unpublished address on dedication of Annual Survey of American Law, Apr. 7, 1983) (on file at New York University Law Review) (proposing the creation of a permanent NCA).
7. See, e.g., Brennan, Some Thoughts on the Supreme Court's Workload, 66 Judicature 230, 231 (1983) ("There is a limit to human endurance" and, taking into account the complexity of the cases, 150 cases "taxes that endurance to its limits.").
8. See, e.g., Burger, Annual Report on the State of the Judiciary, 69 A.B.A. J. 442 (1983).
9. Testimony of Erwin Griswold before the Subcommittee on the Courts of the House Judiciary Committee (February 27, 1986).
10. 106 S. Ct. 1242 (1986).
11. Estreicher & Sexton, A Managerial Theory of the Supreme Court's Responsibilities: An Empirical Study, 59 N.Y.U. L. Rev. 681 (1984).
12. Paul v. Davis, 424 U.S. 693, 698 (1976).

13. See, e.g., Procunier v. Navarette, 434 U.S. 555 (1978); Baker v. McCollan, 443 U.S. 137 (1979); Parratt v. Taylor, 451 U.S. 527 (1981); Daniels v. Williams, 106 S. Ct. 662 (1986).

14. Parratt v. Taylor, 451 U.S. 527 (1981).

15. Daniels v. Williams, 106 S. Ct. 662 (1986).

16. See, e.g., Shaffer v. Heitner, 433 U.S. 186 (1977); Kulko v. Superior Court, 436 U.S. 84 (1978); World-Wide Volkswagen Corp. v. Woodson, 444 U.S. 286 (1980); Rush v. Savchuk, 444 U.S. 320 (1980); Insurance Corp. of Ireland v. Compagnie des Bauxites de Guinée, 456 U.S. 694 (1982); Gillette Co. v. Miner, 459 U.S. 86 (1982); Keeton v. Hustler Magazine, Inc., 465 U.S. 770 (1984); Calder v. Jones, 465 U.S. 783 (1984); Helicopteros Nacionales de Columbia, S.A. v. Hall, 466 U.S. 408 (1984); Burger King Corp. v. Rudzewicz, 105 S. Ct. 2174 (1985); Phillips Petroleum Co. v. Shutts, 105 S. Ct. 2965 (1985).

17. 326 U.S. 310 (1945).

18. 433 U.S. 186 (1977).

Chapter 2: The Evolution of our Present Judicial Structure

1. U.S. Const. art. III, § 1 provides only that "[t]he judicial Power of the United States, shall be vested in one Supreme Court, and in such inferior Courts as the Congress may from time to time ordain and establish."

2. Act of Sept. 24, 1789, ch. 20, 1 Stat. 73. Even this venerable statute, a product of the First Congress, was the subject of debate in the republic's early days. See, e.g., 3 A. Beveridge, The Life of John Marshall 54–55 (1919); R. Ellis, The Jeffersonian Crisis: Courts and Politics in the Young Republic 12–13 (1971); Warren, New Light on the History of the Federal Judiciary Act of 1789, 37 Harv. L. Rev. 49, 52–53 (1923).

3. Act of Sept. 24, 1789, ch. 20, §1, 1 Stat. 73.

4. *Id*. §§3–4.

5. *Id*. §4.

6. *Id*. §§9, 11.

7. H. Carson, The Supreme Court of the United States: Its History 145 (1891).

8. F. Frankfurter & J. Landis, The Business of the Supreme Court 11–13 (1927).

9. J. Goebel, I History of the Supreme Court of the United States: Antecedents and Beginnings to 1801, at 798 (1971).

10. *Id*. at 800.

11. *Id*. at 557.

12. F. Frankfurter & J. Landis, *supra* note 8, at 21–22.

13. Act of Mar. 2, 1793, ch. 22, §1, 1 Stat. 333.

14. Act of Feb. 13, 1801, ch. 4, 2 Stat. 89, repealed by Act of Mar. 8, 1802, ch. 8, 2 Stat. 132.

15. See 1 C. Warren, The Supreme Court in United States History 185–86 (1926).

16. Act of Feb. 13, 1801, ch. 4, §7, 2 Stat. 89, 90.

17. C. Warren, *supra* note 15, at 185–93.

18. Act of Mar. 8, 1802, ch. 8, 2 Stat. 132.

19. Act of Apr. 29, 1802, ch. 1, 2 Stat. 156.

20. F. Frankfurter & J. Landis, *supra* note 8, at 34–35.

21. *Id*. at 34 & n.96.

22. *Id*. at 38–39.

23. Act of Feb. 24, 1807, ch. 16, 2 Stat. 420.

24. Act of Mar. 3, 1837, ch. 34, 5 Stat. 176.

25. Act of Mar. 3, 1863, ch. 100, 12 Stat. 794.

26. Act of July 23, 1866, ch. 210, 14 Stat. 209.

27. See H. Abraham, Justices and Presidents 114–16 (1974).

28. See A. Kelly & W. Harbison, The American Constitution 449–50 (5th ed. 1976).

29. Act of Apr. 10, 1869, ch. 22, 16 Stat. 44.

30. H. Abraham, *supra* note 27, at 118.

31. Act of Apr. 10, 1869, ch. 22, §§2, 4, 16 Stat. 44, 44–45.

32. Griswold, The Supreme Court's Case Load: Civil Rights and Other Problems, 1973 U. Ill. L.F. 615.

33. F. Frankfurter & J. Landis, *supra* note 8, at 60 n.165.

34. *Id*. at 60.

35. Act of Mar. 3, 1875, ch. 137, 18 Stat. 470; see F. Frankfurter & J. Landis, *supra* note 8, at 65.

36. Act of Mar. 3, 1891, ch. 517, 26 Stat. 826.

37. *Id*. §§ 1–2, 6. On the drafting of this statute, see W. King, Melville Weston Fuller 149–51 (1950).

38. A. Mason, William Howard Taft: Chief Justice 89–90 (1965); D. Provine, Case Selection in the United States Supreme Court 10–11 (1980).

39. See A. Mason, *supra* note 38; see also, e.g., Taft, Delays and Defects in the Enforcement of Law in This Country, 187 N. Am. Rev. 851 (1908).

40. F. Frankfurter & J. Landis, *supra* note 8, at 260; see also A. Mason, *supra* note 38, at 109.

41. F. Frankfurter & J. Landis, *supra* note 8, at 260.

42. Act of Feb. 13, 1925, ch. 229, 43 Stat. 936.

43. W. King, *supra* note 37, at 149–51.

44. A. Mason, *supra* note 38, at 108–09.

45. H.R. Rep. No. 1075, 68th Cong., 2d Sess. 2 (1925), quoted in A. Mason, *supra* note 38, at 110.

46. 62 Cong. Rec. 8547 (1922).

47. F. Frankfurter & J. Landis, *supra* note 8, at 276.

48. Frankfurter & Landis, The Supreme Court under the Judiciary Act of 1925, 42 Harv. L. Rev. 1, 18 (1928).

49. F. Frankfurter & J. Landis, *supra* note 8, at 1–2.

50. Frankfurter & Landis, *supra* note 48, at 11.

51. G. Casper & R. Posner, The Workload of the Supreme Court 6 (1976).

52. 52 U.S.L.W. 3025 (July 26, 1983). Although the figure for the 1982 Term had declined slightly, to 4201, the number of filings was still nearly six times what it was in the 1920s.

53. S. Hendel, Charles Evans Hughes and the Supreme Court 249–50 (1951).

54. See Leuchtenburg, The Origins of Franklin D. Roosevelt's "Court-Packing" Plan, 1966 Sup. Ct. Rev. 347.

55. 81 Cong. Rec. 877 (1937), quoted in E. Gerhart, America's Advocate: Robert H. Jackson 106 (1958).

56. 2 M. Pusey, Charles Evans Hughes 753 (1963).

57. *Id.* at 755–56.

58. *Id.* at 756–65.

Chapter 3: Recent Proposals for Change

1. See A. Bickel, The Caseload of the Supreme Court and What, If Anything, to Do About It 6 (1973).

2. Warren & Burger, Retired Chief Justice Warren Attacks, Chief Justice Burger Defends Freund Study Group's Composition and Proposal, 59 A.B.A. J. 721, 723 (1973).

3. See, e.g., Griswold, The Supreme Court's Case Load: Civil Rights and Other Problems, 1973 U. Ill. L.F. 615, 618 (quoting a comment made in 1960 by Justice Stewart); Harlan, Some Aspects of the Judicial Process in the Supreme Court of the United States, 33 Austl. L.J. 108 (1959) (as number of certiorari petitions increases, so does competition between time needed for writing opinions and time required to review petitions).

4. For a comparison of Burger's energetic campaign for restructuring the federal judiciary with Chief Justice Taft's, see A. Bickel, *supra* note 1, at 6.

5. Serving with Freund were the late Alexander M. Bickel of the Yale Law School, Peter D. Ehrenhaft of the District of Columbia Bar, Russell D. Niles of New York University School of Law, Bernard G. Segal of the Pennsylvania Bar, Robert L. Stern of the Illinois Bar, and Charles Alan Wright of the University of Texas Law School. The committee's report was issued in December 1972. Federal Judicial Center, Report of the Study Group on the Caseload of the Supreme Court, 57 F.R.D. 573 (1972) [hereinafter Freund Committee Report].

6. *Id.* at 611–12.

7. *Id.* at 611.

8. *Id.* at 583–90.

9. *Id.* at 589.

10. *Id.* at 611.

11. For a convenient compilation of citations to the vast literature generated by the Freund Committee Report, see Haworth, Circuit Splitting and the "New" National Court of Appeals: Can the Mouse Roar?, 30 Sw. L.J. 839, 856 n.135 (1976). See also pp. 26–27.

12. Act of Oct. 13, 1972, Pub. L. No. 92–489, 86 Stat. 807, amended by Act of Sept. 19, 1974, Pub. L. No. 93–420, 88 Stat. 1153 (codified as amended at 28 U.S.C. § 41 (Supp. V 1975)) (calling for termination of statute 90 days following the submission of the Commission's second report). The Commission had sixteen members. Four were appointed by President Nixon—Emanuel Celler, Roger C. Crampton, Francis R. Kirkham, and Alfred T. Sulmonetti; four by Chief Justice Burger—J. Edward Lumbard, Roger Robb, Bernard G. Segal, and Herbert Wechsler; four by the President pro tempore of the Senate—Quentin N. Burdick, Edward Gurney (later replaced by Hiram L. Fong), Roman L. Hruska (the eventual chairman of the commission), and John L. McClellan; and four by the Speaker of the House—Jack Brooks, Walter Flowers, Edward Hutchinson, and Charles E. Wiggins. Haworth, *supra* note 11, at 839 n.4.

13. Act of Oct. 13, 1972, §1.

14. Haworth, *supra* note 11, at 840–41.

15. Commission on Revision of the Federal Court Appellate System, Structure and Internal Procedures: Recommendations for Change, 67 F.R.D. 195, 236–47 (1975) [hereinafter Hruska Commission Report].

16. *Id.* at 238–39.

17. *Id.* at 239.

18. *Id.* at 240–41.

19. *Id.* at 241.

20. *Id.* at 242.

21. *Id.*

22. *Id.*

23. *Id.* at 246.

24. *Id.* at 237.

25. *Id.* at 238.

26. *Id.* at 237.

27. See, e.g., Alsup, Reservations on the Proposal of the Hruska Commission to Establish a National Court of Appeals, 7 U. Tol. L. Rev. 431 (1976). For a bibliography of articles on the Hruska NCA, see Haworth, *supra* note 11, at 840 n.14.

28. S. 2762, 94th Cong., 1st Sess., 121 Cong. Rec. 39,559 (1975);

H.R. 11218, 94th Cong., 1st Sess. (1975). S. 2762 was later revised and introduced as a new bill. S. 3423, 94th Cong., 2d Sess., 122 Cong. Rec. 13,582–86 (1976).

29. Alsup, *supra* note 27, at 434. The discussion sparked by the Freund Committee and the Hruska Commission did manage to entice several prominent commentators into the fray in favor of a national court of appeals. See, e.g., Griswold, Rationing Justice—The Supreme Court's Caseload and What the Court Does Not Do, 60 Cornell L. Rev. 335, 349–53 (1975) (endorsing a National Court of Appeals to decide approximately 150 cases a year referred to it by the Supreme Court); Leventhal, A Modest Proposal for a Multi-Circuit Court of Appeals, 24 Am. U. L. Rev. 881, 912-17 (1975) (endorsing the Hruska NCA but arguing that it should be staffed by circuit judges chosen by the judiciary rather than new presidential appointments).

30. R. Stern & E. Gressman, Supreme Court Practice, § 1.16, at 46–47 (5th ed. 1978).

31. S. 645, 98th Cong., 1st Sess., §§ 601–07 (1983); see 129 Cong. Rec. S1947–56 (daily ed. Mar. 1, 1983). The proposal for an ICT is set out in title VI of S. 645. Subcommittee approval of the bill is noted in 129 Cong. Rec. D923 (daily ed. June 29, 1983).

32. H.R. 1970, 98th Cong., 1st Sess. (1983). The action of the subcommittee is reported in 130 Cong. Rec. D1142 (daily ed. Sept. 13, 1984). H.R. 1970 is reprinted in The Supreme Court Workload: Hearings on H.R. 1968, 1970 Before the Subcomm. on Courts, Civil Liberties and the Administration of Justice of the House Comm. on the Judiciary, 98th Cong., 1st Sess. 9–18 (1983) [hereinafter Hearings].

33. Burger, Annual Report on the State of the Judiciary, 69 A.B.A. J. 442 (1983).

34. *Id.*

35. *Id.* at 443.

36. *Id.* at 443–44.

37. *Id.* at 447.

38. *Id.*

39. *Id.*

40. Burger, 1984 Year-End Report on the Judiciary 9-10 (1985) (on file at New York University Law Review).

41. *Id.* at 9.

42. A useful summary of most of the public remarks of the sitting Justices is found in Hearings, *supra* note 32, at 306–423.

43. See Handler, What to Do with the Supreme Court's Burgeoning Calendars?, 5 Cardozo L. Rev. 249, 250–58 (1984).

44. Letter from Justice Blackmun to Sen. Roman L. Hruska (May 30, 1975), reprinted in Hearings, *supra* note 32, at 374.

45. Letter from Justice White to Rep. Kastenmeier (March 6, 1984),

reprinted in Hearings, *supra* note 32, at 360; Remarks of Justice Powell to the Eleventh Circuit Conference (May 8–10, 1983), reprinted in Hearings, *supra* note 32, at 375; Letter from Justice Rehnquist to Rep. Kastenmeier (June 8, 1984), reprinted in Hearings, *supra* note 32, at 382 (favoring the creation of the ICT "for somewhat different reasons" from the Chief Justice—"the demonstrated need to increase the capacity of the federal judicial system to decide cases on a nationwide basis"); Letter from Justice O'Connor to Rep. Kastenmeier (June 11, 1984), reprinted in Hearings, *supra* note 32, at 419.

46. White, Challenges for the U.S. Supreme Court and the Bar: Contemporary Reflections, 51 Antitrust L.J. 275 (1982) [hereinafter White, Challenges for the U.S. Supreme Court].

47. Letter from Justice Stevens to Rep. Kastenmeier (Oct. 25, 1983), reprinted in Hearings, *supra* note 32, at 390.

48. Stevens, Some Thoughts on Judicial Restraint, 66 Judicature 177, 181 (1982) [hereinafter Stevens, Judicial Restraint].

49. *Id.* at 181–82.

50. Stevens, The Life Span of a Judge-Made Rule, 58 N.Y.U. L. Rev. 1, 21 (1983) [hereinafter Stevens, Life Span].

51. Brennan, Some Thoughts on the Supreme Court's Workload, 66 Judicature 230 (1983).

52. Remarks of Justice Marshall to the Second Circuit Conference (Sept. 9, 1982), reprinted in Hearings, *supra* note 32, at 372.

53. Brennan, *supra* note 51, at 231.

54. *Id.* at 235.

55. *Id.* at 233–35.

56. Remarks of Justice Marshall, *supra* note 52, at 372; Remarks of Mr. Justice Marshall, Acceptance of Learned Hand Medal 8–9 (May 1, 1975), quoted in N.Y.L.J. May 5, 1975, at 2–3.

57. See, e.g., S. Hufstedler, The Quiet Collapse: The Crumbling of the Federal Appellate Structure 13–17 (unpublished address on dedication of Annual Survey of American Law, Apr. 7, 1983) (on file at New York University Law Review) (proposing the creation of a permanent NCA); see also, e.g., Cameron, Federal Review, Finality of State Court Decisions, and a Proposal for a National Court of Appeals—A State Judge's Solution to a Continuing Problem, 1981 B.Y.U. L. Rev. 545, 558 (advocating the creation of an NCA for state court appeals "with original appellate jurisdiction to review state court decisions, both civil and criminal, in which federal questions have been raised and state remedies exhausted"); Rx for an Overburdened Supreme Court: Is Relief in Sight?, 66 Judicature 394 (1983) (panel discussion including Judges Alvin Rubin and Patrick Higginbotham of the Court of Appeals for the Fifth Circuit, Professor Daniel Meador of the University of Virginia, Profesor Arthur D. Hellman of the University

of Pittsburgh, Robert L. Stern and Paul A. Freund, members of the Freund Committee, and the Hon. Roman L. Hruska, chairman of the Hruska Commission).

58. There is general agreement, however, that one useful approach to the workload problem would be the abolition of the Court's remaining mandatory jurisdiction. See, e.g., Brennan, *supra* note 51, at 232, 235; Stevens, Life Span, *supra* note 50, at 21. Our study suggests that such action will free the Court of approximately 7 percent of the cases it presently decides, and of the burden of having to take some affirmative action (with precedential implications) on all proper appeals. See chapter 8 *infra*.

Chapter 4: The Contours of the Present Debate

1. See Federal Judicial Center, Report of the Study Group on the Caseload of the Supreme Court, 57 F.R.D. 573 (1972) [hereinafter Freund Committee Report]; Commission on Revision of the Federal Court Appellate System, Structure and Internal Procedures: Recommendations for Change, 67 F.R.D. 195 (1975) [hereinafter Hruska Commission Report].

2. See p. 13 *supra*.

3. Freund Committee Report, *supra* note 1, at 578; Hruska Commission Report, *supra* note 1, at 330–32.

4. Freund Committee Report, *supra* note 1, at 578; Hruska Commission Report, *supra* note 1, at 335–44.

5. Freund Committee Report, *supra* note 1, at 581. The Freund Committee was, of course, not the first to raise concern about the Court's ability to tackle its responsibilities. In the early 1950s, Fowler V. Harper and four collaborators analyzed the cases denied certiorari in the 1949, 1950, 1951, and 1952 Terms. Harper & Rosenthal, What the Supreme Court Did Not Do in the 1949 Term: An Appraisal of Certiorari, 99 U. Pa. L. Rev. 293 (1950); Harper & Etherington, What the Supreme Court Did Not Do During the 1950 Term, 100 U. Pa. L. Rev. 354 (1951); Harper & Pratt, What the Supreme Court Did Not Do During the 1951 Term, 101 U. Pa. L. Rev. 439 (1953); Harper & Leibowitz, What the Supreme Court Did Not Do During the 1952 Term, 102 U. Pa. L. Rev. 427 (1954). They estimated that the Supreme Court had denied certiorari in a significant number of cases in which review should have been granted. See Harper & Rosenthal, *supra*, at 323–24; Harper & Etherington, *supra*, at 407–09; Harper & Pratt, *supra*, at 478–79; Harper & Leibowitz, *supra*, at 457. These studies, however, offered no systematic framework for assessing "certworthiness." Nor did they investigate the extent to which the Court granted review in cases in which certiorari should have been denied.

Henry Hart's 1959 article, "The Time Chart of the Justices," approached the workload problem from another perspective, attempting to demonstrate that the growing burden of evaluating applications for review meant that the Justices could not devote enough time and attention to the cases they accepted for review. See Hart, The Supreme Court, 1958 Term—Foreword: The Time Chart of the Justices, 73 Harv. L. Rev. 84 (1959). Hart argued that this burden inevitably affected the quality and usefulness of the Court's opinions. *Id.* at 100–01. Hart's criticism provoked responses by Justice Douglas, who retorted that the Justices were able to make up their minds in the time available, and by former circuit judge Thurman Arnold, who contended that, in any event, the Justices would not be induced to reconsider their votes by additional study or deliberation. See Douglas, The Supreme Court and Its Case Load, 45 Cornell L.Q. 401, 411 (1960) ("I do not recall any time [other than the 1958 Term] in my twenty years or more of service on the Court when we had more time for research, deliberation, debate, and meditation"); Arnold, Professor Hart's Theology, 73 Harv. L. Rev. 1298, 1310–14 (1960). But see Griswold, The Supreme Court, 1959 Term—Foreword: Of Time and Attitudes—Professor Hart and Judge Arnold, 74 Harv. L. Rev. 81, 83–86 (1960) (contending that Hart had the better of the argument).

6. Freund Committee Report, *supra* note 1, at 577–78.

7. See Alsup, A Policy Assessment of the National Court of Appeals, 25 Hastings L.J. 1313, 1332–42 (1974); Blumstein, The Supreme Court's Jurisdiction—Reform Proposals, Discretionary Review, and Writ Dismissals, 26 Vand. L. Rev. 895, 911–20 (1973); Gressman, The National Court of Appeals: A Dissent, 59 A.B.A. J. 253, 255–57 (1973).

8. Warren & Burger, Retired Chief Justice Warren Attacks, Chief Justice Burger Defends Freund Study Group's Composition and Proposal, 59 A.B.A. J. 721, 728 (1973).

9. *Id.* at 725.

10. *Id.* at 725–26.

11. *Id.* at 730.

12. *Id.*

13. S. Hufstedler, The Quiet Collapse: The Crumbling of the Federal Appellate Structure 8 (unpublished address on dedication of Annual Survey of American Law, Apr. 7, 1983) (on file at New York University Law Review).

14. *Id.* at 11–12.

15. Blumstein, *supra* note 7, at 916 (footnote omitted).

16. See, e.g., Alsup, *supra* note 7, at 1335; Brennan, Some Thoughts on the Supreme Court's Workload, 66 Judicature 230, 234 (1983).

17. Hruska Commission Report, *supra* note 1, at 209.

18. *Id.* at 212.

19. *Id.* at 213.

20. *Id.* at 213–14.

21. *Id.* at 217.

22. *Id.* at 217–19.

23. See Swygert, The Proposed National Court of Appeals: A Threat to Judicial Symmetry, 51 Ind. L.J. 327 (1976).

24. See Leventhal, A Modest Proposal for a Multi-Circuit Court of Appeals, 24 Am. U.L. Rev. 881, 882 (1975).

25. See Alsup, Reservations on the Proposal of the Hruska Commission to Establish a National Court of Appeals, 7 U. Tol. L. Rev. 431, 450–51 (1976).

26. *Id.* at 447.

27. *Id.* at 447–48.

28. *Id.* at 448–49.

29. *Id.* at 449–50.

30. See pp. 20–22 *supra.*

31. Meador, A Comment on the Chief Justice's Proposals, 69 A.B.A. J. 448, 448 (1983).

32. *Id.* at 448–49; accord, Cutler, Help for High Court, N.Y. Times, Nov. 1, 1982, at A19; see also The Supreme Court Workload: Hearings on H.R. 1968, 1970 Before the Subcomm. on Courts, Civil Liberties and the Administration of Justice of the House Comm. on the Judiciary, 98th Cong., 1st Sess. 77–81 (1983) [hereinafter Hearings] (statement of John P. Frank).

33. Letter from the Committee on Federal Courts of the Association of the Bar of the City of New York to Sen. Robert Dole 1 (Aug. 19, 1983); accord, Hearings, *supra* note 32, at 155–56 (statement of Chief Judge Wilfred Feinberg) (setting out opposition to an ICT "until other less drastic measures have been tried"); Letter from Judge Henry J. Friendly to Sen. Robert Dole 1 (June 7, 1983) (on file at New York University Law Review).

34. See Hearings, *supra* note 32, at 157–58 (statement of Chief Judge Wilfred Feinberg) (proposing that a specialized court for tax appeals be created and that Congress consider creating a National Law Revision Commission to work with Congress in identifying and disposing of ambiguities in the law giving rise to intercircuit conflicts).

Chapter 5: Assessments of the Court's Workload

1. Brennan, Some Thoughts on the Supreme Court's Workload, 66 Judicature 230, 234 (1983).

2. Federal Judicial Center, Report of the Study Group on the Caseload of the Supreme Court, 57 F.R.D. 573, 613–26 (1972) [hereinafter Freund Committee Report]. The report merely divided the Court's docket into a number of categories to illustrate the source and nature of the cases coming before the Court.

3. See *id.* at 580.

4. Feeney, Conflicts Involving Federal Law: A Review of Cases Presented to the Supreme Court, in Commission on Revision of the Federal Court Appellate System, Structure and Internal Procedures: Recommendations for Change, 67 F.R.D. 195, 301–24 (1975) [hereinafter Hruska Commission Report].

5. Hruska Commission Report, *supra* note 4, at 222.

6. *Id*. at 300.

7. Feeney, *supra* note 4, at 306.

8. *Id*.

9. Hruska Commission Report, *supra* note 4, at 300.

10. Feeney, *supra* note 4, at 317–21.

11. Hruska Commission Report, *supra* note 4, at 233.

12. *Id*. at 281.

13. Feeney, *supra* note 4, at 311.

14. Shenberg, Note, Identification, Tolerability, and Resolution of Intercircuit Conflicts: Reexamining Professor Feeney's Study of Conflicts in Federal Law, 59 N.Y.U. L. Rev. 1007 (1984).

15. This applies with even greater force to Feeney's "strong partial conflict" category, where the conflict, if any, is not over the holdings of cases but over the "implications" of various doctrines.

16. Feeney, *supra* note 4, at 316.

17. See Hruska Commission Report, *supra* note 4, at 361–90.

18. G. Casper & R. Posner, The Workload of the Supreme Court (1976); Casper & Posner, The Caseload of the Supreme Court: 1975 and 1976 Terms, 1977 Sup. Ct. Rev. 87 [hereinafter Casper & Posner, Caseload]. A preliminary version of the Casper and Posner book was published in 1974 as a contribution to the debate touched off by the Freund Committee Report. Casper & Posner, A Study of the Supreme Court's Caseload, 3 J. Legal Stud. 339 (1974).

19. See, e.g., Freund Committee Report, *supra* note 2, at 580 (arguing that the Court's caseload would rise as the population and the economy expanded).

20. G. Casper & R. Posner, The Workload of the Supreme Court 32 (1976).

21. *Id*. at 33–34.

22. *Id*.

23. *Id*. at 41.

24. *Id*. at 61–62 (emphasis in original).

25. *Id*. at 63.

26. *Id*. at 74.

27. *Id*. at 78–79 (emphasis omitted).

28. *Id*. at 85.

29. *Id*.

30. *Id*. at 82–85.

31. *Id*. at 89.

32. *Id.*

33. *Id.* at 92.

34. *Id.* at 8.

35. Casper & Posner, Caseload, *supra* note 18, at 97–98.

36. See R. Posner, The Federal Courts: Crisis and Reform 108 (1985).

Chapter 6: A Managerial Theory of the Supreme Court's Docket

1. This view is changing as the composition of the Supreme Court changes. Increasingly, civil liberties advocates are steering cases away from Supreme Court review by seeking to base decisions on state constitutional grounds. See Brennan, State Constitutions and the Protection of Individual Rights, 90 Harv. L. Rev. 489 (1977). However, even under current circumstances, there remain areas, such as the First Amendment, where the Court is viewed as the forum of choice.

2. See, e.g., S. Hufstedler, The Quiet Collapse: The Crumbling of the Federal Appellate Structure 3 (unpublished address on dedication of Annual Survey of American Law, April 7, 1983) (on file at New York University Law Review); Griswold, The Supreme Court's Case Load: Civil Rights and Other Problems, 1973 U. Ill. L.F. 615, 616–17.

3. See Hufstedler, *supra* note 2; Griswold, *supra* note 2, at 627.

4. Sup. Ct. R. 17. Rule 17 continues: "The same general considerations outlined above will control in respect of petitions for writs of certiorari to review judgments of the Court of Claims, the Court of Customs and Patent Appeals and of any other court whose judgments are reviewable by law or on writ of certiorari."

5. See chapter 8.

6. *Id.*

7. R. Stern & E. Gressman, Supreme Court Practice 263–64 (5th ed. 1978) (footnote omitted) (quoting Harlan, Manning the Dikes, 13 Rec. A.B. City N.Y. 541, 549 (1958)).

8. The Supreme Court's obligatory appellate jurisdiction is defined in 28 U.S.C. §§1252, 1253, 1254(2), 1257 (1982).

9. See generally 17 C. Wright, A. Miller & E. Cooper, Federal Practice and Procedure: Jurisdiction and Related Matters, § 4054, at 196–97 (1978).

10. See R. Posner, The Federal Courts: Crisis and Reform 59–77 (1985).

11. See, e.g., Federal Judicial Center, Report of the Study Group on the Caseload of the Supreme Court, 57 F.R.D. 573, 577–78 (1972) [hereinafter Freund Committee Report].

12. *Id.* at 578.

13. Hufstedler, *supra* note 2, at 3.

14. See Griswold, Rationing Justice—The Supreme Court's Case-

load and What the Court Does Not Do, 60 Cornell L. Rev. 335, 339–49 (1975).

15. See Marcus, Conflicts Among Circuits and Transfers Within the Federal Judicial System, 93 Yale L.J. 677, 686–87 (1984); Vestal, Relitigation by Federal Agencies: Conflict, Concurrence and Synthesis of Judicial Policies, 55 N.C.L. Rev. 123, 141–62 (1977). See also Note, Using Choice of Law Rules to Make Intercircuit Conflicts Tolerable, 59 N.Y.U. L. Rev. 1078 (1984).

16. See Marcus, *supra* note 15, at 686–87.

17. United States v. Mendoza, 464 U.S. 154, 160 (1984).

18. We recognize, of course, that some of the Court's constitutional rulings may be revised by congressional action, such as decisions invalidating state action as a matter of federal preemption or under the "dormant commerce clause" or decisions refusing to find invalidity under the Constitution. See generally Estreicher, Congressional Power and Constitutional Rights: Reflections on Proposed "Human Life" Legislation, 68 Va. L. Rev. 333, 384–412, 443–57 (1982).

19. Brown v. Allen, 344 U.S. 443, 540 (1953) (Jackson, J., concurring).

20. See Cover & Aleinikoff, Dialectical Federalism: Habeas Corpus and the Court, 86 Yale L.J. 1035 (1977).

21. See generally R. Posner, *supra* note 10. See also H. Friendly, Federal Jurisdiction: A General View 186–87 (1973); Currie & Goodman, Judicial Review of Federal Administrative Action: Quest for the Optimum Forum, 75 Colum. L. Rev. 1, 69 (1975); McGarity, Multi-Party Forum Shopping for Appellate Review of Administrative Action, 129 U. Pa. L. Rev. 302, 318–19 (1980).

22. R. Posner, *supra* note 10, at 163.

23. A few disclaimers are in order. In our reliance on structural rather than doctrinal identifiers of priority cases, our approach resembles Congress's efforts over the years to define the Court's appellate jurisdiction in terms of doctrinally neutral indications of significance. Some of the current appellate categories would remain on the priority docket as we conceive of it. Although we favor the abolition of the Court's remaining appellate jurisdiction and acknowledge that the appeals categories have not always generated a list of cases that are worthy of plenary review, we believe the truly problematic appellate category involves cases from the state courts sustaining state legislation against federal challenge. Such cases do not appear on our priority docket.

24. See Restatement (Second) of Judgments §27, comment i (1980). But see United States v. Title Ins. & Trust Co., 265 U.S. 472, 486 (1924) ("[W]here there are two grounds, upon . . . which an appellate court may rest its decision . . . each is the judgment of the court and of equal validity") (quoting Union Pac. R.R. v. Mason City & F.D. R.R., 199 U.S 160, 166 (1905)).

25. See Note, Identification, Tolerability, and Resolution of Inter-circuit Conflicts: Reexamining Professor Feeney's Study of Conflicts in Federal Law, 59 N.Y.U. L. Rev. 1007 (1984), for examples of realignment by the lower courts among the circuit court conflicts identified by Professor Feeney.

26. The "constitutional fact" doctrine presents special difficulties. When the Court has reason to believe that the lower courts are displaying a systematic bias in the findings of fact on which certain constitutional claims turn, there may be justification for discretionary exercise of its supervisory authority. However, cases that turn on the application of the same legal doctrine to a nonrecurring fact, such as the obscenity of a given book, do not pose a square conflict (for purposes of triggering the Court's conflict-resolution role), even if the case is one in which the same book is receiving different treatment in different jurisdictions.

27. Cover & Aleinikoff, *supra* note 20, at 1046–68.

28. See Golsen v. Commissioner, 54 T.C. 742, 757 (1970), *aff'd*, 445 F.2d 985 (10th Cir. 1971).

29. It may be argued that, although conflicts in the criminal law area rarely present forum shopping difficulties, and thus are unlikely candidates for priority treatment on a conflict rationale, in certain situations such conflicts are especially debilitating to respect for law and may be resolved in the absence of consideration by additional circuits. One such situation, it is suggested, occurs when a defendant is held to suffer the stigma of conviction and attendant loss of liberty for conduct that another court of appeals has held not to be criminal, at least where the United States has made clear that it intends to continue to seek prosecutions in the circuit finding liability. In our view, without consideration by a third court or other justification for a discretionary grant, intercircuit disagreement over a point of substantive law is not sufficient, standing alone, to compel Supreme Court review. We also question whether this rationale can really be restricted to criminal substantive law conflicts or indeed to the criminal law area.

30. See Leventhal, A Modest Proposal for a Multi-Circuit Court of Appeals, 24 Am. U. L. Rev. 881, 898–99 (1975).

31. See United States v. Cronic, 675 F.2d 1126 (10th Cir. 1982), *rev'd*, 466 U.S. 648 (1984) (No. 82–660).

32. See Note, Deciding Whether Conflicts with Supreme Court Precedent Warrant Certiorari, 59 N.Y.U. L. Rev. 1104 (1984) (distinguishing the "next case" from a conflict with Supreme Court precedent).

33. Under current practice, a ruling of statutory invalidity must be explicit to occasion an appeal under 28 U.S.C. § 1254(2) (1982). See Silkwood v. Kerr-McGee Corp., 464 U.S. 238, 246–47 (1984) (No. 81–2159).

34. Currently, such a decision is appealable under 28 U.S.C. § 1254(2) (1982).

35. In some situations state legislative action may not rise to a level of significance meriting Supreme Court review, but we have deliberately chosen an overinclusive formulation to facilitate application and to text our hypothesis fully.

36. Currently, such decisions are appealable under 28 U.S.C. § 1257(1) (1982).

37. Currently, such a decision would be appealable under 28 U.S.C. § 1252 (1982).

38. To be placed on the priority docket, the case must turn on the issue of statutory invalidity. For example, in Heckler v. Edwards, 465 U.S. 870 (1984) (No. 82–874), the Supreme Court properly remanded the case to the court of appeals because only the remedy was contested on appeal, not the issue of statutory invalidity. See *id.* at 875–76.

39. 418 U.S. 683 (1974).

40. P. Bator, P. Mishkin, D. Shapiro & H. Wechsler, Hart and Wechsler's The Federal Courts and the Federal System 1628 (2d ed. 1973) [hereinafter Hart and Wechsler].

41. 28 U.S.C. § 1251(a) (1982).

42. See, e.g., West Virginia ex rel. Dyer v. Sims, 341 U.S. 22 (1951).

43. This would be subject, of course, to the Court's forum non conveniens inquiry. See Massachusetts v. Missouri, 308 U.S. 1 (1939).

44. Currently, such decisions are appealable under 28 U.S.C. §1257(2) (1982).

45. Also, where federal habeas review is available, 28 U.S.C. §§2241–55 (1982), the Court should defer consideration of rulings on direct review from state criminal proceedings and await the outcome of the federal habeas review. The habeas process itself serves as a check on state action.

46. See United States v. Mendoza, 464 U.S. 154, 160 (1984).

47. Hart and Wechsler, *supra* note 40, at 1628.

48. 453 U.S. 654 (1981).

49. But see, e.g., Tower v. Glover, 467 U.S. 914, 924 (1984) (Brennan, J., joined by Marshall, Blackmun & Stevens, JJ., concurring in part and concurring in the judgment) (maintaining that it was improper for the majority opinion to point out that decision on a question had been reserved).

50. See, e.g., Roadway Express, Inc. v. Warren, 464 U.S. 988 (1983) (No. 82–1367) (review justified because of failure to achieve majority opinion in Thomas v. Washington Gas & Light Co., 448 U.S. 261 (1980)).

51. 15 U.S.C. § 2 (1982).

52. See, e.g., Bose Corp. v. Consumers Union of United States, Inc., No. 82–1246, 466 U.S. 484 (1984).

53. A classic example is Erie R.R. v. Tompkins, 304 U.S. 64 (1938), in which the Court overruled the doctrine of Swift v. Tyson, 41 U.S. (16 Pet.) 1 (1842), though the issue of the applicability of *Swift* was not even argued in the court below or in the petitions for review. See T. Freyer, Harmony & Dissonance 123–42 (1981).

54. See, e.g., United States v. Carolene Prods. Co., 304 U.S. 144, 152 n.4 (1938), in which the Court signaled a bifurcation in the analysis of substantive due process and equal protection claims. See generally Estreicher, Platonic Guardians of Democracy: John Hart Ely's Role for the Supreme Court in the Constitution's Open Texture, 56 N.Y.U. L. Rev. 547, 552–57 (1981).

55. See, e.g., Calder v. Jones, 465 U.S. 783 (1984) (No. 82–1401) (related to Keeton v. Hustler Magazine, Inc., 465 U.S. 770 (1984) (No. 82–485)).

56. See, e.g., 28 U.S.C. §1295 (1982) (giving Court of Appeals for the Federal Circuit exclusive jurisdiction over appeals from all district courts in patent cases and in certain suits against the United States).

57. For example, cases involving nationally applicable regulations under the Clean Air Act are reviewed exclusively in the Court of Appeals for the District of Columbia Circuit. See 42 U.S.C. §7607(b)(1) (1982).

58. See Sager, Fair Measure: The Legal Status of Underenforced Constitutional Norms, 91 Harv. L. Rev. 1212, 1242–50 (1978).

Chapter 7: Probable Criticisms of the Criteria

1. See, e.g., Federal Judicial Center, Report of the Study Group on the Caseload of the Supreme Court, 57 F.R.D. 573, 578 (1972) (Freund Committee Report).

Chapter 8: The Criteria Applied

1. See generally Anderson, Integration Theory and Attitude Change, 78 Psychological Rev. 171 (1971); Anderson, Functional Measurement and Psychological Judgment, 77 Psychological Rev. 153 (1970); Darley & Fazio, Expectancy Confirmation Processes Arising in the Social Interaction Sequence, 35 Am. Psychologist 867 (1980); Higgins, Rholes & Jones, Category Accessibility and Impression Formation, 13 J. Experimental Soc. Psychology 141 (1977); Wyer & Shull, The Processing of Social Stimulus Information: A Conceptual Integration, in Person Memory: The Cognitive Basis for Social Perception (1980).

2. For example, none of the major cue studies, including Tanenhaus, Shick, Muraskin & Rosen, The Supreme Court's Certiorari Jurisdiction: Cue Theory, *in* Judicial Decision-Making 111 (G. Schubert

ed. 1963), has employed controls for rater bias. See also Songer, Concern for Policy Outputs as a Cue for Supreme Court Decisions in Certiorari, 41 J. Politics 1185 (1979); Ulmer, Hintze & Kirklovsky, The Decision to Grant or Deny Certiorari: Further Considerations of Cue Theory, 6 L. & Society Rev. 637 (1972).

3. Compare Tanenhaus, Shick, Muraskin & Rosen, *supra* note 2, at 123–24 (disagreement defined as variance between the district court and circuit court in the same case), with D. Provine, Case Selection in the United States Supreme Court 199 n.17 (1980) (disagreement as intercircuit conflict). Ironically, both studies were basing their cues on the same statement by Chief Justice Vinson.

4. Throughout this study, all petitions or jurisdictional statements arising out of the same lower court decision are counted as one case.

5. Franchise Tax Bd. v. Construction Laborers Vacation Trust, No. 82–695, 463 U.S. 1 (1983), vacating and remanding 679 F.2d 1307 (9th Cir. 1982), and Arcudi v. Stone & Webster Eng'g Corp., No.82–1085, 463 U.S. 1220 (1983) (mem.), aff'g Stone & Webster Eng'g Corp. v. Ilsley, 690 F.2d 323 (2d Cir. 1982), concerned federal preemption of otherwise valid state statutes. Donovan v. Lone Steer, Inc., No. 82–1684, 464 U.S. 408 (1984), rev'g 565 F. Supp. 229 (D.N.D. 1982), concerned an implicit invalidation of a federal statute.

6. Edward J. DeBartolo Corp. v. NLRB, No. 81–1985, 463 U.S. 147 (1983), vacating and remanding 662 F.2d 264 (4th Cir. 1981), presented a conflict between the Fourth and Eighth Circuits on whether handbills were protected by the National Labor Relations Act's publicity proviso to its secondary boycott prohibition. Newport News Shipbuilding & Dry Dock Co. v. EEOC, No. 82–411, 462 U.S. 669 (1983), aff'g 682 F.2d 113 (4th Cir. 1982), presented a conflict between the Fourth and Ninth Circuits regarding the scope of the Pregnancy Discrimination Act of 1978. Commissioner v. Engle, No. 82–599, 464 U.S. 206 (1984), aff'g 677 F.2d 594 (7th Cir. 1982), and Farmer v. United States, No. 82–774, 464 U.S. 206 (1984), rev'g and remanding 689 F.2d 1017 (Ct. Cl. 1982), presented a conflict between the Seventh Circuit and the Court of Claims regarding the interpretation of the Internal Revenue Code's depletion allowance for oil and gas wells. The fifth case, Arizona v. San Carlos Apache Tribe, No. 81–2147, 463 U.S. 545 (1983), rev'g Navajo Nation v. United States, 668 F.2d 1100 (9th Cir. 1982), presented a two-court conflict over an issue that most likely would be confined to the Ninth and Tenth Circuits. As both of these circuits had addressed the issue, Supreme Court resolution was not premature.

It should be noted that seven additional two-court conflicts have been placed on the discretionary docket. These were appropriate discretionary grants under our criteria; the Court's intervention was not premised solely on the conflict-resolution rationale.

7. For a disingenuous attempt to evade the school desegregation mandate of Brown v. Board of Educ., 347 U.S. 483 (1954), see Stell v. Savannah-Chatham County Bd. of Educ., 220 F. Supp. 667 (S.D. Ga. 1963) (distinguishing *Brown* on grounds that in instant case evidence established that school segregation did not harm pupils), rev'd and remanded, 333 F.2d 55 (5th Cir. 1964).

8. No. 82–195, 463 U.S. 388 (1983), aff'g 676 F.2d 1195 (8th Cir. 1982).

9. Mueller v. Allen, 676 F.2d 1195, 1200–02 (8th Cir. 1982) (citing Rhode Island Fed'n of Teachers v. Norberg, 630 F.2d 855 (1st Cir. 1980)).

10. 413 U.S. 756 (1973).

11. Mueller v. Allen, 676 F.2d 1195, 1203–05 (8th Cir. 1982).

12. No. 82–276, 463 U.S. 646 (1983), rev'g 681 F.2d 824 (D.C. Cir. 1982).

13. 445 U.S. 222 (1980).

14. No. 81–2386, 462 U.S. 151 (1983), rev'g 679 F.2d 879 (4th Cir. 1982).

15. No. 81–2408, 462 U.S. 151 (1983), rev'g 671 F.2d 87 (2d Cir. 1982).

16. 451 U.S. 56 (1981).

17. See *id.* at 60 n.2; *id.* at 71–72 & n.1 (Stevens, J., concurring in part and dissenting in part).

18. 29 U.S.C. §160(b) (1982).

19. See Flowers v. Local 2602, United Steelworkers of Am., 671 F.2d 87, 89–90 (2d Cir. 1982) (*Mitchell* does not apply to employee actions against unions), rev'd, 462 U.S. 151 (1983); Singer v. Flying Tiger Line, 652 F.2d 1349, 1353 (9th Cir. 1981) (*Mitchell* applies to employee actions against unions) (dicta); see also McFarland v. International Bhd. of Teamsters, 535 F. Supp. 970, 973–74 (N.D. Tex. 1982); Fedor v. Hygrade Food Prods. Corp., 533 F. Supp. 269, 271–72 (E.D. Pa.), aff'd per curiam, 687 F.2d 8 (3d Cir. 1982); Kennard v. United Parcel Serv., Inc., 531 F. Supp. 1139, 1145 (E.D. Mich. 1982) (dicta).

20. No. 82–1367, 464 U.S. 988 (1983), dismissing cert. to 163 Ga. App. 759, 295 S.E.2d 743 (1982).

21. 448 U.S. 261 (1980).

22. No. 81–757, 104 S. Ct. 3315 (1984), rev'g 656 F. 2d 820 (D.C. Cir. 1981).

23. No. 82–1260, 467 U.S. 752 (1984), rev'g 691 F.2d 310 (7th Cir. 1982).

24. See, e.g., Areeda, Intraenterprise Conspiracy in Decline, 97 Harv. L. Rev. 451 (1983); Willis & Pitofsky, Antitrust Consequences of Using Corporate Subsidiaries, 43 N.Y.U. L. Rev. 20 (1968).

25. No. 82–432, 467 U.S. 526 (1984), rev'g and remanding 679 F.2d 978 (1st Cir. 1982).

26. 379 U.S. 134 (1964).

27. 29 U.S.C. §§411–15 (1982).

28. *Id*. §§481–83 (1982). See generally Note, Pre-Election Remedies Under the Landrum-Griffin Act, 74 Colum. L. Rev. 1105 (1974).

29. No. 82–23, 463 U.S. 783 (1983), rev'g 675 F.2d 228 (8th Cir. 1982).

30. 403 U.S. 602 (1971).

31. See Copperweld Corp. v. Independence Tube Corp., 467 U.S. 752, 759–77 (1984).

32. No. 82–485, 465 U.S. 770 (1984), rev'g and remanding 682 F. 2d 33 (1st Cir. 1982).

33. No. 82–1401, 465 U.S. 783 (1984), aff'g 138 Cal. App. 3d 128, 187 Cal. Rptr. 825 (1982).

34. Two other cases also involved issues directly related to cases already properly on the priority or discretionary dockets. See Brown v. Thomson, No. 82–65, 462 U.S. 835 (1983), aff'g 536 F. Supp. 780 (D. Wyo. 1982) (three-judge court), and Arizona v. United States Dist. Court, No. 82–675, 459 U.S. 1191 (1983), aff'g 688 F.2d 1297 (9th Cir. 1982).

35. See, e.g., Public Serv. Comm'n v. Mid-Louisiana Gas Co., No. 81–1889, 463 U.S. 319 (1983), vacating and remanding 664 F.2d 530 (5th Cir. 1981); Motor Vehicle Mfrs. Ass'n of the United States, Inc. v. State Farm Mut. Auto Ins. Co, No. 82–354, 463 U.S. 29 (1983), vacating and remanding State Farm Mut. Auto Ins. Co. v. Department of Transp., 680 F.2d 206 (D.C. Cir. 1982).

36. No. 81–2399, 460 U.S. 766 (1983), rev'g 678 F.2d 222 (D.C. Cir. 1982).

37. No. 82–1371, 467 U.S. 104 (1984), vacating and remanding 685 F.2d 19 (2d Cir. 1982).

38. No. 82–500, 465 U.S. 1 (1984), modifying 31 Cal. 3d 584, 645 P.2d 1192, 183 Cal. Rptr. 360 (1982).

39. No. 82–11, 462 U.S. 791 (1983), rev'g and remanding 427 N.E.2d 686 (Ind. App. 1981).

40. 339 U.S. 306 (1950).

41. No. 82–1565, 104 S. Ct. 3049 (1984), rev'g 65 Hawaii 566, 656 P.2d 724 (1982).

42. No. 82–492, 463 U.S. 277 (1983), aff'g 684 F.2d 582 (8th Cir. 1982).

43. 445 U.S. 263 (1980).

44. 454 U.S. 370 (1982) (per curiam).

45. No. 81–2159, 464 U.S. 238 (1984), rev'g 667 F.2d 908 (10th Cir. 1981).

46. No. 81–2257, 461 U.S. 731 (1983), vacating 660 F.2d 1335 (9th Cir. 1981).

47. See generally Fay v. Noia, 372 U.S. 391 (1963); Cover & Aleini-koff, Dialectical Federalism: Habeas Corpus and the Court, 86 Yale L.J. 1035 (1977).

48. See, e.g., Solem v. Bartlett, No. 82–1253, 465 U.S. 463 (1984), aff'g 691 F.2d 420 (8th Cir. 1982).

49. Aluminum Co. of Am. v. Central Lincoln Peoples' Util. Dist., No. 82–1071, 467 U.S. 380 (1984), rev'g 686 F.2d 708 (9th Cir. 1982).

50. No. 82–91, 464 U.S. 183 (1984), rev'g 673 F.2d 1013 (9th Cir. 1982).

51. No. 81–2149, 465 U.S. 638 (1984), rev'g 671 F.2d 1150 (8th Cir. 1982).

52. 451 U.S. 477 (1981).

53. Heckler v. Edwards, No. 82–874, 465 U.S. 870 (1984), vacating Schweiker v. Edwards, No. 82–4156 (9th Cir. July 27, 1982); United States v. Mendoza, No. 82–849, 464 U.S. 154 (1984), rev'g 672 F.2d 1320 (9th Cir. 1982).

54. Process Gas Consumers Group v. Consumers Energy Council of Am., No. 81–2008, 463 U.S. 1216 (1983), aff'g 673 F.2d 425 (D.C. Cir. 1982).

55. 462 U.S. 919 (1983).

56. We suspect, however, that given the sweeping invalidation of the "legislative veto" in INS v. Chadha, 462 U.S. 919 (1983), the Court would not have granted review in Process Gas Consumers Group v. Consumers Energy Council of Am., No. 81–2008, 463 U.S. 1216 (1983), aff'g 673 F.2d 425 (D.C. Cir. 1982), if its obligatory jurisdiction had been abolished.

57. The Supreme Court, 1982 Term, 97 Harv. L. Rev. 70, 300–02 (1983).

58. No. 82–940, 467 U.S. 69 (1984), rev'g 678 F.2d 1022 (11th Cir. 1982).

59. 42 U.S.C. §2000e et seq. (1982).

60. No. 81–1893, 463 U.S. 992 (1983), rev'g 30 Cal. 3d 553, 639 P.2d 908, 180 Cal. Rptr. 266 (1982).

61. No. 82–1135, 465 U.S. 168 (1984), rev'g Wiggins v. Estelle, 681 F.2d 266 (5th Cir. 1982).

62. 422 U.S. 806 (1975).

63. No. 82–1246, 466 U.S. 485 (1984), aff'g 692 F. 2d 189 (1st Cir. 1982).

64. 376 U.S. 254 (1964).

65. 418 U.S. 323 (1974).

66. 456 U.S. 844 (1982).

67. 456 U.S. 273 (1982).

68. No. 82–940, 467 U.S. 69 (1984), rev'g 678 F.2d 1022 (11th Cir. 1982).

69. No. 81–1893, 463 U.S. 992 (1983), rev'g 30 Cal. 3d 553, 639 P.2d 908, 180 Cal. Rptr. 266 (1982).

70. See table 9 *supra*.

71. See Brennan, State Constitutions and the Protection of Individual Rights, 90 Harv. L. Rev. 489 (1977).

72. See, e.g., Michigan v. Long, 463 U.S. 1032, 1065–72 (1983) (Stevens, J., dissenting).

73. See Sager, Fair Measure: The Legal Status of Underenforced Constitutional Norms, 91 Harv. L. Rev. 1212, 1244 (1978).

74. See Florida v. Meyers, 466 U.S. 380, 385 (1984) (Stevens, J., dissenting): "[I]n reviewing the decisions of state courts, the primary role of this Court is to make sure that persons who seek to *vindicate* federal rights have been fairly heard" (quoting Michigan v. Long, 463 U.S. 1032, 1068 (1983) (Stevens, J., dissenting)) (emphasis in original).

75. 1982 Att'y Gen. Ann. Rep. 7 (table II-A).

76. Secretary of the Interior v. California, No. 82–1326 et al., 464 U.S. 312 (1984), rev'g 683 F.2d 1253 (9th Cir. 1982); Ruckelshaus v. Sierra Club, No. 82–242, 463 U.S. 680 (1983), rev'g Sierra Club v. Gorsuch, 672 F.2d 33 (D.C. Cir. 1982); Morrison-Knudsen Constr. Co. v. Director, Office of Workers' Compensation Programs, No. 81–1891, 461 U.S. 624 (1983), rev'g 670 F.2d 208 (D.C. Cir. 1981).

77. United States v. Whiting Pools, Inc., No. 82–215, 462 U.S. 198 (1983), aff'g 674 F.2d 144 (2d Cir. 1982).

78. No. 81–1374, 465 U.S. 866 (1984), aff'g in part and rev'g in part 671 F.2d 493 (2d Cir. 1981).

79. No. 82–271, 462 U.S. 650 (1983), aff'g 681 F.2d 42 (1st Cir. 1982).

80. No. 82–372, 462 U.S. 19 (1983), rev'g 671 F.2d 553 (D.C. Cir. 1982).

81. No. 82–215, 462 U.S. 198 (1983), aff'g 674 F.2d 144 (2d Cir. 1982).

82. No. 81–2169, 462 U.S. 306 (1983), aff'g 667 F.2d 1133 (4th Cir. 1981).

83. No. 82–472, 464 U.S. 16 (1983), aff'g United States v. Martino, 681 F.2d 952 (5th Cir. 1982) (en banc).

84. No. 82–1330, 104 S. Ct. 2916 (1984), aff'g 693 F.2d 132 (5th Cir. 1982).

85. No. 82–1041, 465 U.S. 330 (1984), aff'g 690 F.2d 812 (11th Cir. 1982).

86. No. 82–1453, 464 U.S. 386 (1984), aff'g 693 F.2d 298 (3d Cir. 1982).

87. 447 U.S. 410 (1980).

88. No. 82–52, 463 U.S. 1073 (1983), aff'g in part and rev'g in part 671 F.2d 330 (9th Cir. 1982).

89. No. 82–738, 465 U.S. 75 (1984), vacating and remanding 703 F.2d 564 (6th Cir. 1982).
90. No. 82–1135, 465 U.S. 168 (1984), rev'g Wiggins v. Estelle, 681 F.2d 266 (5th Cir. 1982).
91. No. 82–1095, 465 U.S. 37 (1984), rev'g 692 F.2d 1189 (9th Cir. 1982).
92. 428 U.S. 153 (1976).
93. 428 U.S. 242 (1976).
94. 428 U.S. 262 (1976).
95. No. 82–1246, 466 U.S. 485 (1984), aff'g 692 F.2d 189 (1st Cir. 1982).
96. No. 82–1479, 466 U.S. 294 (1984), rev'g 698 F.2d 1 (1st Cir. 1982).
97. Several cases deemed appropriate discretionary grants because of doctrinal incoherence in the lower courts involved borderline judgments. See, e.g., Jefferson Parish Hosp. Dist. No. 2 v. Hyde, No. 82–1031, 466 U.S. 2 (1984), rev'g and remanding 686 F.2d 286 (5th Cir. 1982); Ellis v. Brotherhood of Ry. Clerks, No. 82–1150, 466 U.S. 435 (1984), aff'g in part and rev'g in part 685 F.2d 1065 (9th Cir. 1982). Some cases were predominantly of local interest. See, e.g., Summa Corp. v. California ex rel. State Lands Comm'n, No. 82–708, 466 U.S. 198 (1984), rev'g and remanding 31 Cal. 3d 288, 644 P.2d 792, 182 Cal. Rptr. 599 (1982).
98. Although we worked closely with the *Review* while formulating the study's case selection criteria, the *Review*'s application of the criteria to particular cases may differ from our own. We report the *Review*'s findings without necessarily approving every case analysis.
Lengthy Notes in the full study in the *New York University Law Review* discuss cases that were difficult to categorize or that presented interesting issues not yet ripe for Supreme Court review. All told, the Notes discuss forty-seven cases, organized by subject. Readers wishing to evaluate the *Review*'s findings should refer to the Notes and to the appendices describing the cases denied review.
99. Note, Identification, Tolerability, and Resolution of Intercircuit Conflicts: Reexamining Professor Feeney's Study of Conflicts in Federal Law, 59 N.Y.U. L. Rev. 1007 (1984).
100. *Id*. at 1040.

Chapter 9: The Avoidable Causes of Overgranting

1. We do not claim that the Justices' perceived workload problem is exclusively the result of overgranting. The Justices, for instance, might be unnecessarily increasing their workload when they grant cases to resolve important issues but then fail to address decisively those issues in their opinion, delaying final resolution until later opinions. See, e.g., Upjohn Co. v. United States, 449 U.S. 383, 389–97 (1981)

(holding that the attorney-client privilege applied in the case before it, but refusing to formulate a general rule of use in future cases); Sexton, A Post-*Upjohn* Consideration of the Corporate Attorney-Client Privilege, 57 N.Y.U. L. Rev. 443 (1982). We do not address this or other reasons because our study focused only on the relationship between overgranting and the Court's workload.

2. Stevens, The Life Span of a Judge-Made Rule, 58 N.Y.U. L. Rev. 1, 10 (1983).

3. Cf. Singleton v. Commissioner, 439 U.S. 940, 942–46 (1978) (Stevens, J.) (asserting that dissents from denials of certiorari are a "totally unnecessary use of the Court's scarce resources"). See generally D. Provine, Case Selection in the United States Supreme Court 41 (1980).

4. Leiman, The Rule of Four, 57 Colum. L. Rev. 975, 981–82 (1957); Stevens, *supra* note 2, at 10, 14–21.

Justice Stevens has suggested that the Rule of Four does not permit four Justices to compel the Court to decide a case on the merits. Although the rule allows four Justices to achieve a grant of certiorari over the objections of their colleagues, it does not control the case's disposition once review has been granted:

> If a majority is convinced after studying the case that its posture, record, or presentation of issues makes it an unwise vehicle for exercising the "gravest and most delicate" function that this Court is called upon to perform, the Rule of Four should not reach so far as to compel the majority to decide the case.
>
> In conclusion, the Rule of Four is a valuable, though not immutable, device for deciding when a case must be argued, but its force is largely spent once the case has been heard. At that point, a more fully informed majority of the Court must decide whether some countervailing principle outweighs the interest in judicial economy in deciding the case.

New York v. Uplinger, 467 U.S. 246, 251 (1984) (Stevens, J., concurring in dismissal of certiorari).

In *Uplinger*, the Court dismissed the writ of certiorari as improvidently granted because the state statute in question appeared to the majority to have been invalidated by the New York Court of Appeals on state law grounds. *Id.* at 248–49. Four Justices dissented, maintaining that the decision below invalidated the statute on federal constitutional grounds. *Id.* at 252.

5. Stevens, *supra* note 2, at 12.

6. D. Provine, *supra* note 3, at 26–30, Stevens, *supra* note 2, at 13.

7. Stevens, *supra* note 2, at 13. D. Provine, *supra* note 3, at 28–29, dates the change from dead list to discuss list as beginning in 1950 with the creation of the Discussion List for Miscellaneous Docket Cases. In recent Terms, this list has expanded to include all cases.

8. In his dissent in Florida v. Meyers, 466 U.S. 380, 383–87 (1984), Justice Stevens noted nineteen cases since the 1981 Term in which the Court summarily disposed of criminal procedure petitions or appeals brought by prosecutors. *Id.* 386 & n.3. In all of these cases, the Court ruled in favor of the Government and restricted the rights of criminal defendants. *Id.* Justice Stevens contended that the Court chose these cases primarily to rule in favor of state prosecutorial authorities. *Id.* at 385–87.

9. See D. Provine, *supra* note 3, at 131–72; Linzer, The Meaning of Certiorari Denials, 79 Colum. L. Rev. 1227, 1299–1302 (1979).

10. Justices Burton and Clark may have been willing to join three-vote combinations because both were naturally "affable and outgoing" and believed strongly in maintaining the Court's collegial atmosphere. D. Provine, *supra* note 3, at 156–57.

11. See *id.* at 33; Linzer, *supra* note 9, at 1249 & n.168.

12. D. Provine, *supra* note 3, at 156.

13. See Note, Disagreement in D.C.: The Relationship Between the Supreme Court and the D.C. Circuit Court and Its Implications for a National Court of Appeals, 59 N.Y.U. L. Rev. 1048, 1064–66 (1984).

14. Linzer, *supra* note 9, at 1280–86.

15. Figures compiled from data in United States Law Week, vols. 47–50.

Chapter 10: Unsuitable Remedies

1. See Swygert, The Proposed National Court of Appeals: A Threat to Judicial Symmetry, 51 Ind. L. J. 327, 329–32 (1976), for a detailed presentation of this objection to the Hruska NCA. This is not the occasion, however, to consider the question of Congress's power to curtail the Supreme Court's appellate jurisdiction. See generally Sager, The Supreme Court, 1980 Term—Foreword: Constitutional Limitations on Congress' Authority to Regulate the Jurisdiction of the Federal Courts, 95 Harv. L. Rev. 17 (1981).

The current proposal for an ICT is vulnerable to many of the same objections raised against the Hruska NCA. Its supporters acknowledge these objections, but justify their ICT proposal by arguing that the Court's workload problem has grown much more acute since the Hruska Commission's proposal. See, e.g., Rehnquist, A Plea for Help: Solutions to Serious Problems Currently Experienced by the Federal Judicial System, 28 St. Louis U.L.J. 1, 2–5 (1984). Rehnquist favors allowing the currently proposed ICT to have the last word on cases referred to it by the Supreme Court, but does not discuss the constitutional question posed by Swygert. See *id.* at 6.

2. See Alsup, Reservations on the Proposal of the Hruska Com-

mission to Establish a National Court of Appeals, 7 U. Tol. L. Rev. 431, 451 (1976).

3. Note, Disagreement in D.C.: The Relationship Between the Supreme Court and the D.C. Circuit Court and Its Implications for a National Court of Appeals, 59 N.Y.U. L. Rev. 1048, 1049 (1984).

4. *Id.* at 1050.

5. See *id.* at 1050–60.

6. *Id.* at 1061.

7. Cf. Motor Vehicle Mfrs. Ass'n of the United States, Inc. v. State Farm Mut. Auto. Ins. Co., 463 U.S. 29 (1983).

8. Burger, Annual Report on the State of the Judiciary, 69 A.B.A. J. 442, 447 (1983).

9. See generally H. Abraham, Justices and Presidents (rev. ed. 1985); L. Tribe, God Save This Honorable Court (1985).

10. See The Supreme Court Workload: Hearings on H.R. 1968, 1970 Before the Subcomm. on Courts, Civil Liberties and the Administration of Justice of the House Comm. on the Judiciary, 98th Cong., 1st Sess. 274–81 (1983) (testimony of Louis Craco for the Association of the Bar of the City of New York).

Chapter 11: Tailoring the Remedy to the Problem

1. During the 1984 Term, the Court did not accept enough cases to fill its 1984–85 hearing schedule. See Busy, Busy, Oops!, N.Y. Times, Jan. 23, 1985, at A20, col. 2.

2. See, e.g., S. 3018, 97th Cong., 2d Sess., 128 Cong. Rec. S13,297 (daily ed. Oct. 1, 1982), introduced by Senator John East, Chairman of the Subcommittee on Separation of Powers of the Senate Judiciary Committee. Senator East's bill would prohibit, among other things, Supreme Court review of claims that a state has abridged "any right secured by the first eight amendments to the Constitution. . . . " *Id.* §111(a). Cf. Sager, The Supreme Court, 1980 Term—Foreword: Constitutional Limitations on Congress' Authority to Regulate the Jurisdiction of the Federal Courts, 95 Harv. L. Rev. 17, 18 & nn.3 & 5 (1981) (detailing legislative attempts to undo federal court "mischief" by stripping the federal judiciary of jurisdiction to decide cases concerning abortion, prayer in public schools, and busing to achieve racial integration).

3. See Kurland & Hutchinson, The Business of the Supreme Court, O.T. 1982, 50 U. Chi. L. Rev. 628, 639–43 (1983).

4. See generally Eisenberg, Congressional Authority to Restrict Lower Federal Court Jurisdiction, 83 Yale L.J. 498 (1974); Hart, The Power of Congress to Limit the Jurisdiction of Federal Courts: An Exercise in Dialectic, 66 Harv. L. Rev. 1362 (1953); Sager, *supra* note 2.

5. See Coleman, The Supreme Court of the United States: Managing Its Caseload to Achieve Its Constitutional Purpose, 52 Fordham L. Rev. 1, 24–33 (1983); Handler, What to Do with the Supreme Court's Burgeoning Calendars?, 5 Cardozo L. Rev. 249, 250–58 (1984); Kurland & Hutchinson, *supra* note 3, at 648–50.

6. Coleman, *supra* note 5, at 17 & n.88.

7. See pp. 60–61 *supra*.

8. See, e.g., Anderson v. Celebreze, 460 U.S. 780, 784 & n.5 (1983) (summary dispositions by Court should be accorded "limited precedential effect"); Sporhase v. Nebraska ex rel. Douglas, 458 U.S. 941, 949 (1982) (affirmance indicates only Court's agreement with result reached by lower court).

9. See, e.g., Hicks v. Miranda, 422 U.S. 332, 344 (1975) (describing summary dismissal of appeal in Miller v. California, 418 U.S. 915 (1974), as decision on merits); see also Mandel v. Bradley, 432 U.S. 173, 176 (1977) (per curiam).

10. See, e.g., 16 C. Wright, A. Miller, E. Cooper & E. Gressman, Federal Practice and Procedure: Jurisdiction §4003 (1977).

11. See, e.g., Edelman v. Jordan, 415 U.S. 651 (1974).

12. See Supreme Court Jurisdiction Act of 1978: Hearings on S. 3100 Before the Subcomm. on Improvements in Judicial Machinery of the Senate Comm. on the Judiciary, 95th Cong., 2d Sess. 40 (1978) (letter signed by all nine sitting Justices); *id.* at 2 (statement of Solicitor General McCree, quoting Justice Stevens); *id.* at 32 (statement of Professor Hellman).

13. See G. Gunther, Cases and Materials on Constitutional Law 71 (10th ed. 1980) (Court's unpredictable grants of certiorari encourage filing of petitions); Handler, *supra* note 5, at 261 ("The Court's certiorari rule is itself partly responsible for encouraging the filing of groundless petitions.").

14. Kurland and Hutchinson have suggested that the large number of unmeritorious claims is the product of an irresponsible bar: attorneys can rarely bill clients for unwritten certiorari petitions. Kurland & Hutchinson, *supra* note 3, at 646. Similarly, some unscrupulous petitioners may draw out the appellate process solely to delay execution of a money judgment. A stay of judgment of execution pending an application for certiorari may be granted either by a judge of the court rendering judgment or by a Justice of the Supreme Court. 28 U.S.C. §2101(f) (1982); 11 C. Wright & A. Miller, Federal Practice and Procedure: Civil § 2908 (1973). Naturally, the development of clear case selection criteria is at best half the battle. To enforce those criteria, the Court should fine attorneys who consistently file frivolous petitions. See also Sup. Ct. R. 56(4) (authorizing award of "reasonable damages").

15. Kurland & Hutchinson, *supra* note 3, at 646.

16. Handler, *supra* note 5, at 266–67.

17. Kurland & Hutchinson, *supra* note 3, at 628.

18. 459 U.S. 86 (1982); see Note, Procedural Law, 59 N.Y.U. L. Rev. 1343, 1388 (1984).

19. 466 U.S. 521 (1984).

20. 462 U.S. 213, 217 (1983) (Rehnquist, J.) ("We decide today, with apologies to all, that the issue we framed for the parties was not presented to the Illinois courts and, accordingly, [we] do not address it").

21. See, e.g., Edwards, The Rising Work Load and Perceived "Bureaucracy" of the Federal Courts: A Causation-Based Approach to the Search for Appropriate Remedies, 68 Iowa L. Rev. 871, 879–89 (1983); Higginbotham, Bureaucracy—The Carcinoma of the Federal Judiciary, 31 Ala. L. Rev. 261 (1980); Hoffman, The Bureaucratic Sphere: Newest Challenges to the Court, 66 Judicature 60 (1982); McCree, Bureaucratic Justice: An Early Warning, 129 U. Pa. L. Rev. 777 (1981); Rubin, Bureaucratization of the Federal Courts: The Tension Between Justice and Efficiency, 55 Notre Dame Law. 648 (1980); Vining, Justice, Bureaucracy, and Legal Method, 80 Mich. L. Rev. 248 (1981).

22. Coleman, *supra* note 5, at 27; see also Handler, *supra* note 5, at 277–85.

23. Contra, Handler, *supra* note 5, at 263–64.

24. For useful discussion of venue proposals to reduce forum shopping, see McGarity, Multi-Party Forum Shopping for Appellate Review of Administrative Action, 129 U. Pa. L. Rev. 302 (1980); Sunstein, Participation, Public Law, and Venue Reform, 49 U. Chi. L. Rev. 976 (1982); Note, Venue for Judicial Review of Administrative Actions: A New Approach, 93 Harv. L. Rev. 1735 (1980).

25. Van Dusen v. Barrack, 376 U.S. 612 (1964).

26. For a contrary view, see Marcus, Conflicts Among Circuits and Transfers Within the Federal Judicial System, 93 Yale L.J. 677 (1984).

27. See Note, Using Choice of Law Rules to Make Intercircuit Conflicts Tolerable, 59 N.Y.U. L. Rev. 1078 (1984). This Note argues that it is possible to develop fairly clear-cut, manageable rules that refer either to the law of the circuit where the claim or cause of action arose or to the law of the circuit of the defendant's principal place of business or residence.

28. See, e.g., Handler, *supra* note 5, at 269; Kurland & Hutchinson, *supra* note 3, at 645–46; Stevens, The Life Span of a Judge-Made Rule, 58 N.Y.U. L. Rev. 1, 10–21 (1983).

29. See White, Challenges for the U.S. Supreme Court and the Bar: Contemporary Reflections, 51 Antitrust L.J. 275 (1982); accord, Note, Securing Uniformity in National Law: A Proposal for National Stare

Decisis in the Courts of Appeals, 87 Yale L.J. 1219, 1238–40 (1978); see also Handler, *supra* note 5, at 273 & nn.80–82. Walter Schaefer would go even further. He argues that the first *panel* decision of a circuit court should bind all other circuit courts unless it is overruled by any circuit court sitting en banc or by the Supreme Court. See Schaefer, Reducing Circuit Conflicts, 69 A.B.A. J. 452, 455 (1983).

30. Coleman, *supra* note 5, at 18–20.

31. *Id.* at 18–19 (footnotes omitted).

32. See, e.g., Griswold, Rationing Justice—The Supreme Court's Caseload and What the Court Does Not Do, 60 Cornell L. Rev. 335, 350–51 (1975).

33. Feinberg, A National Court of Appeals? 42 Brooklyn L. Rev. 611, 627 (1976); Friendly, The Gap in Lawmaking—Judges Who Can't and Legislators Who Won't, 63 Colum. L. Rev. 787, 802–07 (1963).

34. See Hellman, Error Correcting, Lawmaking, and the Supreme Court's Exercise of Discretionary Review, 44 U. Pitt. L. Rev. 795, 801–02 (1983); Hellman, The Business of the Supreme Court Under the Judiciary Act of 1925: The Plenary Docket in the 1970's, 91 Harv. L. Rev. 1709, 1800 (1978).

35. See, e.g., Griswold, The Need for a Court of Tax Appeals, 57 Harv. L. Rev. 1153 (1944); Handler, *supra* note 5, at 274–75; Jordan, Should Litigants Have a Choice Between Specialized Courts and Courts of General Jurisdiction?, 66 Judicature 14 (1982); Rifkind, A Special Court for Patent Litigation? The Danger of a Specialized Judiciary, 37 A.B.A. J. 425 (1951); Wald, Judicial Review of Complex Administrative Agency Decisions, 462 Annals 72, 74–75 (1982).

36. See, e.g., Ginsburg, Making Tax Law Through the Judicial Process, 70 A.B.A. J. 74 (1984); Griswold, *supra* note 35; Handler, *supra* note 5, at 275.

37. E.g., Rifkind, *supra* note 35; see also Edwards, *supra* note 21, at 919 (arguing that such proposals might result in segregation of disfavored classes of litigation).

38. See Blonder-Tongue Laboratories, Inc. v. University of Ill. Found., 402 U.S. 313, 328 (1971).

39. See Federal Courts Improvement Act of 1982, 28 U.S.C. § 1295 (1982). The Federal Courts Improvement Act provides for the merger of the Court of Customs and Patent Appeals and the Court of Claims into the twelve-judge United States Court of Appeals for the Federal Circuit. Section 127 of the Act provides that the new court shall retain substantially all of the jurisdiction of the two courts abolished in the merger. This includes jurisdiction over such matters as appeals in suits against the Government and appeals from the Patent and Trademark Office, the Court of International Trade, the Merit Systems Protection Board, and the boards of contract appeals. It also includes jurisdiction over patent appeals from the district courts, ap-

peals from final determinations of the United States International
Trade Commission relating to unfair practices in import trade, appeals
from certain findings of the Secretary of Commerce, and appeals
arising under the Plant Variety Protection Act, 28 U.S.C. § 1245
(1982). The legislative history indicates that the Act was intended to
create an appellate forum capable of exercising nationwide jurisdiction over appeals in areas of the law in which there was a particular
need for nationwide uniformity. S. Rep. No. 275, 97th Cong., 2d
Sess. 2, reprinted in 1982 U.S. Code Cong. & Ad. News 11, 12. Of
particular concern was the practice of forum shopping characteristic
of patent litigation, which often resulted in different appellate courts
reaching diametrically opposed conclusions from identical or nearly
identical facts. *Id.* at 15.

40. The Court granted certiorari in sixteen tax cases in the 1982
Term, although not all addressed technical aspects of the Internal
Revenue Code. See, e.g., Allen v. Wright, 104 S. Ct. 3315 (1984)
(black parents of school-age children lack standing to challenge IRS
procedures that determine tax-exempt status for racially discriminatory
private schools). See generally Note, Tax Law, 59 N.Y.U. L. Rev.
1394 (1984).

41. Note, *supra* note 40, at 1395–1401.

Chapter 12: Implications and Conclusions

1. 5 U.S. (1 Cranch) 137, 177–78 (1803).

2. Until 1889, criminal cases were reviewable by the Court only in
the event of a division in the circuit court on a question of law or within
a limited range of issues that could be raised by habeas corpus. The Act
of February 6, 1889, §6, 25 Stat. 655, 656, authorized a writ of error to
the Court in capital cases only; the Evarts Act of March 3, 1891, 26
Stat. 826, extended the Court's appellate jurisdiction to "otherwise
infamous crime[s]." See P. Bator, P. Mishkin, D. Shapiro & H. Wechsler, Hart and Wechsler's The Federal Courts and the Federal System
1839–40 (2d ed. 1973) [hereinafter Hart and Wechsler].

3. From 1789 until the Act of December 23, 1914, ch. 2, 38 Stat.
790, the Court could not review a state court decision that upheld the
federal claim and found a state act invalid. See Hart and Wechsler,
supra note 2, at 440; C. Wright, Law of Federal Courts 737–38 (4th ed.
1983); Sager, Fair Measure: The Legal Status of Underenforced Constitutional Norms, 91 Harv. L. Rev. 1212, 1242–43 (1978).

4. Indeed, intermediate appellate courts on the state level are a
relatively recent phenomenon; the first intermediate court specializing
in appellate work was Ohio's, established in 1883, and until 1958, only
13 states had such intermediate courts. See S. Wasby, T. Marvell & A.
Aikman, Volume and Delay in State Appellate Courts: Problems and

Responses 51 (1979). Creation of intermediate courts has often been coupled with a transformation of the state high court's role from one of mandatory to discretionary jurisdiction, although early in this century some state supreme courts had a largely discretionary jurisdiction even in the absence of an intermediate tier of mandatory appeals. See *id.* at 57.

5. To consult with noncourt personnel without notifying the parties may constitute a breach of judicial ethics. See Code of Judicial Conduct for United States Judges 3A(4) (1973); Weinstein & Bonvillian, A Part-Time Clerkship Program in Federal Courts for Law Students, 68 F.R.D. 265, 273 (1975).

6. 433 U.S. 186 (1977). See Silberman, *Shaffer v. Heitner*: The End of an Era, 53 N.Y.U. L. Rev. 33 (1978).

7. 452 U.S. 666 (1981). See Harper, Leveling the Road from *Borg-Warner* to *First National Maintenance*: The Scope of Mandatory Bargaining, 68 Va. L. Rev. 1447 (1982).

8. Cf. Thomas v. Arn, 106 S. Ct. 466, 470–71 (1985).

9. See R. Posner, The Federal Courts: Crisis and Reform 120–29 (1985); Reynolds & Richman, An Evaluation of Limited Publication in the United States Court of Appeals: The Price of Reform, 48 U. Chi. L. Rev. 573 (1981); Reynolds & Richman, the Non-Precedential Precedent—Limited Publication and No-Citation Rules in the United States Court of Appeals, 78 Colum. L. Rev. 1167 (1978).

10. See R. Posner, *supra* note 9, at 101 (visiting or senior judges sat on 31 percent of the panels in 1983, compared to 22 percent in 1960); Green & Atkins, Designated Judges: How Well Do They Perform?, 61 Judicature 358, 363 (March 1978) (visiting, senior, or district judges sat on 47.3 percent of all panels between 1965 and 1969).

11. See Wasby, Inconsistency in the United States Court of Appeals: Dimensions Mechanisms for Resolution, 32 Vand. L. Rev. 1343 (1979).

12. See R. Posner, *supra* note 9, at 100–02 (rehearing en banc is unwieldly corrective device particularly after 1982 law permitting senior judges to participate in en bancs). Statistics collected by the Administrative Office of the United States Courts reveal that in the twelve-month period ending June 30, 1983, 13,217 appeals were decided by panels, yet only 66 (fewer than 1 in 200) were reheard en banc. Administrative Office of the United States Courts, Federal Case Management Statistics 15–18 (1983). In the Second Circuit, 1193 appeals were decided during the same period, yet only one case was reheard en banc. *Id.* at 3.

13. See generally R. Leflar, Internal Operating Procedures of Appellate Courts (1976).

14. *Id.* at 60.

15. See, e.g., Alabama Power Co. v. Costle, 606 F.2d 1068, superseded by 636 F.2d 323 (D.C. Cir. 1979) (Leventhal, J.); see generally

Saeta, Tentative Opinions: Letting a Little Sunshine into Appellate Decision Making, Judges' Journal, Summer 1981, at 20.

16. But cf. Monaghan, The Supreme Court, 1974 Term—Foreword: Constitutional Common Law, 89 Harv. L. Rev. 1 (1975).

17. California v. Krivda, 409 U.S. 33 (1972).

Appendix A

1. No. 81–1374, 465 U.S. 886 (1984), aff'g in part, rev'g in part 671 F.2d 493 (2d Cir. 1981).

2. No. 81–1843, 463 U.S. 765 (1983), rev'g 100 Ill. App. 3d 396, 426 N.E.2d 1078 (1981).

3. No. 81–1857, 462 U.S. 1039 (1983), rev'g 54 Ore. App. 949, 636 P.2d 1011 (1981).

4. 384 U.S. 436 (1966).

5. 451 U.S. 477 (1981).

6. No. 81–1859, 462 U.S. 640 (1983), rev'g 99 Ill. App. 3d 830, 425 N.E.2d 1383 (1981).

7. 433 U.S. 1 (1977).

8. No. 81–1891, 461 U.S. 624 (1983), rev'g 670 F.2d 208 (D.C. Cir. 1981).

9. 33 U.S.C. § 902(13) (1982).

10. No. 81–1893, 463 U.S. 992 (1983), rev'g 30 Cal. 3d 553, 639 P.2d 908, 180 Cal. Rptr. 266 (1982).

11. 391 U.S. 510 (1968).

12. 428 U.S. 262 (1976).

13. No. 81–2066, 459 U.S. 4 (1982) (per curiam), rev'g 664 F.2d 610 (6th Cir. 1981).

14. 442 U.S. 510 (1979).

15. No. 81–2169, 462 U.S. 306 (1983), aff'g 667 F.2d 1133 (4th Cir. 1981).

16. 42 U.S.C. §1983 (1982).

17. Metros v. United States Dist. Court, 441 F.2d 313 (10th Cir. 1970).

18. Restatement (Second) of Judgments, Section 85, comment a (1980); see A. Amsterdam, Trial Manual for the Defense of Criminal Cases 195 (1984).

19. No. 81–2318, 462 U.S. 637 (1983) (per curiam), dismissing as improvidently granted 410 So. 2d 152 (Fla. 1982).

20. See 462 U.S. at 638 (Burger, C.J., concurring).

21. No. 81–2332, 464 U.S. 30 (1983), rev'g 674 F.2d 298 (4th Cir. 1982).

22. 42 U.S.C. §§4601–55 (1982).

23. No. 82–39, 459 U.S. 801 (1982), aff'g 536 F. Supp. 578 (E.D. Pa. 1982) (three-judge court).

24. No. 82–52, 463 U.S. 1073 (1983) (per curiam), aff'g in part and rev'g in part 671 F.2d 330 (9th Cir. 1982).

25. 435 U.S. 702 (1978).

26. No. 82–63, 463 U.S. 239 (1983), rev'g 385 Mass. 772, 434 N.E.2d 185 (1982).

27. 429 U.S. 97 (1976).

28. 441 U.S. 520 (1979).

29. 430 U.S. 651 (1977).

30. No. 82–215, 462 U.S. 198 (1983), aff'g 674 F.2d 144 (2d Cir. 1982).

31. The Second Circuit remanded on this issue. See United States v. Whiting Pools, Inc., 674 F.2d 144, 160 (2d Cir. 1982).

32. No. 82–242, 463 U.S. 680 (1983), rev'g Sierra Club v. Gorsuch, 672 F.2d 33 (D.C. Cir. 1982).

33. 42 U.S.C. §7607(f) (1982).

34. No. 82–271, 462 U.S. 650 (1983), aff'g 681 F.2d 42 (1st Cir. 1982).

35. 42 U.S.C. §1983 (1982).

36. Id. §1988.

37. 446 U.S. 478 (1980).

38. 414 U.S. 538 (1974).

39. 5 U.S.C. §156 (1982).

40. No. 82–284, 459 U.S. 983 (1982) (per curiam), aff'g 678 F.2d 1092 (D.C. Cir. 1982) (en banc).

41. 2 U.S.C. §§431–56 (1982).

42. No. 82–357, 464 U.S. 287 (1984), aff'g No. 58278 (Mich. Ct. App. Mar. 30, 1982).

43. 436 U.S. 499 (1978).

44. No. 82–360, 459 U.S. 961 (1982), aff'g 543 F. Supp. 235 (M.D. Ala. 1982) (three-judge court).

45. 42 U.S.C. §1973c (1982).

46. No. 82–372, 462 U.S. 19 (1983), rev'g 671 F.2d 553 (D.C. Cir. 1982).

47. 5 U.S.C. §552(b)(5) (1982).

48. 443 U.S. 340 (1979).

49. Id. at 354–55, 362–63. But cf. NLRB v. Sears, Roebuck & Co., 421 U.S. 132, 148–49 (1975).

50. No. 82–1616, 465 U.S. 792 (1984), rev'g 688 F.2d 638 (9th Cir. 1982).

51. No. 82–472, 464 U.S. 16 (1983), aff'g United States v. Martino, 681 F.2d 952 (5th Cir. 1982) (en banc).

52. 18 U.S.C. §1963(a)(1) (1982).

53. See United States v. Godoy, 678 F.2d 84 (9th Cir. 1982), cert. denied, 464 U.S. 959 (1983); United States v. Marubeni Am. Corp., 611 F.2d 763 (9th Cir. 1980).

54. No. 82–738, 465 U.S. 75 (1984), vacating and remanding 703 F.2d 564 (6th Cir. 1982).

55. 42 U.S.C. §1983 (1982).

56. 449 U.S. 90 (1980).

57. *Id.* at 96–101.

58. No. 82–940, 467 U.S. 69 (1984), rev'g 678 F.2d 1022 (11th Cir. 1982).

59. 42 U.S.C. §2000e et seq. (1982).

60. No. 82–945, 467 U.S. 883 (1984), aff'g in part and rev'g in part 672 F.2d 592 (7th Cir. 1982).

61. No. 82–952 et al., 460 U.S. 1001 (1983) (per curiam), aff'g United States v. American Tel. & Tel. Co., 552 F. Supp. 131 (D.D.C. 1982).

62. No. 82–958, 464 U.S. 548 (1984), rev'g 687 F.2d 338 (10th Cir. 1982).

63. No. 82–1080, 463 U.S. 1219 (1983), aff'g In re Pennsylvania Congressional Dist. Reapportionment Cases, 535 F. Supp. 191 (M.D. Pa. 1982) (per curiam) (three-judge court).

64. No. 82–1041, 465 U.S. 330 (1983), aff'g 690 F.2d 812 (11th Cir. 1982).

65. No. 82–1095, 465 U.S. 37 (1984), rev'g 692 F.2d 1189 (9th Cir. 1982).

66. Petition for Certiorari at 42–46 (citing Brooks v. Estelle, 697 F.2d 586 (5th Cir.), cert. denied, 459 U.S. 106 (1982)).

67. Brooks v. Estelle, 697 F.2d 586, 588 (5th Cir.), cert. denied, 459 U.S. 106 (1982).

68. 428 U.S. 153 (1976) (Stewart, Powell & Stevens, JJ.).

69. 428 U.S. 242 (1976) (Stewart, Powell & Stevens, JJ.).

70. 428 U.S. 262 (1976) (Stewart, Powell & Stevens, JJ.).

71. No. 82–1135, 465 U.S. 168 (1984), rev'g Wiggins v. Estelle, 681 F.2d 266 (5th Cir. 1982).

72. 422 U.S. 806 (1975).

73. *Id.* at 834 n.46.

74. No. 82–1141, 461 U.S. 911 (1983), aff'g 574 F. Supp. 672 (D.D.C. 1982) (three-judge court).

75. No. 82–1246, 466 U.S. 485 (1984), aff'g 692 F.2d 189 (1st Cir. 1982).

76. 376 U.S. 254 (1964).

77. 456 U.S. 844 (1982).

78. 456 U.S. 273 (1982).

79. See, e.g., Gertz v. Robert Welch, Inc., 418 U.S. 323 (1974).

80. No. 82–1326, 464 U.S. 312 (1984), rev'g 683 F.2d 1253 (9th Cir. 1982).

81. 16 U.S.C. §§1451–64 (1982).

82. No. 82–1330, 104 S. Ct. 2916 (1984), aff'g 693 F.2d 132 (5th Cir. 1982).

83. 447 U.S. 410 (1980).
84. Cutshall v. State, 191 Miss. 764, 4 So. 2d 289 (1941).
85. 417 U.S. 21 (1974).
86. No. 82–1408, 462 U.S. 111 (1983) (per curiam), rev'g 692 F.2d 354 (5th Cir. 1982).
87. No. 82–1432, 466 U.S. 522 (1984), aff'g 690 F.2d 376 (4th Cir. 1982).
88. 42 U.S.C. §1988 (1982).
89. 446 U.S. 719 (1980).
90. No. 82–1453, 464 U.S. 386 (1984), aff'g 693 F.2d 298 (3d Cir. 1982).
91. 26 U.S.C. §6501(a) (1982).
92. No. 82–1479, 466 U.S. 294 (1984), rev'g 698 F.2d 1 (1st Cir. 1982).
93. 437 U.S. 1 (1978) (double jeopardy bars retrial when conviction reversed because of insufficient evidence).
94. 427 U.S. 618 (1976).
95. No. 82–1496, 461 U.S. 571 (1983) (per curiam), rev'g 692 F.2d 765 (9th Cir. 1982) (mem.).

Appendix B: The Unresolved Conflicts Denied Review

1. No. 81–2240, 463 U.S. 1229 (1983), denying cert. to 671 F.2d 1299 (11th Cir. 1982). See Note, Criminal Law I, 59 N.Y.U. L. Rev. 1227, 1227–31 (1984).
2. 671 F.2d at 1300–02; accord, Passmore v. Estelle, 607 F.2d 662 (5th Cir. 1979) (per curiam), cert. denied, 446 U.S. 937 (1980).
3. Hill v. Page, 454 F.2d 679 (10th Cir. 1971).
4. See, e.g., Strickland v. Washington, 466 U.S. 668 (1984); United States v. Cronic, 466 U.S. 648 (1984); Jones v. Barnes, 463 U.S. 745 (1983).
5. No. 81–2273, 459 U.S. 976 (1982), denying cert. to 411 So. 2d 13 (La. 1982); see Note, *supra* note 1, at 1231–34.
6. Cooper v. United States, 594 F.2d 12 (4th Cir. 1979).
7. 707 F.2d 323 (8th Cir. 1983), rev'd, 467 U.S. 504 (1984).
8. No. 81–2343, 459 U.S. 948 (1982), denying cert. to Riley v. Gray, 674 F.2d 522 (6th Cir. 1982); see Note, Criminal Law III, 59 N.Y.U. L. Rev. 1272, 1272–74 (1984).
9. 428 U.S. 465 (1976).
10. Williams v. Brown, 609 F.2d 216 (5th Cir. 1980).
11. Gamble v. Oklahoma, 583 F.2d 1161 (10th Cir. 1978).
12. No. 82–72, 459 U.S. 906 (1982), denying cert. to 677 F.2d 998 (4th Cir. 1982); see Note, Procedural Law, 59 N.Y.U. L. Rev. 1343, 1345–52 (1984).
13. 28 U.S.C. §2401(b) (1982).

14. *Wilkinson* held that the statute was not so tolled. 677 F.2d at 1001.

15. See Brown Transp. Corp. v. Atcon, Inc., 439 U.S. 1014, 1017–19 (1978) (White, J., dissenting from denial of certiorari).

16. No. 82–194, 459 U.S. 883 (1982), denying cert. to 685 F.2d 436 (8th Cir. 1982).

17. See Note, *supra* note 12, at 1379–86.

18. No. 82–949, 460 U.S. 1011 (1983), denying cert. to 684 F.2d 1126 (5th Cir. 1982).

19. 442 U.S. 510 (1979). *Sandstrom* held that a jury instruction violates due process if it contains a presumption that shifts the burden of proof on an essential element of a crime to the defendant. *Id.* at 524. In *Fricke*, as in *Sandstrom*, the trial judge instructed that defendants are presumed to intend the ordinary consequences of their acts. See Note, *supra* note 1, at 1240–42.

20. See Note, *supra* note 1, at 1234–42.

21. 684 F.2d at 1129.

22. 460 U.S. 73 (1983).

23. 466 U.S. 1 (1984).

24. 467 U.S. 1225 (1984).

25. No. 82–1007, 460 U.S. 1022 (1983), denying cert. to Nieszner v. Mark, 684 F.2d 562 (8th Cir. 1982).

26. See Note, Constitutional Law I, 59 N.Y.U. L. Rev. 1179, 1179 n.1 (1984).

27. No. 82–1161, 460 U.S. 1023 (1983), denying cert. to 683 F.2d 154 (6th Cir. 1982).

28. See Note, Labor Law, 59 N.Y.U. L. Rev. 1301, 1328–42 (1984).

29. 683 F.2d at 155.

30. No. 82–1322, 460 U.S. 1052 (1983), denying cert. to 689 F.2d 865 (9th Cir. 1982).

31. See Note, Administrative Law, 59 N.Y.U. L. Rev. 1150, 1151–57 (1984).

32. 26 U.S.C. §6103(b)(2) (1982).

33. King v. Commissioner, 688 F.2d 488, 491 (7th Cir. 1982).

34. No. 82–1531, 462 U.S. 1119 (1983), denying cert. to 691 F.2d 1384 (11th Cir. 1982).

35. 691 F.2d at 1387 & n.5.

36. See In re Grand Jury Proceedings, 486 F.2d 85, 89 (3d Cir. 1973).

37. *Bank of Nova Scotia* rejected the foreign illegality defense. 691 F.2d at 1388–91.

38. See Note, *supra* note 12, at 1353–62.

39. No. 82–1838, 462 U.S. 1134 (1983), denying cert. to 416 Mich. 1581, 331 N.W.2d 707 (1982).

40. See p. 155 *supra*.

41. See Note, *supra* note 1, at 1237–38.

42. No. 82–1801, 462 U.S. 1108 (1983), denying cert. to 702 F.2d 33 (2d Cir. 1983) (per curiam).

43. See Note, Criminal Law II, 59 N.Y.U. L. Rev. 1243, 1250–56 (1984).

44. United States v. Radeker, 664 F.2d 242 (10th Cir. 1981).

45. No. 82–1089, 461 U.S. 905 (1983), denying cert. to 674 F.2d 1377 (11th Cir. 1982); see Note, *supra* note 26, at 1179 n.1.

46. No. 82–2026, 459 U.S. 967 (1982), denying cert. to 657 F.2d 750 (5th Cir. 1981).

47. 450 U.S. 248 (1981).

48. 657 F.2d 1322, 1333–35 (3d Cir. 1981) (en banc).

49. 662 F.2d 975, 991 (3d Cir. 1981) (en banc).

50. See Note, *supra* note 28, at 1304–08.

51. No. 82–494, 459 U.S. 1127 (1983), denying cert. to Simpson v. Director, Office of Workmen's Compensation Programs, 681 F.2d 82 (1st Cir. 1982).

52. 370 U.S. 114 (1962).

53. 33 U.S.C. §§901–50 (1982).

54. 681 F.2d at 84–91.

55. Shea v. Texas Employers Ins. Ass'n, 383 F.2d 16 (5th Cir. 1967).

56. See Note, *supra* note 12, at 1343 n.1.

57. No. 82–623, 459 U.S. 1183 (1983), denying cert. to United States v. Hartley, 678 F.2d 961 (11th Cir. 1982).

58. 18 U.S.C. §§1962–65 (1982).

59. See Note, *supra* note 43, at 1260–68.

60. United States v. Hartley, 678 F.2d 961, 989–90 (11th Cir. 1982), cert. denied, 459 U.S. 1183 (1983).

61. See Note, *supra* note 43, at 1263–68.

62. No. 82–798, 459 U.S. 1202 (1983), denying cert. to 682 F.2d 820 (9th Cir. 1982).

63. 682 F.2d at 824.

64. United States v. Perez-Hernandez, 672 F.2d 1380 (11th Cir. 1982) (per curiam).

65. See Note, *supra* note 8, at 1284 n.108.

66. No. 82–1464, 462 U.S. 1118 (1983), denying cert. to 696 F.2d 231 (3d Cir. 1982).

67. See 28 U.S.C. §455(a) (1982).

68. See Note, *supra* note 12, at 1343–44 n.1.

69. No. 82–1510, 463 U.S. 1207 (1983), denying cert. to 690 F.2d 470 (5th Cir. 1982).

70. See Note, *supra* note 8, at 1274–78.

71. 105 S. Ct. 733 (1985).

72. No. 81–2344, 459 U.S. 1021 (1982), denying cert. to 641 P.2d 1222 (Wyo. 1982).

73. See Note, Constitutional Law II, 59 N.Y.U. L. Rev. 1196, 1219–26 (1984).